FLORIDA STATE
UNIVERSITY LIBRARIES

NOV 17 1997

TALLAHASSEE, FLORIDA

# Rationality and Structure

SOUTH FLORIDA STUDIES IN THE HISTORY OF JUDAISM

Edited by
Jacob Neusner
Bruce D. Chilton, Darrell J. Fasching, William Scott Green,
Sara Mandell, James F. Strange

Number 144
RATIONALITY AND STRUCTURE
The Bavli's Anomalous Juxtapositions

by
Jacob Neusner

# Rationality and Structure

## The Bavli's Anomalous Juxtapositions

by
Jacob Neusner

Scholars Press
Atlanta, Georgia

# RATIONALITY AND STRUCTURE
## The Bavli's Anomalous Juxtapositions

by
Jacob Neusner

©1997
University of South Florida

Publication of this book was made possible by a grant from the Tisch Family Foundation, New York City. The University of South Florida acknowledges with thanks this important support for its scholarly projects.

**Library of Congress Cataloging in Publication Data**

Neusner, Jacob, 1932–
    Rationality and structure : the Bavli's anomalous juxtapositions / by Jacob Neusner.
        p.    cm — (South Florida studies in the history of Judaism ; no. 144)
    ISBN 0-7885-0340-5 (alk. paper)
    1. Talmud—Criticism, Redaction.  2. Talmud—Sources. I. Title. II. Series.  III. Series: South Florida studies in the history of Judaism ; 144.
BM503.6.N488   1997
296.1'25066—dc21                                        97-3557
                                                                           CIP

Printed in the United States of America
on acid-free paper

## Table of Contents

Preface ..................................................................................... v

| | | |
|---|---|---|
| I. | The Structure of Babylonian Talmud Berakhot | 1 |
| II. | The Structure of Babylonian Talmud Shabbat | 9 |
| III. | The Structure of Babylonian Talmud Erubin | 19 |
| IV. | The Structure of Babylonian Talmud Pesahim | 23 |
| V. | The Structure of Babylonian Talmud Yoma | 29 |
| VI. | The Structure of Babylonian Talmud Sukkah | 39 |
| VII. | The Structure of Babylonian Talmud Besah | 45 |
| VIII. | The Structure of Babylonian Talmud Rosh Hashanah | 51 |
| IX. | The Structure of Babylonian Talmud Taanit | 55 |
| X. | The Structure of Babylonian Talmud Megillah | 59 |
| XI. | The Structure of Babylonian Talmud Moed Qatan | 63 |
| XII. | The Structure of Babylonian Talmud Hagigah | 71 |
| XIII. | The Structure of Babylonian Talmud Yebamot | 77 |
| XIV. | The Structure of Babylonian Talmud Ketubot | 81 |
| XV. | The Structure of Babylonian Talmud Nedarim | 85 |
| XVI. | The Structure of Babylonian Talmud Nazir | 89 |
| XVII. | The Structure of Babylonian Talmud Sotah | 91 |
| XVIII. | The Structure of Babylonian Talmud Gittin | 97 |
| XIX. | The Structure of Babylonian Talmud Qiddushin | 101 |
| XX. | The Structure of Babylonian Talmud Baba Qamma | 105 |
| XXI. | The Structure of Babylonian Talmud Baba Mesia | 111 |
| XXII. | The Structure of Babylonian Talmud Baba Batra | 117 |
| XXIII. | The Structure of Babylonian Talmud Sanhedrin | 125 |
| XXIV. | The Structure of Babylonian Talmud Makkot | 131 |
| XXV. | The Structure of Babylonian Talmud Shebuot | 139 |
| XXVI. | The Structure of Babylonian Talmud Abodah Zarah | 143 |
| XXVII. | The Structure of Babylonian Talmud Horayot | 155 |
| XXVIII. | The Structure of Babylonian Talmud Zebahim | 161 |
| XXIX. | The Structure of Babylonian Talmud Menahot | 165 |
| XXX. | The Structure of Babylonian Talmud Hullin | 169 |
| XXXI. | The Structure of Babylonian Talmud Bekhorot | 173 |
| XXXII. | The Structure of Babylonian Talmud Arakhin | 177 |
| XXXIII. | The Structure of Babylonian Talmud Temurah | 183 |
| XXXIV. | The Structure of Babylonian Talmud Keritot | 187 |
| XXXV. | The Structure of Babylonian Talmud Meilah | 195 |
| XXXVI. | The Structure of Babylonian Talmud Tamid | 197 |
| XXXVII. | The Structure of Babylonian Talmud Niddah | 199 |

# Preface

The Talmud of Babylonia, a.k.a., the Bavli, takes shape as a commentary to the Mishnah, but encompasses sizable composites of materials that focus on their own topic, collecting sayings and stories about said topic, but that do not serve the document's principal purpose of exegesis of the Mishnah and analysis of the law. When these topical composites are inserted, they create a jarring interruption in the steady course of Mishnah-exegesis and legal exposition and analysis, and they also constitute anomalies in the exegetical and analytical large-scale program of the document. But, I maintain and here demonstrate, to the compilers of the Bavli a clear rationality guided the inclusion of the exposition a topical. What appears to impede the work enriches it, and an account of the structure of the Talmud, its sequence of exegetical problems and its palpable requirement of supplementary topical information, shows the rationality of inserting discussions of topics not required by the labor of Mishnah-exposition.

The stakes prove formidable, for to the proposition that the Talmud of Babylonia forms a coherent commentary to the Mishnah, the document's miscellaneous character poses a considerable objection. Everyone who has studied a complete tractate or perhaps even an entire chapter, start to finish, will point to two important traits that call into question the claim that the document follows a rational program. The first is the presence of large composites that do not serve the purpose of commenting on the Mishnah, and the second, the intrusion of such composites into the very heart of the work of Mishnah-exegesis. These miscellaneous composites of materials on a given topic, lacking all argument and proposition, not only intrude but disrupt. Not only so, but it is not always easy to explain why a given composite is inserted where it is; juxtapositions of Mishnah-exegesis and a topical miscellany — a composite of materials on a given subject that the Mishnah, for its part, has not introduced, or of materials that vastly exceed what is required for the explanation of a reference in the Mishnah — prove jarring. What has one thing to do with another — wheat with straw, so to speak?

Accordingly, to sustain the case that the Talmud of Babylonia adheres to a governing rationality, that defined by the logic of Mishnah-exegesis and amplification, I have to identify these anomalous constructions and propose a theory of why they are inserted where they are, and what the framer of the document accomplished in including in his exposition of the Mishnah and its law rather formidable topical composites that bear no obvious relationship to the tasks of Mishnah-commentary.

This book recapitulates my account of the way in which these free-standing composites, most of them organized around a given topic but not centered on proving a particular proposition in connection with said topic, find a position in the Talmud's unfolding, flowing discourse. At issue is the rationality of the Talmud's compilers: if (as I allege) they were preparing a commentary, what made them utilize the topical composites that take a place in the Talmud? How the whole holds together at any one passage then is what requires explanation. And that means, what has one thing got to do with some other. Here, in acute detail, I explain how topics that on the surface do not intersect in fact fit together very nicely and by their juxtaposition convey a message in tandem that on their own the respective parts do not deliver or even adumbrate.[1]

The question, what has this to do with that, finds its answer here in these pages for every point in the Talmud at which — so my outline of the Bavli shows — the subject takes an unexpected turn. Juxtapositions that jar and disrupt turn out to bear an entirely pertinent, even urgent, message for the larger discourse in which they take their place. Indeed, these topical composites themselves commonly constitute a comment upon the paramount subject of the Mishnah-tractate at the very point at which they find their position — if only by highlighting what belongs but has been omitted. Properly understood, the topical miscellanies do not jar and do not violate the document's prevailing rationality. In these pages I therefore represent our Talmud as the best of all possible talmuds, insisting upon the rationality of the document at its most puzzling and perplexing passages — thus the title of the book: *Rationality and Structure: The Bavli's Anomalous Juxtapositions.*

How to set forth the evidence and argument that sustains my proposition? Through my analytical outlines of the Talmud I claim to have penetrated into that rationality that made this fit very well with that, and that rationality that at the same time excluded the other thing. When we know the principles of association, of making connections and drawing conclusions, then we can define the logic, the rationality, that governs throughout. That takes shape in the (to the compilers of the document) self-evident principle of coherence that holds the whole together, even (or especially) where the sequence of completed cogent discourses appears to disintegrate into a haphazard and incoherent collection of unrelated sayings and stories about nothing in particular.

---

[1] Certainly one of the critical problems in the study of the history of the formation of Judaism is the relationship of the Talmud's system to the Mishnah's, and that means, what does the Talmud have to say about the topical program of the Mishnah when it does more than paraphrase and clarify the Mishnah's message: when is the Talmud talmudic? I struggled with that problem in my *The Talmud of the Land of Israel. A Preliminary Translation and Explanation.* Chicago: The University of Chicago Press: 1983. XXXV. *Introduction. Taxonomy*, and it is the subtext of my Form-History for Volumes VI and VII.

*Preface* vii

Two issues intersect, the structure of the document, on the one side, the rationality of those inserted discourses that seem to violate the rules of structure and order that otherwise govern throughout, on the other. Questions of structure pertain to how the document is put together and is so framed as to convey its framers' messages in consistent forms. These privileged forms define the document, and I have now fully identified and richly catalogued them in the companion work to this study, *The Documentary Form-History of Rabbinic Judaism,* Volume VII (bibliographical data of which are given below). The coherent formal program contains ample indication of the character and purpose of any given detailed analytical discussion. What we have is a commentary, and the forms of the document leave no doubt whatsoever about that fact. Then the topical miscellanies, composites that do not advance the work of Mishnah-exegesis, require our attention — so much for structure.

Questions of system encompass the matters of rationality, principles of self-evidence, laws of list-making. These then concern the points of emphasis and current stress, the agenda that comes to expression in whatever topic is subject to analysis. The framers of the composites that comprise the document pursue a uniform analytical program throughout. Here too, they never leave us in doubt as to what they wish to discover or demonstrate. By explaining the coherence of the whole through the identification of the parts and the systematic specification of what links one part to another, I mean to show the Talmud for what it is. And that is, a document that — like all enduring works of intellect — in a monotonous voice says the same thing about many things and changes the subject only to re-present the original subject itself.

This insistence upon the rationality of jarring juxtapositions, as I said at the outset, runs counter to the view of the Talmud that prevails even among those who claim to know the document well, and that is because of the way in which it is studied. The Talmud up to now has been understood within the processes of philological inquiry and phrase by phrase exegesis conducted in other than academic settings, yeshivas and Jewish seminaries for example. In recent times, the Talmud is not studied in its own terms at all, but texts selected by reason of their common topic will be studied in their own framework. So students do not even master the Talmud in the way in which its framers and compilers created it. Whether people study isolated passages, losing track of the whole, or whether to begin with they ignore the whole for congruent parts, the result is the same: the impression that the document is just a collection of this and that, not a purposive and well-crafted piece of writing to be mastered through its own disciplines — a mere scrapbook.

Questions of coherence, order, rationality of discourse under such conditions do not command attention, for if people concentrate on words and phrases and small, whole units out of all larger context, they are unlikely to ask, what has this to do with that? In that setting the Talmud serves as a source of information, opinion, authoritative fact out of all context, but it is rarely perceived as a cogent and systematic (and I argue, systemic) statement overall. Issues of detail overwhelm concerns of structure and order. The received exegetical tradition, essential in its theological and political setting of faith and useful also in the academic one, yields a mass of detail, but no coherent account formed of the details. People quote sayings but grasp little of their broader intellectual context. Setting forth bits and pieces while never gaining sight of the whole (and in recent times even saying there is no whole, only parts to be detached and reassembled as one likes), the received exegetical and philological tradition addresses few questions of serious academic concern. But it forms the basis for this next step in a centuries-old labor of mediation. On its successes, we build. Responding to questions it did not address, we move forward.

No mere arguments joined to examples can suffice to overcome a prevailing attitude toward a widely-studied document. That is why I do not offer general arguments but detailed treatments of every piece of data in all thirty-seven tractates of the Bavli. This I systematically carried out in my *Academic Commentary* to the Bavli (and the Yerushalmi), where at each point I systematically addressed issues of coherence. There I defined the Talmud's definitive character as a commentary, through visual signals portraying the whole in a process of large-scale description, analysis, and interpretation. I further identified and defined the components, beyond Mishnah-commentary. The path I took carried me through a detailed, line by line rereading of the document, with a uniform program of questions always guiding our progress. Since Mishnah-exegesis defines the Talmud's purpose, though not its character, I identified, then frame my discussion around, the Talmud's definitive units of discourse, which are those organized around Mishnah-paragraphs.[2] The commentary on the Talmud's structure then asked how the Mishnah-paragraph

---

[2] These are, in general, to be divided into two types, sources and traditions, as I have defined the basic taxonomy of types of compositions of the Bavli in my *Sources and Traditions. Types of Composition in the Talmud of Babylonia.* Atlanta, 1992: Scholars Press for South Florida Studies in the History of Judaism; and note also the following: *The Bavli's One Voice: Types and Forms of Analytical Discourse and their Fixed Order of Appearance.* Atlanta, 1991: Scholars Press for South Florida Studies in the History of Judaism.*The Bavli's Massive Miscellanies. The Problem of Agglutinative Discourse in the Talmud of Babylonia.* Atlanta, 1992: Scholars Press for South Florida Studies in the History of Judaism.*The Bavli's Primary Discourse. Mishnah Commentary, its Rhetorical Paradigms and their Theological Implications in the Talmud of Babylonia Tractate Moed Qatan.* Atlanta, 1992: Scholars Press for South Florida Studies in the History of Judaism. I have provided a systematic and detailed account of the other theories, both earlier and contemporary, of the same matter in *The Modern Study of the Mishnah.* Leiden, 1973: Brill, and *The Formation of the Babylonian Talmud. Studies on the Achievements of Late Nineteenth and Twentieth Century Historical and Literary-Critical Research.* Leiden, 1970: Brill. In addition, my discussion of the literary-historical and exegetical theories of David W. Halivni, in addition to the treatment of his work in those two volumes, is presented in *Sources and Traditions.* Note also the section edited by me concerning Halivni's ideas in comparison to those of Shamma Friedman in *Literature as Law,* ed. William Scott Green (= *Semeia* Volume ??).

*Preface*                                                                 ix

before us has been analyzed, and whether that analysis has then dictated the introduction of further discussion. The question of structural cogency is answered by the information produced by a description of the Talmud as Mishnah-commentary. But the Talmud commonly moves beyond the limits of the Mishnah-paragraph that defines the starting point of its discussion.

The essential work of that academic commentary — showing how things cohere, when they do, or pointing out their incoherence, when they do not hold together — thus came into view, yielding the problem taken up here. In the commentary, after I had set forth the tractates, I made a complete outline of the whole, showing how the successive clauses of the Mishnah formed the main beams of structure and system for the document, then pointing up both the points of coherence and also the various anomalies. My task then was to explain where that further discussion that the Bavli introduces has led us and, if we can, also to account for the cogency of the result. For the critical issue of structure centers upon coherence and cogency: the whole that is made up of the parts, and that, in this context, exceeds the sum of the parts. If, as I said at the outset, we can explain how connections are made, then we can describe, also, those principles of reasoning that lead us to link this to that, but not to the other thing. And when we can define the principles of making selections and imputing connections, we also can identify bases for drawing the coherent conclusions from selecting those connections. That is to say, through the uniformities of selection, connection, and conclusion, we may define that governing system that the structure's cogency both supports and also expresses in formal language. The results of that inquiry are recapitulated here.

This produced a very systematic and comprehensive examination of the Bavli's massive miscellanies.[3] In my outlines I accounted for each completed unit of discourse in the tractate, showing its relationship either to the requirement of Mishnah-exegesis or to the needs of secondary expansion and generalization of the law portrayed by the Mishnah. That outline, in each case, then focused attention upon the large-scale composites that provide information on a topic but do not propose to clarify a rule of the Mishnah; these I called topical appendices, or topical miscellanies (as the case required). At the end of the outline of the tractate, I raised questions: of structure and system, and this I did in the same manner for all tractates. The questions I pursued are spelled out at tractate Moed Qatan, my starting point, roughly in the following way (revised to remove what is particular to that tractate).

---

[3] *The Bavli's Massive Miscellanies,* cited above.

POINTS OF STRUCTURE

1. DOES THE BABYLONIAN TALMUD-TRACTATE THAT IS UNDER STUDY FOLLOW A COHERENT OUTLINE GOVERNED BY A CONSISTENT RULES?

The answer to that question consistently demonstrated that the Talmud-tractate follows a coherent outline — that supplied by the Mishnah-chapters at their successive paragraphs; at remarkably few points was I unable to account for the position and purpose of a complete composition, one with a beginning, middle, and end. I could identify few, if any, such compositions that do not relate to the composite of which they form a part, and I can point to not a single composites without a clear purpose in the tractate's large-scale constructions. The outline I was able to construct from one tractate to the next ordinarily followed a simple order: topic sentence, ordinarily a sentence of the Mishnah-tractate, at some points a subject or proposition not supplied by it; analytical discussion of the topic-sentence; propositions generated by the topic-sentences. Where the compilers wish to provide both analysis and illustrative cases, the order is, first, analysis, then illustration.

2. WHAT ARE THE SALIENT TRAITS OF ITS STRUCTURE?

The outline of the Talmud-tractate follows the outline of the Mishnah-tractate, but extends beyond the Mishnah-tractate in two ways. First, important statements of the Mishnah-tractate are not analyzed at all. Second, important propositions not set forth in the Mishnah-tractate are examined, and significant topical composites are inserted without regard to the Mishnah-tractate's program but in addition to it. The rules that the outline reveals present no surprises. In examining any sentence of the Mishnah or of a comparable Tannaite document, [1] the compilers first discuss the formulation, authorities, or scriptural foundations for the Mishnah's or other Tannaite document's statement. Then [2] secondary augmentation will begin, whether through an extension of the rule to other cases, or an investigation of the implicit principle of the rule and its intersection with other types of cases altogether. Following comes [3] the consideration of Tannaite formulations of rules that pertain in theme or problem or principle, and these will be subjected to the same sequence and type of analytical questions that have already been brought to bear upon the Mishnah.

3. WHAT IS THE RATIONALITY OF THE STRUCTURE?

We proceed from the particular — the Mishnah's rule — to the general. We first deal with the details of the particular, then we move outward to theoretical considerations. We deal with rules accorded Tannaite origin or sponsorship, first found in the Mishnah, then found in the Tosefta (not so firm a rule), and finally given a signal of Tannaite but not found in a compilation of Tannaite statements now in our hands (e. g., Tenno rabbanon, Tanné and the like). These procedures emerged inductively, through an account of one tractate after another, and, within the tractates, the successive chapters. I did not give a few examples and a broad generalization, I did the exact opposite: every detail, start to finish, and from the

*Preface* xi

details, the claim to set forth the rationality of the document found its sustaining validation.

4. WHERE ARE THE POINTS OF IRRATIONALITY IN THE STRUCTURE?

Here we reach the issue of this book: the compositions and composites that violate the document's principles of structure. The foregoing account of the orderly structure of the Talmud-tractate under study then requires attention to those composites that violated the demonstrated structure and therefore contradict its rationality — that is, in context, irrational intrusions. With only the Mishnah-tractate in hand, we should have no basis for predicting the topics of the composites that provide other than Mishnah-exegesis, augmentation, and extension. Only when we ask why a given topical composite, extrinsic to the Mishnah-tractate, has been positioned where it is, and whether or not said composite can have occupied a position elsewhere in the Talmud-tractate or have been omitted with a significant loss of meaning.

The answers to these four questions then lead me, tractate by tractate, to the inquiry into the system of said tractate. By "system" in this context I mean, how does the Talmud's reading of the Mishnah-tractate impost upon the Mishnah-tractate a viewpoint or a logic of its own: do we understand the Mishnah-tractate under study in a different way from the way we should without the Talmud's commentary? The inquiry into where and how the Talmud's own system, its logic, has reshaped the presentation of the topic to which the Mishnah-tractate is devoted takes the form of asking another set of questions, three in all. These are as follows.

POINTS OF SYSTEM

1. DOES THE BABYLONIAN TALMUD-TRACTATE THAT IS UNDER STUDY SERVE ONLY AS A RE-PRESENTATION OF THE MISHNAH-TRACTATE OF THE SAME NAME?

For negative and positive reasons, the answer to this question in general, though not always, is one-sidedly negative. The negative reason is that Talmud-tractate does not re-present Mishnah-tractate that is under study, because it omits consideration of sizable passages of the Mishnah-tractate. I can conceive of no way to predict what the Talmud-tractate's framers will omit; I see no pattern, nor can I explain why, in the same set of sentences, a given sentence will attract extensive consideration and another will not. But it suffices to say that the Talmud-tractate in no way pretends to cover every clause of the Mishnah. I further have formed the subjective impression that at no point do the framers of compositions concerning clauses of the Mishnah strain to find something to fill up space where they have nothing to say. I can rarely point to a passage that strikes me as extraneous or fabricated for the occasion. That subjective impression gains a measure of objective standing when we observe that the same types of discussion accorded to a given Mishnah-clause recur throughout. A coherent and cogent program of Mishnah-exegesis governs everywhere. That seems to me to bear the implication that the framers of the Talmud-tractate do not acknowledge the task of filling up space by making statements where they have nothing interesting to say. My tentative hypothesis is that where a sentence of the Mishnah attracts no analytical inquiry, it is because it contains nothing that the framers of our Talmud-tractate found problematic; where they say nothing, it is because they have nothing to say. But to test that hypothesis we should have to pursue the question of the sources of the Talmud-tractate, that is, the resources upon which the compilers of composites drew, or the authors of compositions devoted to Mishnah-exegesis wrote up. That is not a question that concerns me here, since the answer tells us nothing about structure and system, explaining what we do not have, not what we do.

The positive reason is that the Talmud-tractate that is under study includes presentation of topics and principles and propositions that the Mishnah-tractate does not present. These I then catalogued. The proportion of the tractate represented by the freestanding topical composites is accurately estimated only by a word count, that is, the number of words in the listed composites as against the number of words in the tractate as a whole. Without making such a word-count, I believe readers will concur in the simple judgment that the important topical composites extrinsic to Mishnah-exegesis and yet primary in the Talmud-tractate form a substantial component of the whole. These extrinsic composites and compositions take shape around their own subjects or propositions or problems, and they do not respond to those of the Mishnah-tractate. But, as we shall now see, they do change the re-presentation of the Mishnah-tractate in important ways, to which we now turn.

2. How do the topical composites fit into the Talmud-tractate Under Study and what do they contribute that the Mishnah-tractate of the same name would lack without them?

Here we come to the crux of the matter: how the Talmud recasts the Mishnah's treatment of the Mishnah's own topic. That is done by introducing systematic presentations of topics beyond those covered by the Mishnah but in the context of the exposition of those of the Mishnah. To answer this question, I examined each composite and asked how it fit into the tractate under study. The topical composites fit in in two distinct ways. First, some of them greatly expand the scope of the Mishnah-rule, introducing a level of abstraction that Mishnah-exegesis does not require. Mishnah-exegesis is made to set the stage for a much broader consideration of principles that transcend cases and recast rules into representations of underlying conceptions of a high order of generalization. In this first type of topical composite, the Mishnah's rule is re-presented as an indicator of a deeper, compelling problem of thought, often of a philosophical, rather than a narrowly-legal character.

Second, and more strikingly, the larger number of the topical composite change the face of the Mishnah-tractate by raising to prominence subjects treated by the Mishnah only incidentally and in a subordinate status.

*Preface*

3. CAN WE STATE WHAT THE COMPILERS OF THIS DOCUMENT PROPOSE TO ACCOMPLISH IN PRODUCING THIS COMPLETE, ORGANIZED PIECE OF WRITING THAT WE NOW HAVE (THAT IS, MY THESIS THAT IN OUR HANDS WE POSSESS THE BEST OF ALL POSSIBLE TALMUDS?

The answer to this question lies in explaining the connection between topics laid out by the Mishnah-tractate and those introduced by the Talmud's insertion of topical composites or miscellanies. I asked, What made sages conceive that the latter should find a comfortable and capacious place amid the former? This lead to systematic discussions on the connections between topics that sages found self-evident — and that, in the nature of things, a merely topical program of exegesis must find jarring. Once we ask, what has one thing to do with the other — the Mishnah's topic with the Talmud's insertion of an extraneous, therefore anomalous topic — the issue of making connections and drawing conclusions — the self-evidence of list-making — comes to the fore. A substantive, ultimately theological, explanation is required, and it is contained in the answer to a simple question. Precisely what has this topic unheralded by the Mishnah to do with that topic that the Mishnah has assigned for exegesis? The principal mode of thought of the Mishnah is that of comparison and contrast. Something is like something else, therefore follows its rule; or unlike, therefore follows the opposite of the rule governing the something else.

So as a matter of hypothesis, let us assume that the framers of Talmud-tractate that is under study found self-evidently valid the modes of thought that they learned from the Mishnah and so made connections between things that were alike, on the one side, or things that were opposite, on the other. Then, if the contrast proves obvious, the point of comparison — how are these things similar, and what rule pertains to both — emerges with equal facility. So in establishing the connection, through treating the categories as equivalent and counterpart to one another, what have our sages in Talmud-tractate that is under study said in their own behalf, not about the Mishnah but through their re-presentation of the Mishnah? They make the connection between the one and the other. When we can explain that connection, we are also able to account for the character of the Talmud — not only its systematic commentary to the Mishnah, which imparts to the whole the character of coherence and cogency — but also its jarring juxtapositions. In the structure that the outline reveals, we discern a rationality that makes juxtapositions logical and rational — and deeply meaningful.

My general introduction to the literature and history of formative Judaism is summarized elsewhere.[4] This book, in particular, carries forward the issues of three others, *the Academic Commentary* and *the Complete Outline*. That is because

---

[4] *The Doubleday Anchor Reference Library Introduction to Rabbinic Literature.* N.Y., 1994: Doubleday, and *Rabbinic Judaism. The Documentary History of the Formative Age.* Bethesda, 1994: CDL Press, and *Rabbinic Judaism. Its Structure and its System in the Formative Age.* Minneapolis, 1995: Fortress Press.

I decided those results when scattered among the several tractates do not make the impact that they should when seen all together and all at once, as they are here. The present volume collects and summarizes the results of two prior studies, which are as follows:

*The Talmud of Babylonia. An Academic Commentary.* Atlanta, 1994-6: Scholars Press for *USF Academic Commentary Series.*

| | |
|---|---|
| I. | *Bavli Tractate Berakhot* |
| II.A | *Bavli Tractate Shabbat. Chapters One through Twelve* |
| II.B | *Bavli Tractate Shabbat. Chapters Thirteen through Twenty-Four* |
| III.A | *Bavli Tractate Erubin. Chapters One through Five* |
| III.B | *Bavli Tractate Erubin. Chapters Six through Eleven* |
| IV.A | *Bavli Tractate Pesahim. Chapters One through Seven.* |
| IV.B | *Bavli Tractate Pesahim. Chapters Eight through Eleven.* |
| V. | *Bavli Tractate Yoma* |
| VI. | *Bavli Tractate Sukkah* |
| VII. | *Bavli Tractate Besah* |
| VIII. | *Bavli Tractate Rosh Hashanah* |
| IX. | *Bavli Tractate Taanit* [Outline only] |
| X. | *Bavli Tractate Megillah* |
| XI. | *Bavli Tractate Moed Qatan* |
| XII. | *Bavli Tractate Hagigah* |
| XIII.A | *Bavli Tractate Yebamot. Chapters One through Eight* |
| XIII.B | *Bavli Tractate Yebamot. Chapters Nine through Seventeen* |
| XIV.A | *Bavli Tractate Ketubot. Chapters One through Six* |
| XIV.B | *Bavli Tractate Ketubot. Chapters Seven through Fourteen* |
| XV. | *Bavli Tractate Nedarim* |
| XVI. | *Bavli Tractate Nazir* [Outline only.] |
| XVII. | *Bavli Tractate Sotah* |
| XVIII. | *Bavli Tractate Gittin* |
| XIX. | *Bavli Tractate Qiddushin* |
| XX. | *Bavli Tractate Baba Qamma* |
| XXI.A | *Bavli Tractate Baba Mesia. Chapters One through Six* |
| XXI.B | *Bavli Tractate Baba Mesia. Chapters Seven through Eleven* |
| XXII.A | *Bavli Tractate Baba Batra. Chapters One through Six* |
| XXII.B | *Bavli Tractate Baba Batra. Chapters Seven through Eleven* |
| XXIII.A | *Bavli Tractate Sanhedrin. Chapters One through Seven* |
| XXIII.B | *Bavli Tractate Sanhedrin. Chapters Eight through Twelve* |
| XXIV. | *Bavli Tractate Makkot* |
| XXV. | *Bavli Tractate Abodah Zarah* |
| XXVI. | *Bavli Tractate Horayot* |

| | |
|---|---|
| XXVII. | *Bavli Tractate Shebuot* |
| XXVIII.A | *Bavli Tractate Zebahim. Chapters One through Seven* |
| XXVIII.B | *Bavli Tractate Zebahim. Chapters Eight through Fifteen* |
| XXIX.A | *Bavli Tractate Menahot. Chapters One through Six* |
| XXIX.B | *Bavli Tractate Menahot. Chapters Seven through Fourteen* |
| XXX. | *Bavli Tractate Hullin* |
| XXXI. | *Bavli Tractate Bekhorot* |
| XXXII. | *Bavli Tractate Arakhin* |
| XXXIII. | *Bavli Tractate Temurah* |
| XXXIV. | *Bavli Tractate Keritot* |
| XXXV. | *Bavli Tractate Meilah and Tamid* |
| XXXVI. | *Bavli Tractate Niddah* |

Second, the *Complete Outline* allows us immediately to identify the entire corpus of relevant compositions and composites, and a systematic classification of those items and their indicative traits will certainly tell us what we do not now know about the preparation of the Bavli's other-than-Mishnah-exegetical compositions and composites.

*The Talmud of Babylonia. A Complete Outline.* Atlanta, 1995-6: Scholars Press for *USF Academic Commentary Series.*

| | |
|---|---|
| I.A | *Tractate Berakhot and the Division of Appointed Times. Berakhot, Shabbat, and Erubin.* |
| I.B | *Tractate Berakhot and the Division of Appointed Times. Pesahim through Hagigah.* |
| II.A. | *The Division of Women. Yebamot through Ketubot* |
| II.B. | *The Division of Women. Nedarim through Qiddushin* |
| III.A | *The Division of Damages. Baba Qamma through Baba Batra* |
| III.B | *The Division of Damages. Sanhedrin through Horayot* |
| IV.A | *The Division of Holy Things and Tractate Niddah. Zebahim through Hullin* |
| IV.B | *The Division of Holy Things and Tractate Niddah. Bekhorot through Niddah* |

Furthermore, the study takes its place alongside the form-historical project that is now complete, and that once more highlighted the important position in the Bavli of the topical composite that stands outside the framework of Mishnah-exegesis. But the topical miscellany proved a more important form than I realized when I worked on the Bavli in isolation from other documents and ignored form-historical considerations altogether. It was only when I reached the end of the following project that the truly formidable position accorded to the topical miscellany in the whole of Rabbinic literature made its impression on me. Then I determined to call attention to results that at the time struck me as interesting but not demanding systematic recapitulation. The form-history is as follows:

*The Documentary Form-History of Rabbinic Literature.* I. *The Documentary Forms of the Mishnah.* Atlanta, 1997: Scholars Press for South Florida Studies in the History of Judaism.

*The Documentary Form-History of Rabbinic Literature* II. *The Aggadic Sector: Tractate Abot, Abot deRabbi Natan, Sifra, Sifré to Numbers, and Sifré to Deuteronomy.* Atlanta, 1997: Scholars Press for South Florida Studies in the History of Judaism.

*The Documentary Form-History of Rabbinic Literature* III. *The Aggadic Sector:.Mekhilta Attributed to R. Ishmael and Genesis Rabbah.* Atlanta, 1997: Scholars Press for South Florida Studies in the History of Judaism.

*The Documentary Form-History of Rabbinic Literature* IV. *The Aggadic Sector:.Leviticus Rabbah, and Pesiqta deRab Kahana.* Atlanta, 1997: Scholars Press for South Florida Studies in the History of Judaism.

*The Documentary Form-History of Rabbinic Literature* V. *The Aggadic Sector: Song of Songs Rabbah, Ruth Rabbah, Lamentations Rabbati, and Esther Rabbah I.* Atlanta, 1997: Scholars Press for South Florida Studies in the History of Judaism.

*The Documentary Form-History of Rabbinic Literature.* VI. *The Halakhic Sector. The Talmud of the Land of Israel.* A. *Berakhot and Shabbat through Taanit.* Atlanta, 1997: Scholars Press for South Florida Studies in the History of Judaism.

*The Documentary Form-History of Rabbinic Literature.* VI. *The Halakhic Sector. The Talmud of the Land of Israel.* B. *Megillah through Qiddushin.* Atlanta, 1997: Scholars Press for South Florida Studies in the History of Judaism.

*The Documentary Form-History of Rabbinic Literature.* VI. *The Halakhic Sector. The Talmud of the Land of Israel.* C. *Sotah through Horayot and Niddah.* Atlanta, 1997: Scholars Press for South Florida Studies in the History of Judaism.

*The Documentary Form-History of Rabbinic Literature.* VII. *The Halakhic Sector. The Talmud of Babylonia.* A. *Tractates Berakhot and Shabbat through Pesahim.* Atlanta, 1997: Scholars Press for South Florida Studies in the History of Judaism.

*The Documentary Form-History of Rabbinic Literature.* VII. *The Halakhic Sector. The Talmud of Babylonia.* B. *Tractates Yoma through Ketubot.* Atlanta, 1997: Scholars Press for South Florida Studies in the History of Judaism.

*The Documentary Form-History of Rabbinic Literature.* VII. *The Halakhic Sector. The Talmud of Babylonia.* C. *Tractates Nedarim through Baba Mesia.* Atlanta, 1997: Scholars Press for South Florida Studies in the History of Judaism.

*The Documentary Form-History of Rabbinic Literature.* VII. *The Halakhic Sector. The Talmud of Babylonia.* D. *Tractates Baba Batra through Horayot.* Atlanta, 1997: Scholars Press for South Florida Studies in the History of Judaism.

*The Documentary Form-History of Rabbinic Literature.* VII. *The Halakhic Sector. The Talmud of Babylonia.* E. *Tractates Zebahim through Bekhorot.* Atlanta, 1997: Scholars Press for South Florida Studies in the History of Judaism.

*The Documentary Form-History of Rabbinic Literature.* VII. *The Halakhic Sector. The Talmud of Babylonia.* F. *Tractates Arakhin through Niddah. And Conclusions.* Atlanta, 1997: Scholars Press for South Florida Studies in the History of Judaism.

How do I explain the resort to the topical miscellany or composite? While these do not play a role in the exposition of a cogent thought set forth as Mishnah-commentary or propositional composition, they do supply important data for the advancement of the purposes of the framers of a commentary or a composition or a composite. In our own day we know might relegate much of the material collected in the topical miscellany into footnotes and appendices. But I think the topical miscellany takes a more integral part in the exposition of the Mishnah or its law and theology than an appendix of interesting information would have done. In our context a footnote adds information that is relevant to a proposition but that in the context of an exposition would interrupt the flow of the statement. An appendix sets forth a sizable block of information that the author deems necessary to the presentation, but that can find no economical location in the shank of a book. Since the authors of compositions and the framers of composites did not possess the technical capacity for subordinating information into footnotes or appendices, they inserted into the body of their text materials that interrupt the exposition at hand. I discovered the systematic intrusion of what in another context we should now call footnotes and appendices only late in my work of translation, that was one of the reasons that persuaded me to redo the entire translation in my Academic Commentary. That permits us to see with great perspicacity the precise components of a given composite and how they are put together.[5] Then comes the theological consequences, as new work will show in due course: how people made connections and drew conclusions. Form-analysis proves essential to any theological description that claims to originate in the canonical writings, not in contemporary theological category-formations.

---

[5] This matter is spelled out in *The Rules of Composition of the Talmud of Babylonia. The Cogency of the Bavli's Composite.* Atlanta, 1991: Scholars Press for South Florida Studies in the History of Judaism.

No one in the academic world enjoys more favorable circumstances for scholarship than I do here in Florida. I did most of the project of which this work is part at the University of South Florida as Distinguished Research Professor in the Florida State University System. I express my thanks for not only the advantage of a Distinguished Research Professorship in the Florida state university system, which for a scholar must be the best job in the world, but also of a substantial research expense fund, ample research time, and stimulating, straight-forward, and cordial colleagues, many of whom also are cherished friends.

I did this part of the commentary at Christchurch, New Zealand, where I served as Canterbury Visiting Fellow at the University of Canterbury. I express thanks to my friends and colleagues there, who made the visit a happy and productive one for both myself and my wife.

JACOB NEUSNER

DISTINGUISHED RESEARCH PROFESSOR OF RELIGIOUS STUDIES
UNIVERSITY OF SOUTH FLORIDA
TAMPA, FLORIDA 33620-5550 U.S.A.

# I

# The Structure of Babylonian Talmud Berakhot

### POINTS OF STRUCTURE

1  DOES BABYLONIAN TALMUD-TRACTATE BERAKHOT FOLLOW A COHERENT OUTLINE GOVERNED BY A CONSISTENT RULES?

The answer to this question for the thirty-six other tractates of the Bavli is simple. All but this one depend principally upon the Mishnah-tractate at hand for structure and order, and most, though not all, of the main units of discourse — large-scale discussions of a given topic, marked in my outlines by a capital letter — coincide with statements of the Mishnah, systematically expounded. Upon first impression, Bavli-tractate Berakhot appears to violate the rules of structure and cogency that predominate, and it seems to draw back from that insistence upon the privileging of the Mishnah that governs elsewhere.

More to the point, the composites that comprise these main units of discourse ordinarily appeal for cogency to Mishnah-exposition, the secondary expansion and amplification of the Mishnah's topics or the Mishnah's legal principles, and exposition of verses of Scripture deemed relevant to the Mishnah. An examination of the outlines of these other thirty-six tractates will show, therefore, that those tractates, and most of their large-scale composites, are formed around the requirements of Mishnah-exegesis. True, the proportions of the Mishnah's treatment of given topics may not govern; some tractates expand mightily upon what, in the Mishnah's discussion, is a mere detail. But, over all, we may say that all of the work of Talmud-compilation, and the larger part of the work of formation of composites used for the compilation, responds to the discipline imposed by the Mishnah.

That upon first glance, but for good and substantial reasons, is not the case with Bavli-tractate Berakhot, where the exposition of the Mishnah forms only one of the compilers' goals. In addition, they have included not only a number of topical composites related only tenuously to the Mishnah, an entirely familiar phenomenon, as a glance at, e.g., Menahot, will show, but also composites in no way required either for the purpose of Mishnah-amplification or even for the purpose of topical extension. These additional, anomalous composites include cogent propositional units, parachuted down without regard to Mishnah-exegesis but for some other reason involved in the framers' tractate-building. An example is the concluding unit, on the sages' virtues. But other composites are built upon principles that do not ordinarily take a prominent place in the Bavli.

First, we see composites that are formed around the repetition of attributive formula, e.g., said X said Y, lacking all other point of cogency.

Second, we find composites joining a shared attributive formula to a shared theme or even proposition.

Third, composites framed around a scriptural theme make their appearance, which is a phenomenon familiar in other tractates, but such composites may have little or nothing to do with the context into which they find their way, which is uncommon elsewhere.

Fourth, topics take a prominent place in the Talmud that the Mishnah-tractate at hand scarcely knows. Linking some of the topical composites to the Mishnah's program requires more than routine inquiry.

Of all of the anomalous composites, the one I find most difficult to accommodate within the theory of a purposive work of composition of composites and compilation thereof is the composite based solely on a single attributive formula. Where elsewhere these occur, and they do, the secondary and tertiary units of a given attributive-composite add up to a small aggregate at worst; here, they turn out to form a principal filler and they give to vast tracts of this tractate a random and episodic character. The case for the Talmud as a coherent statement expressed in a cogent form, made up of materials that in the aggregate are compiled to serve the document's main purposes, in Talmud tractate Berakhot competes only with difficulty with the case against that proposition.

The upshot is, the normal rules for composite-making for the Talmud that govern elsewhere — primary interest in Mishnah-exegesis and in the analysis of principles of law introduced in the Mishnah, secondary interest in topical exposition, lacking propositional cogency, of subjects introduced in the Mishnah, tertiary interest in systematic exposition of verses of Scripture in some way introduced in the work of Mishnah-exegesis, whether at the primary or secondary levels — those rules govern only in part. For use in Bavli-tractate Berakhot the compilers have selected, in addition, from types of composites that figure seldom, and never in such proportion, in other tractates. In the end, it is a matter of proportion, and the disproportionate utilization of composites of an other-than-Mishnah or legal or Mishnah-topical character, composites formed around other rationales of cogency entirely than the one that privileges the Mishnah, calls into question the thesis of this Outline overall. Not only so, but the smaller-than-usual proportion of systematic analytical inquiry, the near-absence, for pages at a time, of the rigorous inspection of logic, both exegetical logic and analytical logic, further differentiates this tractate from all of its companions. The presence of composites of an anomalous character

Chapter One. The Structure of Babylonian Talmud Berakhot 3

and proportion finds its match in the absence of the kind of dialectical-analytical composites that predominate in all other tractates. In a moment, we shall find reason to qualify these judgments, but, for the present, they define the problematic of our analysis, since they underscore the anomalous character of the Talmud's opening tractate.

2. WHAT ARE THE SALIENT TRAITS OF ITS STRUCTURE?

The tractate nonetheless finds its definitive organizing program in the Mishnah, and there is no other, competing program at all. The inclusion of large-scale composites of various types that bear no relationship to the requirements of Mishnah-exegesis or even exposition of the Mishnah's topics follows no rules I can discern. The prolix character of the tractate overall still leaves obvious the main lines of structure and order, which derive from the Mishnah-tractate. A comparison of Chapters Six and Eight, both of which exhibit the rest of the Talmud's admirable economy of analysis and discipline of focus, with, e.g., Chapters One and Nine tells the whole story. The latter chapters, which prove more typical of the tractate than the former, exhibit a prolix and promiscuous character, not so much organizing their composites and the larger compilation made of them by appeal to some theme other than Mishnah-exegesis as not organizing those compositions and the larger compilation at all.

3. WHAT IS THE RATIONALITY OF THE STRUCTURE?

Speaking from first impressions, some chapters conform to the rationality that predominates in the other tractates, and some do not. Specifically, for two chapters, Six and Eight, the rationality is the familiar one, Mishnah-exegesis, pure and simple. For two others, One and Nine, I discern no rationality at all. Hence, having already introduced the necessary qualification for that judgment, we shall once more appeal to the task of Mishnah-exegesis as the criterion of structure and order.

4. WHERE ARE THE POINTS OF IRRATIONALITY IN THE STRUCTURE?

Enough has been said already to answer that question. It suffices to underscore that criteria for irrationality (from the perspective of a document that privileges the Mishnah) are two: divergence from the discipline of Mishnah-exegesis for large-scale compilations, divergence from the principle of topical cogency for small-scale composites. My outline has already made provision for both criteria of irrationality. These are systematically catalogued presently, and our task is to refine and localize the judgments spelled out just now.

POINTS OF SYSTEM

1. DOES THE BABYLONIAN TALMUD-TRACTATE BERAKHOT SERVE ONLY AS A RE-PRESENTATION OF THE MISHNAH-TRACTATE OF THE SAME NAME?

The Mishnah-tractate follows a simple and orderly thematic program, making no important points of about those themes. The topics go over the rules of conduct in prayer, covering three subjects: first, the Shema, second, The Prayer, and third, Grace before and after Meals, with an appendix in Chapter Nine on blessings for other occasions. The Mishnah-tractate's presentation of these subjects focuses on the presentation of rules and information; no effort is made to discern within the subject a governing principle (one may hardly identify as more than obvious the principle that one must conduct one's liturgical life in a properly respectful manner). No generative problematic emerges from the presentation of the topic and imposes an unanticipated agenda of issues upon that topic.

The Talmud then takes a merely-informative, intellectually uncomplicated Mishnah-tractate, and, over all adds a great deal of information to the Mishnah's information, but in no way, and at no point, accomplishes that remarkable intellectual feat widely performed elsewhere of making the whole add up to more than the sum of the parts. For two reasons the answer is negative. The lesser is, some Mishnah-statements are not analyzed at all. The greater is, a disproportionate sector of the tractate as a whole has found both its problematic and its inner cogency in some provocation other than Mishnah-exegesis.

2. How do the topical composites fit into the Talmud-tractate Berakhot and what do they contribute that the Mishnah-tractate of the same name would lack without them?

This question is formulated in response to the character of all tractates but this one, since it takes for granted that composites that do not respond to the work of Mishnah-exegesis nonetheless will exhibit a topical principle of coherence, and that is not the case with important composites in this tractate. I present the account in three sections. On the left hand margin are important propositional composites that do not address the Mishnah's propositions but do affect them. Identify these items and distinguishing them from those on the right hand margin involve a measure of subjectivity, and for that reason, I have tried to impose the most rigorous and narrowest possible definition of what is both free-standing and also affective of the rest. In the center I give those utterly anomalous composites that ignore the principle of propositional or at least topical cogency altogether. At the right are the composites that complement the Mishnah's statements with topically relevant amplifications or that carry forward the Mishnah's principle to new data. Finally, I underline and also position in the center column large composites that strike me as entirely out of phase with the Mishnah, lacking all point of contact, whether topical or in principle or even theme, broadly construed.

What we shall now see seriously qualifies the first impression of the tractate, spelled out above.

# Chapter One. The Structure of Babylonian Talmud Berakhot

I.C: Topical Appendix on
the Division of the Night

I.E: Composite on Psalm 145

I.F: Miscellaneous Item, Out of Phase with its Context

I.G: Reciting the Shema on One's Bed

I.H: If a person sees that sufferings afflict him,
let him examine his deeds

I.I: The Tefillin of the Holy One, Blessed be He.
God's Presence in the Synagogue

I.J: Composite of Sayings of
Yohanan in the Name of Simeon b. Yohai

I.K: Composite of Sayings of
Hiyya bar Ammi in the Name of Ulla

I.L: Proper Conduct in
Synagogue Worship;
Proper Conduct
when the Torah is read

I.Q: Topical Composite
Concerning the Exodus

II.B: Topical Appendix on
Beruriah, Meir's Wife

II.C: Interpretation of
Diverse Verses of Scripture

IV.B: Exposition of M. Tamid 5:1

IV.D: Sayings of Rabbah bar Hinena, the elder,
in the name of Rab

VI.B: Topical Composite of Rules
on the Recitation of the Shema

IX.C: Various Prayers for
Special Occasions

X.B: The Honor Owing to the Deceased.
Do the Dead Communicate with the Living?

X.G: Giving One's Life for
the Sanctification of the Divine Name

XI.F: The Obligations of Women
to Carry Out various Commandments

XII.B: Sayings of Judah on
Grace after Meals and Other Prayers

XII.D: Topical Appendix on
the Status of One Who Has Had
a Seminal Emission

XIII.B: Topical Appendix on
Not Saying the Prayer When
One's Bodily Needs Intervene
XIX.B: The Prayer of Hannah
and What We Learn Therefrom
XIX.C: Thematic Appendix on Insolence
toward Heaven, with Special Reference to Moses
XIX.D: Thematic Composite on How to Pray;
the Value of Prayer;
and Other Liturgical Topics
XXIV.C: Miscellany of Interstitial Items
and the Blessings Assigned to Them
XXX.B: Topical Composite:
The Rules and Regulations of a Meal
XXX.N: Composite on How a Quorum
Is Reached for the Purposes of Prayer
XXX.O: Further Rules on Saying Grace
XXXII.D: The Proper and Appropriate
Handling of Bread
XXXII:E: Forgetting to Recite a Blessing
XXXII:F: The Matter of
Asparagus-Brew
XXXII.G: The Cup of Blessing
Prior to Recitation of Grace
XXIV:B: Topical Composite Concerning
Dreams and their Interpretation
XXXIV.S: Proper Conduct with Women
XXXIV.T: The Impulse to Do Evil
XXXIV.W: Rules of Conduct in the Privy
XXXIV.X: David's Conduct When Saul Was Defecating
XXIV.CC: Disquisitions on Hospitality
XXXIV.DD: Disquisition on the Virtues of Discipleship

3. Can we state what the compilers of this document propose to accomplish in producing this complete, organized piece of writing?

Our catalogue of a-rational or irrational composites yields an unanticipated result. Most, though not all, of the topical appendices that give the tractate the appearance of intellectual promiscuity occur in Chapters One and Nine, and some of the very largest of these and the most isolated from their larger context are in Chapter Nine, e.g., the immense composite concerning dreams. The anomalous composites made up around attributive formulas tend to concentrate in Chapter One; these prove few, though their irritating quality is not mitigated by their small

## Chapter One. The Structure of Babylonian Talmud Berakhot

proportion of the whole. Were we to examine only Chapters Two through Eight, we should find an essentially normal tractate, with few composites that are not devoted to Mishnah-exegesis or the amplification of the results or implications of Mishnah-exegesis.

The really interesting data emerge at the right hand column. What we have is a substantial volume of topical appendices, a much larger than usual collection of composites that, in my view, do little more than expand upon topics introduced, or at least invited, by the Mishnah's own topical program. Some obviously relate to the Mishnah's themes, if not its precise topics. Others are secondary to these (e.g., David's conduct when Saul was defecating obviously is subordinate to rules of conduct in the privy). Now at some points the judgment that we deal with topical appendices to the Mishnah's own topics or secondary developments upon the Mishnah's themes is hardy subjective. For example, once we deal with a Mishnah-rule about seemly conduct on the Temple mountain, then further expositions of seemly conduct in other special circumstances will find their place. Other inclusions in the right hand column may invite debate, and the case in favor of my classification may be outweighed by the case against.

Two conclusions emerge. First, the two composites that seriously revise our definition of the topic and even the principles of Mishnah-tractate Berakhot, while few, prove weighty. The first of the two makes the point that we control our destiny, and that our deeds govern. The second makes the complementary point that one may decide to give his or her life for the sanctification of God's name. Both points impart profound theological weight to the tractate's subject matter. But neither presents any surprises.

The second conclusion is that while, compared with other tractates' counterparts, the corpus of topical appendices proves disproportionately large, the appendices simply add information to information. Not only so, but where the tractate's exposition substantially departs from the Mishnah's program and seriously challenges the proposition that the Talmud in the aggregate comprises little more than a systematic exegesis and amplification of the Mishnah, the identified composites, inclusive of anomalous ones, collect in two chapters, and leave most of the rest of the tractate intact, standard and familiar re-presentations of the Mishnah within the basic hermeneutic dictated by the decision to privilege the Mishnah.

# II

# The Structure of Babylonian Talmud Shabbat

### Points of Structure

1. Does Babylonian Talmud-tractate Shabbat follow a coherent outline governed by a consistent rules?

While the tractate contains a number of compositions and composites formed around a program other than that of Mishnah-commentary and legal theory, the structure of the Talmud finds its framework in the Mishnah-tractate, and most sizable composites take shape around the work of Mishnah-commentary, exceptions being listed presently.

2. What are the salient traits of its structure?

The framers of the tractate consistently investigate the properties, formal and propositional, of the Mishnah-tractate; only when that work has been fully accomplished do they insert composites that address other concerns than those of Mishnah-exegesis, and, in that connection, they give priority to composites devoted to topics that intersect with those of the Mishnah or of Mishnah-exegesis over those that do not.

3. What is the Rationality of the structure?

What imparts coherence to the tractate is the Mishnah's statements, read in sequence, and the tractate overall is devoted to the task of Mishnah-exegesis; the principle of cogency derives solely from that work.

4. Where are the points of irrationality in the structure?

We find a variety of composites that originally coalesced around other topics than those introduced by the Mishnah, all the more so around other tasks than phrase-by-phrase Mishnah-exegesis. Some of these composites are formed around a common attributive formula, some around a common attributive formula and a common theme, many around a common theme or problem, and some few around the exegesis of successive verses of Scripture. In this tractate we find a number of composites made up of rules governing Sabbath observance; some of these exhibit a certain miscellaneous quality. Finally, some of the topical composites hold together by addressing a common theological proposition (few), or topic (many).

Seen all together, these diverse composites of an other-than-Mishnah-exegetical character form a sizable body but in no way affect the overall character of the tractate as organized around the Mishnah. Given the sheer volume of the Talmud, moreover, they do not vastly change the picture of the whole. The reason for that judgment is simple. We are able to specify the rules of agglutination (e.g., attributive formulas) or aggregation (e.g., topical coherence) that accounts for the formation of these anomalous composites, but, more to the point, we also are able to explain, case by case, why the framer of the Talmud found a place for a given anomalous composite. The upshot is, there are no "massive miscellanies" in our tractate, even though, viewed in their own terms, some of these anomalous composites do give the impression of a certain miscellaneous character. In the second rubric below we consider each item and its impact upon the tractate as a whole.

### POINTS OF SYSTEM

1. DOES THE BABYLONIAN TALMUD-TRACTATE SHABBAT SERVE ONLY AS A RE-PRESENTATION OF THE MISHNAH-TRACTATE OF THE SAME NAME?

The tractate's framers have dealt with most, though not all, of the statements of the Mishnah; they have included a fair number of composites that form topical or formal supplements to their principal ones. For these two, contradictory reasons, the answer to the question is a qualified negative. The tractate serves mainly as a systematic re-presentation of the Mishnah-tractate of the same name.

2. HOW DO THE TOPICAL COMPOSITES FIT INTO THE TALMUD-TRACTATE AND WHAT DO THEY CONTRIBUTE THAT THE MISHNAH-TRACTATE OF THE SAME NAME WOULD LACK WITHOUT THEM?

I present the account in three sections. On the left hand margin are important propositional composites that do not address the Mishnah's propositions but do affect them. Identifying these items and distinguishing them from those on the right hand margin involve a measure of subjectivity, and for that reason, I have tried to impose the most rigorous and narrowest possible definition of what is both free-standing and also affective of the rest. In the center I give those utterly anomalous composites that ignore the principle of propositional or at least topical cogency altogether. These often find cogency in a shared attributive formula, as indicated. At the right are the composites that complement the Mishnah's statements with topically relevant amplifications or that carry forward the Mishnah's principle to new data. Some of these entries complement a composite devoted to the Mishnah by taking up a subordinate theme and exploring that theme. Finally, I underline and also position in the center column large composites that strike me as entirely

## Chapter Two. The Structure of Babylonian Talmud Shabbat

out of phase with the Mishnah, lacking all point of contact, whether topical or in principle or even theme, broadly construed. These items further do not link up to composites that relate to the Mishnah and therefore from the perspective of my claim that the tractate takes shape as Mishnah-commentary and further extends from that purpose to some other, are totally free-standing. We can often explain why a given item is parachuted down, but we cannot show a rational link of any compelling sort between that item and its context.

II.F COMPOSITE OF SAYINGS IN THE ATTRIBUTIVE, AND SAID RABA BAR MEHASAYYA SAID R. HAMA BAR GURIA SAID RAB

VI.J THE HANUKKAH LAMP. THE FESTIVAL OF HANUKKAH [attached to the discussion of the Sabbath Lamp: They do not kindle the Sabbath light with them' are also not used for kindling the Hanukkah lamp, either on the Sabbath or on weekdays]

VI.L: HANUKKAH IN THE LITURGY

XI.B: TOPICAL APPENDIX: THE STATUS OF THE BOOKS OF QOHELET AND PROVERBS [The prior unit makes reference to pertinent verses, which provide the slender basis for including this sizable composite; the principle of composition is agglutinative; a tangential reference then validates the insertion of what amounts to a ready-made appendix]

XI.C: ANSWER NOT A FOOL ACCORDING TO HIS FOLLY. THE IMPORTANCE OF HUMILITY. Whether or not this item continues XI.B settles the question of classification, either as a continuation of the foregoing or as a completely anomalous intrusion; I am inclined to prefer the former alternative, but it is surely a matter of judgment.

XI.D.MISCELLANY: THE STUDY OF THE TORAH AND THE PRESENCE OF GOD. However we classify the foregoing, the present item must be treated as miscellaneous and not really cogent, and also as inserted for no clear reason of a formal, let alone a substantive, character.

XXX.M Taking Responsibility for What Happens in the Community
This item certainly glosses the one to which it is attached, which says that one is responsible for something that he could have prevented.

XXXIII.E: Topical Composite on the Theme of Women Who Indulge Themselves in Luxury
The reference in the Mishnah to a woman's carrying a perfume flask accounts for the inclusion of this item.

XXXIV.C: Disciples of Sages; Torah Study and its Value.
The Mishnah's dispute on the status of weapons of war provokes the insertion of this item, which complements the discussion of what is ugly in man with what is beautiful, thus, study of the Torah, with special emphasis on conflict over the Torah, as in the opening item, "Two disciples of sages sharpen one another in law. Thus the insertion is pointed and specific to its context and provides an important comment on the implications of sages' position in the Mishnah: appropriate conflict, which is for the sake of Heaven. Here there is a defensible claim that the composite forms a wry comment on the Mishnah and imparts to its rule a dimension otherwise absent.

XXXIV:E: The Susceptibility to Uncleanness of Woven Material

XXXIV.F: "And we have brought the Lord's offering, what each man has gotten of jewels of gold, ankle chains, and bracelets, signet rings and ear rings and armlets" (Num. 31:50) This is not completely out of phase with the Mishnah's topical program, but it hardly supplements the Mishnah in any ordinary way.

XXXVIII.B: What Is Bad, Good for Health. Includes a Common attributive: Said Abin bar Huna said R. Hama bar Guria, but that does not predominate throughout.

XLV.D: Composite on Antidotes and Remedies

XLVIII:D: Utilization of Stones to Clean Up after Defecating. This item adds another reason for carrying stones on the Sabbath.

LIII:B: Topical Appendix on the Revelation at Sinai

LXIV:B: Topical Appendix on Clay Utensils

LXV:B: Topical Appendix on the Wood-Gatherer of Num. 15:32. This item complements the Mishnah-amplification that precedes it.

LXV:D: The Boards of the Tabernacle in the Wilderness Like the foregoing, this is integral to the Mishnah-exegesis that invokes the generative analogy of building the tabernacle in the wilderness.

LXXIV:C: Topical Appendix on the Meanings of Letters of the Alphabet

LXXVIII:B: Topical Composite on Mourning for a Sage. Once more we introduce to a general topic a particular perspective deriving from sages' concerns.

LXXIX:A. COMMENT ON AN
INTERSECTING MISHNAH-PASSAGE
This composite is inserted for essentially formal reasons
LXXXII:E: TOPICAL APPENDIX ON
MATERIALS USED FOR PHYLACTERIES
The question, What is the law on writing phylacteries
on the skin of a clean fish? is hardly required in context,
and so far as I can see, it also does not contribute
to a different perspective on the Mishnah's rule.
LXXXIII:C: TOPICAL APPENDIX
ON DISEASES AND THE
USE ON THE SABBATH
OF THEIR REMEDIES
Once we deal with materials used for healing,
the appendix is a natural next step
LXXXIX.B: COMPOSITE ON RUTH,
BEGINNING WITH HER PREPARATION
OF PROPER GARMENTS FOR THE SABBATH
The reason for including this composite
is made explicit in context. The connection
is substantive but still tangential to the aggregation
of the composite itself.

LXXXIX:C: FURTHER
ON PROPER DRESS
ON THE SABBATH
This propositional composite is integral
to the context of the Mishnah-rule.
XCI:A: FREE-STANDING DISCUSSION WHICH
INVOKES OUR MISHNAH-RULE AS A SUBORDINATED FACT
IN ITS ANALYTICAL ARGUMENT.
Because there is a clear point of intersection,
I do not see this item as irrational (within the
present sense of the word) but as peripheral.
XCII:C: THE PLEASURES OF THE SABBATH
AND THE REWARDS FOR OBSERVING ITS SANCTITY
This free-standing composite is one of several
to place into context the Mishnah-tractate's burden
of detailed rules, underscoring the main point of
Sabbath-observance.

XCII:D: A Further Miscellany: On What Count Do People Achieve Merit to Enjoy Other Benefits; Further Rewards for Keeping the Sabbath. Punishment for failure to Keep the Sabbath

XCVI:C: Miscellany on Disposition on the Sabbath of Objects in the Household of Rabbi
<u>I have no idea why this item is introduced or placed where it is.</u>

CV:C: Hospitality. Giving People the Benefit of the Doubt
The topic is introduced by the Mishnah-rule, but is treated in its own terms.

CVII:C: On the Matter of Bloodletting
This is a free-standing composite, introduced because it intersects with its context in the Talmud.

CVIII:C: The Importance of Circumcision
Accommodated by the topical context.

CXIV:D: Topical Appendix on the Proposition that the Torah is destined to be forgotten in Israel:
This is invited by its context as an expansion on the proposition, which is stated explicitly in the immediately-preceding passage.

CXVI:B: Composite of Rulings on the Sabbath in Hisda's Name, joined to begin with as a gloss to the foregoing

CXVIII:B: Miscellaneous Rulings on Sabbath Conduct
<u>This composite has absolutely no bearing on the Mishnah-paragraph with which it is situated, in detail or even in general.</u>

CXXIII:C: FREE-STANDING COMPOSITION,
INSERTED BECAUSE IT INTERSECTS WITH
A SUBORDINATE DETAIL IN THE PRIOR COMPOSITION.
CXXVIII:D: FURTHER EXEGESIS OF
"HOW ARE YOU YOU FALLEN FROM HEAVEN,
DAY STAR, SON OF THE MORNING?
HOW ARE YOU CUT DOWN TO THE GROUND,
YOU WHO CAST LOTS THE SAME WORD
AS OCCURS HERE OVER THE NATIONS" (ISA. 14:12)
CXXXII:B: MISCELLANEOUS
SAYING ON THE TOPIC OF DEATH.
Invited by the Mishnah's topic.
CXXXII:C: SAYINGS AND
STORIES ON OLD AGE
Continues the foregoing, in a general way.
CXXXII.D: BEHAVIOR IN
THE PRESENCE OF
THE CORPSE. THE SOUL
CXXXV:D: COMPOSITE ON ASTROLOGY.
ATTACHED FOR FORMAL REASON
"IT WAS WRITTEN IN THE NOTEBOOK OF "

3.  CAN WE STATE WHAT THE COMPILERS OF THIS DOCUMENT PROPOSE TO ACCOMPLISH IN PRODUCING THIS COMPLETE, ORGANIZED PIECE OF WRITING?

The three columns yield one conclusion. The tractate's principal program of Mishnah-exegesis has not prevented the compilers from inserting a variety of composites that in no way contribute to the realization of the basic program. The composites that may impart to the Mishnah-tractate a meaning not present but invited through the proper juxtaposition of contrast or complement are few and typical, mostly invocations of the perspective on all things deriving from the sponsorship of the project, disciples of sages themselves. The composites that are inserted as topical appendices in no way change the character of the tractate overall. They really serve only to add to its bulk, but in that way they place the compilers well within the framework of everyday authors known through history, who for the sake of completeness write longer books than absolutely required. What I learn from the middle column is that available to the compilers, and occasionally utilized by them, were a number of composites framed for purposes other than those of Mishnah-commentary and expansion or legal inquiry; I do not see how these odd entries vastly change the face of the tractate. They attest only to lapses of judgment of compilers who, overall, have given us a Talmud remarkable for its cogency. Of these entries into the middle column, those framed around a common attributive prove easiest to accommodate within the theory of a coherent and purposeful

Talmud; those formulated around a common theme or even proposition, curiously, the least cogent. In these latter cases, the difficulty we have in explaining why a given composite is located where it is and not somewhere else is telling. By contrast, we can answer the critical question of location of every composite and secondary composition in the entire tractate but for these few. And that makes the case.

The really interesting problem emerges when, these results in hand, we ask ourselves precisely where and how the framers speak for their own perspective and in their own account and not merely as the extenuating voices of the Mishnah. We cannot identify their distinctive viewpoint at any point at which the compilers or writers propose to amplify the Mishnah's sense. That is by definition; and, I should claim, to make the case that the Mishnah-exegetes vastly revised the clear intent and program of the Mishnah will prove difficult indeed, if the data of this tractate (among many) are supposed to register. Not only so, but so vast a proportion of the tractate's compositions is devoted to Mishnah-exegesis that the framers or compilers clearly exhibit slight concern for leaving for themselves space for a free-standing message. Since it is the fact that the Judaic system put forth by the Talmud radically recasts the inherited one, we shall have for the moment to entertain the hypothesis that the work of formulating ideas that do not merely paraphrase those of the Mishnah went on elsewhere than in the circles that privileged the Mishnah and imposed its priority upon all other writings; or went on in these same circles, but only at another level of their writing.

Those other circles of writers, or those other opportunities of writing, then provided the occasion for stating ideas of a fresh and original character and not simply meant to recapitulate those of the Mishnah. Then, in the secondary results before us, in the extensions and supplements to the Mishnah in our Talmud, in the composites framed around propositions not supplied by the Mishnah and formulated for a purpose other than that of Mishnah-exegesis, these writers found their own voice. These the compilers then insinuated into their primary document, sometimes in autonomous settings, but mostly, in the very center of Mishnah-commentary itself.

# III

## The Structure of Babylonian Talmud Erubin

### POINTS OF STRUCTURE

1. DOES BABYLONIAN TALMUD-TRACTATE ERUBIN FOLLOW A COHERENT OUTLINE GOVERNED BY A CONSISTENT RULES?

The outline of the Mishnah encompasses nearly all of the composites of the Talmud, and the Talmud lays out its composites in accord with the topical and propositional program of the Mishnah-tractate.

2. WHAT ARE THE SALIENT TRAITS OF ITS STRUCTURE?

The order and logical progress of the Mishnah-tractate account for the place and swequence of nearly all of the Talmud's composites.

3. WHAT IS THE RATIONALITY OF THE STRUCTURE?

The principles of cogency and coherence derive from the Mishnah-tractate's sense of the same matters.

4. WHERE ARE THE POINTS OF IRRATIONALITY IN THE STRUCTURE?

I see two points of irrationality. First, we have compositions in which a problem quite external to our Mishnah-tractate is investigated; a passage of our Mishnah-tractate is introduced in a subordinate way because the facts therein contained contribute to the solution of the problem around which said composition takes shape. These compositions do not contribute to the exposition of our Mishnah-tractate. Second, a few composites follow their own program and in no way respond to that of the Mishnah-tractate or take up propositions or even themes provoked by its contents. These are given below.

### POINTS OF SYSTEM

1. DOES THE BABYLONIAN TALMUD-TRACTATE ERUBIN SERVE ONLY AS A RE-PRESENTATION OF THE MISHNAH-TRACTATE OF THE SAME NAME?

A few Mishnah-sentences are not discussed; some composites ignore the Mishnah-tractate's principles of coherence; but in the main, what we have, and all we have, is a commentary to the Mishnah-tractate.

2. How do the topical composites fit into the Talmud-tractate and what do they contribute that the Mishnah-tractate of the same name would lack without them?

I present the account in three sections. On the left hand margin are important propositional composites that do not address the Mishnah's propositions but do affect them. Identifying these items and distinguishing them from those on the right hand margin involve a measure of subjectivity, and for that reason, I have tried to impose the most rigorous and narrowest possible definition of what is both free-standing and also affective of the rest. In the center I give those utterly anomalous composites that ignore the principle of propositional or at least topical cogency altogether. At the right are the composites that complement the Mishnah's statements with topically relevant amplifications or that carry forward the Mishnah's principle to new data. Finally, I underline and also position in the center column large composites that strike me as entirely out of phase with the Mishnah, lacking all point of contact, whether topical or in principle or even theme, broadly construed.

                                                II.F: Topical Appendix on Meir
                                  II:G: Topical Appendix on Disputes
                                                      of the Houses

                  VI:C: Free-standing composite
                                      IX:: Topical Appendix on Woman
                                  and Correct Behavior with Women

XXXI:A: Large-Scale Composite on the
Importance of Memorizing Words and
Traditions in a Precise Way;
Mnemonics; Orthography;
The Role of Mnemonics in Torah-Study
                                      XXXI:D: The Impact of Ecology
                                                        on Residence
                                XXXI:E: Measuring the Space of a Town

XXXVIII:B: Topical Appendix
on Decision-Making:
Masters and Disciples
XXXVIII:D: The Affects of Strong Drink
on Giving Decisions, Praying, and the Like
                              LXXIV:C: Appendix of Sayings
                                  in the Attributive Formula,
                     Said R. Ammi bar Abba said R. Assi

## Chapter Three. The Structure of Babylonian Talmud Erubin 21

3. CAN WE STATE WHAT THE COMPILERS OF THIS DOCUMENT PROPOSE TO ACCOMPLISH IN PRODUCING THIS COMPLETE, ORGANIZED PIECE OF WRITING?

There is some disorganization, with the systematic and orderly exegesis of the Mishnah-passage interrupted by inserted compositions, as at unit XXXVIII. But these are exceptional in this tractate, and rarer still in others. That is all the more reason to identify this tractate as standard and routine in its Talmud: a systematic commentary to the Mishnah, bearing a few composites that take shape around problems are than those of Mishnah-exegesis. of these, the ones in the left-hand line, that is, those imparting a dimension to the reading of the Mishnah that, on its own, the Mishnah-tractate does not evince, take up as their principal issue the interests of disciples of sages, how they master the Torah, how they make decision, proper conduct, and the like. Those that simply complement with further information subjects introduced by the Talmud in the amplification of the Mishnah need not detain us. And a few, those centered in the foregoing catalogue, show us principles of the formation of composites that derive from conceptions of cogency other than those of topic and logic, mostly notions of coherence of a formal, rather than a topical character.

I see no way in which Bavli-tractate Erubin distinguishes itself from the norm. Where the framers insert composites that, in my judgment, materially affect the presentation of the Mishnah-tractate's topic, these have to do with the special interests of sages themselves. Otherwise, all we have are some secondary additions of information deemed somehow supplementary to the main labor of Mishnah-exegesis, and a handful of composites formed by appeal to considerations of aggregation other than those held rational by the authors of most of our composites and compilers of the Talmud-tractate overall. The principles of rational discourse and of cogent connection that govern, of making connections and drawing conclusions, are those that are standard for cogent discourse governed by Graeco-Roman, therefore Western thought: logic, topical order, connection between like things and differentiation of the unlike, and coherence of a substantive, as distinct from a formal, character.

# IV

# The Structure of Babylonian Talmud Pesahim

## POINTS OF STRUCTURE

1. DOES BABYLONIAN TALMUD-TRACTATE PESAHIM FOLLOW A COHERENT OUTLINE GOVERNED BY A CONSISTENT RULES?

The framers of the tractate have given a systematic commentary to the Mishnah-tractate assigned to them, omitting reference to only a few lines. The coherent outline is governed by the Mishnah-tractate. I see only occasional sequences of compositions (all the more so composites) in which a single coherent problem other than Mishnah-commentary governs the discussion of a Mishnah-rule. There are, to be sure, free-standing composites, not formed around the requirement of Mishnah-analysis or secondary expansion, but these are few and occur episodically and not in accord with a large-scale redactional program. The sole redactional principle of sequence, order, and cogency derives from the Mishnah-tractate.

2. WHAT ARE THE SALIENT TRAITS OF ITS STRUCTURE?

The Mishnah's phrases, clauses, or rules dictate the order and program of the Talmud's compositions and composites, with the Tosefta's or an external Tannaite rule's phrases or propositions occasionally contributing to the same. Secondary expansion then fills up the bulk of the tractate, e.g., analysis of a proposition, testing of a proposed solution, or exposition of the exegesis of the written Torah that underpins the rule at hand.

3. WHAT IS THE RATIONALITY OF THE STRUCTURE?

The Mishnah's rules, in the sequence in which they occur, tell the framers what comes first and what must follow, on the one side, and how one thing holds together with another, on the other side.

4. WHERE ARE THE POINTS OF IRRATIONALITY IN THE STRUCTURE?

A number of free-standing composites, formed around topics or problems not contributed by the Mishnah-tractate, occur. These are dealt with below.

## Points of System

1. Does the Babylonian Talmud-tractate Pesahim serve only as a re-presentation of the Mishnah-tractate of the same name?

The answer is qualifiedly affirmative, since not every line of the Mishnah is supplied with a gloss, and, further, the free-standing composites lead in directions not to be predicted on the basis of the Mishnah's materials. But the omitted sentences of the Mishnah are few, and the proportion of free-standing composites negligible. The Talmud-tractate is formed with the purpose of commenting on the Mishnah and accomplishes that purpose, and, seen whole, it accomplishes no other purpose.

2. How do the topical composites fit into the Talmud-tractate and what do they contribute that the Mishnah-tractate of the same name would lack without them?

I present the account in three sections. On the left hand margin are important propositional composites that do not address the Mishnah's propositions but do affect them. At the right are the composites that complement the Mishnah's statements with topically relevant amplifications or that carry forward the Mishnah's principle to new data. Finally, I underline and also position in the center column large composites that strike me as entirely out of phase with the Mishnah, lacking all point of contact, whether topical or in principle or even theme, broadly construed. Identifying these items and distinguishing them from those on the right hand margin involve a measure of subjectivity, and for that reason, I have tried to impose the most rigorous and narrowest possible definition of what is both free-standing and also affective of the rest. In the center I give those utterly anomalous composites that ignore the principle of propositional or at least topical cogency altogether.

> I.B: Composite on the Use of Refined Language and Euphemisms in General. The Problem of word-choices is expanded and made a matter of morality.
> I.F: Those who are agents to carry out a religious duty are not injured either when they go or when they come back. Secondary observation in connection with a Mishnah-Rule.
> X.B: Topical Appendix on Rules governing the Misappropriation of Food in the state of Heave-Offering. Free-Standing Analysis Utilizing the Mishnah-Rule

XI.I: Topical Appendix Concerning
the definition of Bread-Dough
XVIII.B: Free-Standing Composite
Inserted for Formal Reasons

XXII.B: A Meal as a Religious Duty.
Marriage to a Disciple of a Sage.
The Unlettered Person and
the Disciple of the Sage. The Mishnah-rule
augmented here is shifted to stress on the
particular merit accruing to the disciple
of a sage.
XXIII.C: Thematic Composite:
Sloth, The Correct Attitude to Work
and to Religious Duties. This places
the Mishnah-rule in a new context.

XV.B: Topical Composite on
the Sabbath Light
XXV.C: Formal Composite
Supplementing the Foregoing
XXXI.D: Topical and
Formal Supplement
XXXVI.C:Composite on the Resurrection
of the Dead, Inserted in Extension of II:2
This is included for solely formal
reasons and has no relationship
to its broader context, fore or aft.
LII.B: Composite on Daughters and Wives,
with Special Reference to Hosea
LII.C: The Exile and Hosea's Prophecy
LXII.B: Composite on the
Dimensions of the World
LXX.B: Topical Composite on Eating toward
the Time of the Daily Whole-Offering
of the Afternoon. The Order of Blessings
at the End of the Sabbath and Festivals.
LXX.C: Sanctifying the Sabbath Day with Wine
LXX.G: Topical Appendix:
Drinking in Pairs; the Danger of
Doing Deeds in Pairs
LXX.H: Composite on
the Danger of Shade. Demons

LXX.J: Appendix on Wise Counsel of
Sages to their Sons and Disciples
LXXV.C, E: Topical Composite on the Great Hallel
LXXV.D: Topical Composite on the
Difficulty of Making a Living

The bulk of the composites not devoted to Mishnah-exegesis are formulated around free-standing topics and inserted as topical supplements to composites devoted to Mishnah-exegesis and amplification. A handful are formulated around formal, and not substantive, principles of aggregation and cohesion; but as usual, these prove negligible in number and unimportant in proportion. Determining which, if any, free-standing composites actually affect the sense or meaning of the Mishnah or require us to read a rule of the Mishnah in an unanticipated context proves remarkable subjective, and thoughtful readers may well assign to the right hand column every item that strikes me as belonging to the re-visioning of the Mishnah-tractate. I bring to the matter the experience acquired in the analysis of other tractates, where the imposition of the dimension of Torah-study and sages' particular concerns clearly reshapes our reading of the topic of the Mishnah (e.g., Moed Qatan), in a way in which, in this tractate, we are scarcely required to concede. So, in all I see the bulk of the autonomous composites as topical in formulation — lacking important and sustaining propositions — and bearing slight affect upon the presentation of the Mishnah-tractate. The composites that I have identified as essentially distinct from the labor of Mishnah-exegesis and amplification turn out to leave untouched the Talmud's reading of the Mishnah.

3. CAN WE STATE WHAT THE COMPILERS OF THIS DOCUMENT PROPOSE TO ACCOMPLISH IN PRODUCING THIS COMPLETE, ORGANIZED PIECE OF WRITING?

Some tractates of the Mishnah provide information on a topic, others explore the inner logic and deeper dimensions of that same topic. The comparison between Mishnah-tractate Rosh Hashanah, which is informative but hardly sustained by a profound problematic of a theoretical character, and Mishnah-tractate Besah suffices to exemplify the distinction at hand; numerous other contrasts can serve with equal effect, e.g., Mishnah-tractates Terumot, Ohalot, and Tohorot as against Mishnah-tractates Sanhedrin, Berakhot, and Negaim.[1] Overall, I should point to the Divisions of Agriculture and Purities as comprising mostly tractates of a

---

[1] *A History of the Mishnaic Law of Purities* (Leiden, 1974ff.: E. J. Brill) etc., in forty-three volumes, and *Judaism. The Evidence of the Mishnah*. Chicago, 1981: University of Chicago Press. Second edition, augmented: Atlanta, 1987: Scholars Press for Brown Judaic Studies, suffice to spell out the point that the tractates of the Mishnah vary in important and profound ways and can be classified by objective traits; some are merely informative concerning their topic, others profoundly speculative concerning theirs.

## Chapter Four. The Structure of Babylonian Talmud Pesahim

profoundly theoretical character, and to the Divisions of Appointed Times and Women as made up mostly of tractates that inform but hardly provoke deep, abstract thought. The hypothesis I wish now to propose is, in intellectual ambition the Talmud-tractates match the Mishnah-tractates.

In that context we may take up the Talmud as well, with the present tractate as our example. Clearly, the Mishnah-tractate includes only a few provocative and profound passages but a great many merely informative ones; Chapter Ten provides a fine example of a chapter that is intellectually inert, even though rich in theological and ritual statements. Now what I find striking is that where we are given composites not required for Mishnah-exegesis, most of them prove merely informative; they collect a great many statements of a topical character, but none of them vastly changes the sense, context, or meaning of the Mishnah-tractate, either as to its specific rulings, or, more to the point, as to its deeper dimensions of meaning. Just as Mishnah-tractate Sanhedrin amasses vast composites of information, so its Talmud, completing the exposition of the Mishnah's topics, enriches those topics with more information; but the theoretical reading of the subject-matter of the tractate is untouched. And the same is so here. Where, by contrast, the Mishnah-tractate pursues a topic in such a way as to expose its theoretical complexity, there the appended, free-standing composites will carry forward the complete re-presentation of the Mishnah-tractate, the cases of Moed Qatan and Besah sufficing to exemplify the point.

Masters of the Talmud quite rightly insist that the tractates are all pretty much the same, and that is the fact when matters of a formal character are examined. The coherence and cogency of the Talmud overall strike anyone who moves from one tractate to another. These derive from the rigid forms of rhetoric and philosophical argument that prevail throughou. *The Talmud when reading the Mishnah finds* the way to say the same thing about many different things, and that forms part of its remarkable power of coherent discourse. But the tractates, devoted to the Mishnah's various topics, themselves lay claim to a careful analysis in their own terms, and, when they get it, they turn out to exhibit quite diverse traits of mind and capacity of intellect, some providing a recapitulation of the Mishnah's topic in its own terms, others asking us to imagine the Mishnah's topic in another context and manner altogether. The present tractate, with its burden of topical appendices that add masses of information but hardly reshape the face of things, shows us how a given Mishnah-tractate's own intellectual limitations will be replicated, and, I think, vastly magnified, by the Talmud's Mishnah-exegetes. These masters — surely the same figures, or, at any rate, bearing the same names from one tractate to another — prove brilliant where brilliance is required, mundane and merely informed and informative where mere erudition suffices.

# V

# The Structure of Babylonian Talmud Yoma

## Points of Structure

1. Does Babylonian Talmud-tractate Yoma follow a coherent outline governed by a consistent rules?

The Mishnah-tractate dictates the Talmud's treatment of its topic, and seen whole, the Bavli-tractate belongs in the classification of a commentary. The order of topics demonstrates that fact, since at only a very few points are we unable to relate a large-scale composite to the topical program of Mishnah-tractate Yoma. And, as those who have reviewed the tractates now in print will have noted, other tractates do not even demand that we recognize exceptions of any kind. Indeed, this tractate derives much of its power from its elaborate presentations of topics that in the Mishnah receive only a little attention, or none at all. But for that same reason it proves exceptional when compared to the tractates that address only the Mishnah's propositions, or the Mishnah's topics seen as themes, rather than as the occasion for propositional exercises at all.

2. What are the salient traits of its structure?

Overall, we find two distinct components of the structure of the Talmud-tractate: comments on the Mishnah, generally episodic if also systematic, and also large-scale composites.

3. What is the Rationality of the structure?

The rationality of the document finds its definition in the principles of Mishnah-exegesis, on the one side, and the program of Mishnah-re-presentation on the other. That is to say, if we were to remove all of the compositions and composites not linked to Mishnah-amplification in one form or the other, we should find little left of the tractate as we know it.

4. Where are the points of irrationality in the structure?

I identify these asymptomatic entries: I.A, B, E, G, VII.D, VIII.A, XII.G, XIV.B, D, XV.E, XVIII.F, XIX.C, E, XX.B, XXXV.B, C, D, E, G, XXXVI.B, C, H, I, XL.C, XLI.D, H. Now the issue is, how have these entries changed the face of the Bavli-tractate's re-presentation of the Mishnah-tractate?

## POINTS OF SYSTEM

1. DOES THE BABYLONIAN TALMUD-TRACTATE YOMA SERVE ONLY AS A REPRESENTATION OF THE MISHNAH-TRACTATE OF THE SAME NAME?

This question finds its answer in two facts. First, how many compositions of the Mishnah-tractate altogether lack Talmud-discussions? The answer is, few, and these prove episodic. We cannot predict which Mishnah-paragraphs will lack Talmud-compositions or propose a theory on the traits that would characterize the Mishnah-sentences that are treated or those that are not. The matter appears to me to be random. Second, and perhaps of greater interest, how many composites in the Talmud stand completely out of relationship with the Mishnah? That question is answered in the next rubric.

2. HOW DO THE TOPICAL COMPOSITES FIT INTO THE TALMUD-TRACTATE YOMA AND WHAT DO THEY CONTRIBUTE THAT THE MISHNAH-TRACTATE OF THE SAME NAME WOULD LACK WITHOUT THEM?

The tractate is formidable in size, and it carries with it a large and important component of free-standing composites, some of which intersect with the Mishnah in topic, others of which bear upon the theme of the tractate but make no contribution to the amplification of anything that the Mishnah-tractate has to say about that theme. We know that the compilers undertake an initiative of weight when we find jarring juxtapositions. We may suppose that the compilers mean only to provide information, not an occasion for reflection through startling points of intersection, when a topic introduced in the Mishnah in a tangential way is given an exposition lacking all argument or coherent point. The difference then is the mixing of things ordinarily kept distinct as against the provision of information on a subject. This becomes clear in the exposition that follows.

I.A: The framers begin with a remarkable conception, which is to compare the rite of the Day of Atonement with another rite, so placing Leviticus Sixteen into relationship with other systematic Pentateuchal expositions of the most distinguish offerings of the cultic calendar. In selecting another rite for comparison, what guided them? I see three distinct considerations. First is the formal one, which is articulated: rites that demand that the high priest prepare for a week in advance. But there are more than formal considerations. For, second, the compilers surely reflected on critical cultic occasions that brought the cult outside the walls of the Temple. Since a major step in the order of service here is to send forth the scapegoat, it is quite natural to take up a comparable occasion on which a sacrifice is made outside of the Temple. For that purpose, the rite of burning the red cow to produce ashes for purification water, in line with the rite described at Numbers Chapter Nineteen, comes to mind; that offering is not in the Temple but on Mount of Olives. What draws these two offerings into

## Chapter Five. The Structure of Babylonian Talmud Yoma 31

alignment is a third quality. The scapegoat carries with it the sins of the people; the purification-water bears the classification of *hat'at,* translated both purification- and sin. In the present context, therefore, by raising the question of how rites compare, two rites of atonement, one for uncleanness, the other for sin, are drawn into alignment for purposes of comparison and contrast. But having moved beyond the limits of the Talmud's presentation, I note at the end the formal consideration obviously governs, even though the substantive effect — introducing the notion of rites that take up conduct outside of the cult — is to direct attention from the inner to the outer dimensions of the Day. This initiative at the formal level finds its counterpart in substantive ways, as we shall see, when the Talmud insists in its re-presentation of the topic of the Day of Atonement upon asking about considerations external to the Temple and its cult but critical to the life of Israel and its sanctification and salvation.

I.B: The initiative at the opening composite is carried forward on a still larger scale at I.B: what makes the requirement of the Day of Atonement unique, and how we relate the rules governing that day with those governing another comparable occasion, the consecration of the Tent of Meeting. The upshot is that in the majestic opening reading, the Mishnah's simple, factual account is left behind, as the topic, the rite of the Day of Atonement, is addressed in its own, much larger setting of comparable rites, first, the burning of the red cow, second, the consecration of the tent of meeting. Only at I.C, D, do we come back to the high priesthood.

I.E: As if I.A, B, did not suffice to draw attention from the Mishnah's facts to the context, I.E really revises the entire matter, and the composite does so in a dramatic way. Now the entire face of the presentation by the Mishnah changes. From purification of sin and uncleanness, on the one side, and the formation of the tabernacle/Temple, on the other, we proceed to what is always the critical issue in the Rabbinic system, the destruction of the Temple. This is now set forth as the result of the corruption of the priesthood, particularly the high priesthood. So the Day of Atonement calls to mind [1] sin, [2] the Temple and its cult, and [3] the power of sin to destroy the Temple and its cult. The treatment of the third theme seems to me miscellaneous, and the upshot is, what we have is the theme alone, not an exposition that makes some stunning point in the way that I.A, and B do. The upshot, however, is the same, and that is, the definition of an entirely fresh context in which the theme of the Mishnah-tractate, the Day of Atonement, is going to be expounded. Indeed, once we have worked our way through I.A and B, we can scarcely see as definitive for the topic the Mishnah-tractate's identification of its program of exposition — Leviticus Chapter Sixteen, point by point. What the Mishnah-tractate's authors found important about the Day of Atonement the Bavli-tractate's compilers chose to treat as subsidiary and incidental to the points they wished to register at the very beginning of their tractate.

I.G: Why should the topic of the councillors' chamber, I.F, should call to mind the requirement of putting a mezuzah on the doorposts of all Israelites' houses — gates of houses, courts, provinces, cities? The juxtaposition of subjects is jarring. But if we remember where we started — finding contexts in which to interpret the order of service of the Day of Atonement — the answer presents itself quite readily. We begin by moving from the Temple outward: rites comparable in that preparation outside of the cult (the high priest's separation) and beyond the limits of the Temple (the scapegoat, the red cow). We proceeded to a clear statement that the reason the Temple was destroyed was the sins of the priesthood and of Israel. Now we treat as comparable the sanctity of the dwellings of all Israel and the sanctity of the Temple and its chambers. The mezuzah marks off Israel's dwellings as holy, a counterpart to the Temple's very walls and hangings. The presentation, by contrast with the topic, proves once more miscellaneous; I see no point at which anything is said, beyond the introduction of the topic itself, that bears meaning, let alone a clear and relevant proposition.

VII.D: Saul is introduced because he violated the prohibition of taking a census; but then he provides the occasion to underscore the power of sin, however small, to yield weighty consequences. Still, it seems to me this topical appendix does not vastly change the face of the setting in which it is presented.

VIII.A: The exposition of the general procedure of the lottery simply spells out details of the Mishnah's topic.

XII.G: The secondary amplification of facts and rules relevant to the Mishnah's topic seems to me inert.

XIV.B: The wonderful composite at XIV.B really clarifies the presentation of the Mishnah's topic; it does not introduce an unanticipated topic, let alone a problem out of alignment with the Mishnah's, but only works in its own way through the very information that the Mishnah has already given. The improvement upon the Mishnah's presentation nonetheless is particularly talmudic: a more systematic and orderly account of what has already been laid out in a systematic manner.

XIV.D: The richly glossed account of the proper order of the daily priestly rites — by contrast to that of the Day of Atonement — enriches in a factual way the Mishnah's own presentation. I do not discern a single point at which a not-to-be-predicted subject makes an appearance.

XV.E: Now we come to a small but important insertion. We have been told that priests could spend their own money on enhancing the rites. Now we are told, in a huge composition of obvious artistic merit, how riches and

Chapter Five. The Structure of Babylonian Talmud Yoma        33

poverty and good looks are fundamentally irrelevant to Torah-study. Whether one is rich or poor, handsome or ugly, all are obligated to Torah-study. This composition forms a subtle but powerful comment on the topic of the Mishnah-composite before us, the kind of editorial insertion that changes the face of the whole.

XVIII.F: Once more, we have a startling juxtaposition, one that the Mishnah-composite accommodates but hardly requires. That is, the exposition of the Mishnah-composition is complete in its own terms. Then we have a massive composite on the righteous and the wicked in general. But while in the Mishnah, attention focuses upon those who contributed to the cult or refused to do so, here we deal with issues of personal morality, on the one side, and the power of the righteous to save the world, on the other. The conduct in the cult now recedes into the background, and conduct in the social order of holy Israel comes to the fore. The comment made by placing this remarkable composite here is then unmistakable. Virtue in everyday affairs forms the primary consideration, and Israelites who wish to do what is right take priority over those whose virtue involves only cultic activities. Since the Mishnah has cited Prov. 10:7 in the setting of those who were remembered favorably or unfavorably for their activities in the Temple, while the Talmud wishes to read the same verse in the setting of Israel's everyday life, the intent is obvious. Here is a fine example of how the Talmud's compositors make their statement through the juxtaposition of distinct composites, and the comparison and contrast of those composites' themes or even propositions, respectively.

XIX.C: I see this entry as topical; nothing is jarring here, since we have dealt with the outcome of the lottery, and the composite on Simeon begins with that subject. The composite has been assembled for its own purpose, which is to present Simeon the Righteous, but fits in quite well as a supplement to the Mishnah's rule, nothing more.

XIX.E: The question of whether the rite under discussion is essential or merely recommended in no way changes the Mishnah's presentation of the subject.

XX.B: Here we find a reprise of the opening exercise in comparison of the rite of the Day of Atonement, the rite of burning the Red Cow, and other, cognate rituals, now the purification rite involving thread. The composite is a very sizable one, but I am unable to identify in it any proposition, or even a theme, that leads us to take up a position outside of the framework of the factual repertoire of the Mishnah. Here is a lost occasion for theological reflection, sharpening by contrast the quite remarkable character of the juxtapositions that make their own, fresh statement.

[XXII.C: *We note a substantial composite of questions raised by Pappa, C.4ff.; but these fit well into the topical program of XXII.C and in no way form a distinct composite with its own principle of selection and coherence.*]

XXXV.B: The topic of the Mishnah — the high priest's garments — accounts for the inclusion of this composite.

XXXV.C: The same goes for this composite. But the next items change the picture.

XXXV.D: We move from rules on the disposition of the sacred objects to moral lessons to be drawn from verses that deal with the utensils and furniture of the Temple. The moral lessons are commonplaces; what is interesting is only that at this point a set of sayings is introduced to impart to the Mishnah's topic a set of meanings that the Mishnah does not require.

XXXV.E: Here we find the jarring juxtaposition that bears the Talmud's statement upon the Mishnah's topic or proposition, not only the Talmud's restatement thereof. We move from moral lessons deriving from Scripture's account of the Temple's appurtenances to Torah-study sayings pertinent to those same matters. The moral sayings now are recast as lessons for disciples of sages, and the important lesson is that the sage's disciple must be sincere in his convictions and conduct, his inside corresponding to his outside.

XXXV.G: Here we have a topical composite to supplement the Mishnah's exposition.

XXXVI.B: Now we come to Talmud's most remarkable theological statement. We begin with a preparatory composite on the affliction of souls through fasting. This is important because it introduces the theme of hunger as affliction. And that raises to the surface a question that invites the stunning juxtaposition of the next entry.

XXXVI.C: A verse invites our interest in manna, which is, "Who fed you in the wilderness with manna...that he might afflict you" (Dt. 8:16). So we turn to a huge and coherent exposition of manna as a form of affliction, on the one side, but grace, on the other. What happens when the subject of manna is introduced? The issue of fasting for Heaven is given its counterpart: Heaven feeding Israel. So the topic, fasting on the Day of Atonement, is given a new dimension of meaning, we give to Heaven, but Heaven has fed us, and feeds us, so the transaction is reciprocal. When humanity fasts and shows its humility and contrition, Heaven responds with the realization of grace that is provided through supernatural food. Fasting, a deed in the natural world, evokes in Heaven a supernatural response. Now the activities of the Day of Atonement are set into a fresh context and recast in cosmic dimensions. The cultic program for the Day recedes in consequence; the activities of the private person take over. God's interest and response address what all Israel does. Nothing in the Mishnah's presentation of the holy day, it goes without saying, has prepared us for such an amazing interjection of a theme that is at once unanticipated and alien, and, once introduced, also quite natural.

XXXVI.H: What we have here is a repertoire of relevant facts.

XXXVI.I: The same is so here. The face of the Mishnah is unaffected.
XL.C: This brief appendix treats the topic of the Mishnah.
XLI.D: The composite on repentance carries forward the Mishnah's theme; I see here nothing that will have surprised the Mishnah's own framers in context. Nor do I find any proposition that vastly revises the standard picture of the subject. We therefore see how critical to the making of the Talmud's own statement is the intrusion of the unanticipated topic — that principally, possible even, that alone.
XLI.H: This composite stands out of all relationship to the Mishnah-paragraph that stands at the head of its Talmud-unit. It is rare in the Talmud to come across a discussion so out of phase with the Mishnah-context as the present item. The real question is, why has the compositor of XVI.D not included the composite in his presentation of the high priest's confession. If I were making the Talmud over, that is the point to which I would move XLI.H. As it is, it is not only out of place but also fails to make the point that, in the right position, it can have made. It suffices to observe that, in the dozen and a half tractates to date, I have found no other composite that both stands out of relationship to its larger context, whether Mishnaic or Talmudic, and also fails to make the contribution that it ought to have made in its proper context, in the way that this one does. That exception to the rule of brilliant composition forms a mark of the Talmud's compositors' amazing intellectual rigor.

3. CAN WE STATE WHAT THE COMPILERS OF THIS DOCUMENT PROPOSE TO ACCOMPLISH IN PRODUCING THIS COMPLETE, ORGANIZED PIECE OF WRITING?

To understand what our compilers have accomplished, we have to call to mind the fundamental program of the Mishnah-tractate. Even a simple glance at the Mishnah-tractate suffices to show that all chapters but the final one are devoted to an exposition of the Temple rite on the Day of Atonement. Only the last chapter of the Mishnah-tractate addresses the situation of the individual Israelite, not in the Temple cult, and how he observes the occasion. The Mishnah-tractate therefore closely follows the presentation of the Day of Atonement at Leviticus Chapter Sixteen, which carefully catalogues the activities of the high priest on the holy day, but in a sentence or two suffices to tell ordinary folk how they are to conduct themselves. The challenge facing the Talmud-tractate framers, therefore, is to place the facts of the Mishnah's first seven chapters into a framework that accords proportion and balance to the re-presentation of the Mishnah-tractate. That is to say, along with the exposition of the facts of Leviticus Chapter Sixteen as the Mishnah lays them out and complements them, the meaning of the Day of Atonement in the holy life of Israel the people has to be set forth.

Now, when the compilers of the Bavli address the Mishnah, they define for themselves three tasks. First and paramount, they identify what they deemed to be the Mishnah's problematic, that is, what the Mishnah states that they deem to require amplification. So they clarify the Mishnah's words and phrases; they find Scriptural bases for the Mishnah's rules; they ask about the authority behind an anonymous ruling and make an effort to show that rulings belonging to a given authority may be accepted even by those who oppose his position on a parallel matter. Second, they add some sizable complexes of materials that address a topic of the Mishnah, rather than the problematic thereof, and as we now have seen, they organize sizable compositions into composites that supplement the Mishnah's inclusion of a topic with more information about that topic. These composites so far as I can see lack any proposition and accomplish little more than the recapitulation of marginally interesting facts. They fill space, they do not impart structure or add sense. And, third, as we now have seen, the Bavli's framers make us see the Mishnah's topic in a very different way from the way that we would understand that topic absent their work. This they do at critical points in the tractate.

Let us quickly review the main points that we derive from the massive composites that stand wholly outside of the exposition of our Mishnah-tractate and even of our Mishnah-tractate's topic:

1. the rites of the Day of Atonement fall into the larger framework of Israel's rites of purification and atonement for sin; these take place outside of the cult, as much as inside the Temple; they require of the high priest a higher level of sanctification through purification than the Temple's internal cult requires

2. the rite of sanctification of the tent of meeting — also in the world beyond the Temple walls — is comparable to the rite of the Day of Atonement

3. the world intruded on the Temple by reason of Israel's (unatoned-for) sin, which brought about the destruction of the Temple and the cessation of its cult — all the more reason to atone for sin on the Day of Atonement

4. the Temple's points of domestic sanctity, its special chambers, are comparable in their holiness to Israel's points of sanctity, its homes, towns, and cities, all of which are encompassed in the signs of sanctification that apply both in the holy place and also in the homes and towns of holy Israel

5. the Temple requires high priests who can invest their own funds in its rites; the study of Torah is obligatory on all Israel equally, without regard to wealth or poverty, beauty or ugliness

6. Righteous people in this world strengthen their capacity to do what is right; they can avoid the influence of wicked neighbors; even on account of a single righteous man is the world created; a righteous man does not take his leave from the world before another righteous man like him is created the Holy One, blessed be he, saw that the righteous are few. He went and planted some of them in every generation; even for the sake of a single righteous man the world endures; when a man has lived out the better part of his years and has not sinned, he will not likely sin again. And we are responsible for what we make of ourselves, specifically: if someone comes to make himself unclean, they open the way to him, but if he

## Chapter Five. The Structure of Babylonian Talmud Yoma 37

comes to purify himself, they assist him, but transgression dulls the heart of man.; if a person makes himself a bit unclean, he is made very unclean; if someone sanctifies himself a bit, he is made abundantly sanctified.

7. The propositions prominent in the exposition of the theme of the manna treats the manna as Heaven's response to self-affliction for sin. Thus "Who fed you in the wilderness with manna...that he might afflict you" (Dt. 8:16): Just as the prophet told the Israelites what was to be found in clefts or holes, so manna would reveal to Israelites what was in the clefts and holes. Meat, for which they asked not in the right way, was given to them at the wrong time. Bread, for which they asked in the right way, was given to them at the right time. "While the meat was yet between their teeth" (Num. 11:33). And it is written, "But a whole month" (Num. 11:20) — The middling folk died on the spot, the wicked suffered pain for a whole month. When the righteous eat the quail, it is at ease, but when the wicked eat it, it is like thorns for them. "Man did eat the bread of the mighty" (Ps. 78:25) — "It is the bread that the ministering angels eat." The manna marked Israel as supernatural — and so does its fasting.

These important additions, in the form of large-scale composites, introduce into the representation of the theme of the Day of Atonement conceptions and considerations of which the Mishnah scarcely takes cognizance. While the conception of Heaven's response to afflicting oneself by fasting is providing manna in the wilderness — the bread that the angels eat! — strikes me as the single most remarkable initiative, the other propositions before us prove equally striking. Seen as a group, they yield the following proposition: the Day of Atonement, which the Torah lays out as principally a Temple occasion, overspreads the world. That is not a merely-moral statement but one of cultic consequence, since we see the rite itself as one affecting the world beyond the Temple walls in the way in which the one analogous in its careful concern for the high priest's purification, the burning of the red cow, does. Israel's sin in the world intrudes into the cult, because the Temple, the mark of divine favor, was lost on account of Israel's sin. But Israel's virtue, the virtue of self-affliction through fasting, can win Heaven's cordial response, analogous to the provision of manna in the wilderness. That is because Israel's ordinary life compares with the Temple's sanctification; even as the Temple space is sanctified, so Israel's space is marked off by signs of the holy. Just as the Temple's priests display their riches in the ample cult, so Israel's sages display their resources of virtue and intellect in the service of the mind and heart, study of the Torah. And, it must follow, the righteousness represented by a life fearful of sin and rich in repentance, which comes to its climax on the Day of Atonement, infuses the entire people of Israel, not only the priesthood in the Temple on that same holy day.

The upshot is, the Mishnah's presentation of the Day of Atonement, its recapitulation of the themes of Leviticus Chapter Sixteen in the proportions of Scripture's treatment of that topic, is both replicated and revised. What for Leviticus and Mishnah-tractate Yoma forms a cultic occasion, in which Israel participates as bystanders, emerges in Bavli-tractate Yoma as an event in the life of holy Israel, in which all Israel bears tasks of the weight and consequence that, on that holy day, the High Priest uniquely carries out. On the Day of Atonement, holy Israel joins the high priest in the Holy of Holies; this they do on that day by afflicting themselves through fasting and other forms of abstinence, recalling how with Heaven's favor they would eat the bread of angels; this they do on the other days of the year by entering into the disciplines of the Torah; this they do through their lives of virtue. The Day of Atonement, the occasion on which the high priest conducts the rite in the privacy of the Holy of Holies, emerges transformed: the rites are private, but the event is public; the liturgy is conducted in the holy Temple, with sins sent forth through the scapegoat, but the event bears its consequences in holy Israel, where sins are atoned for in the setting of the everyday and and the here and now. What is singular and distinct — the rites of atonement on the holiest day of the year in the holiest place in the world — now makes its statement about what takes place on every day of the year in the ordinary life of holy Israel.

And that is how the Day of Atonement would make its way through time, not the sacrificial rite of the high priest in the Temple, but the atonement-celebration of all Israel in the world. What mattered to the compilers of Leviticus and the Mishnah alike was the timeless rite of atonement through the bloody rites of the Temple What captured the attention of the framers of the Bavli-tractate, by contrast, was the personal discipline of atonement through repentance on the Day of Atonement and a life of virtue and Torah-learning on the rest of the days of the year. They took out of the Holy of Holies and brought into the homes and streets of the holy people that very mysterious rite of atonement that the Day of Atonement called forth. When the compilers of our Talmud moved beyond the limits of the Mishnah-tractate, they transformed the presentation the day and its meaning, transcending its cultic limits. And it was their vision, and not the vision of Leviticus Sixteen and the Mishnah's tractate, that would prove definitive.

The irony comes to expression in the fact that, from antiquity to our own day, the Day of Atonement would enjoy the loyalty of holy Israel come what may, and everywhere, gaining the standing of Judaism's single most widely observed occasion. That fact attests to the power of the distinctive ideas set forth by the framers of the Bavli to transform a sacerdotal narrative into a medium of the inner, moral sanctification for Israel, the holy people in utopia entering into the status of the holy priest and the locus of the Temple's inner sanctum. But that reframing of the rite defines the Bavli-tractate's compilers intent, since, after all, it turns out to form the very first point that the framers of the Bavli make when they commence their exposition of the Mishnah-tractate. The opening composite turns out to bear the entire message, just as it should.

# VI

## The Structure of Babylonian Talmud Sukkah

### POINTS OF STRUCTURE

1. DOES BABYLONIAN TALMUD-TRACTATE SUKKAH FOLLOW A COHERENT OUTLINE GOVERNED BY A CONSISTENT RULES?

Outlining the Mishnah-tractate supplies a coherent outline, also, for nearly the whole of the Talmud-tractate. The general order of inquiry is [1] relationship of a Mishnah-rule in this tractate to one in some other; [2] explanation of words and phrases in the Mishnah-tractate; [3] the sources in Scripture for the Mishnah's rule; [4] theoretical problems precipitated by the facts set forth in the Mishnah's rule. Most of the composites of the tractate fall into those four categories.

2. WHAT ARE THE SALIENT TRAITS OF ITS STRUCTURE?

The coherent outline just now adumbrated also identifies the salient traits of the tractate. Where we have long theoretical compositions, they ordinarily commence with a given of the Mishnah and raise an interstitial problem contained thereby.

3. WHAT IS THE RATIONALITY OF THE STRUCTURE?

It follows that the Talmud-tractate finds coherent in comments on selected sentences or paragraphs of the Mishnah-tractate, and that the bulk of the comments identify as their point of departure a proposition or an implicit principle of the Mishnah.

4. WHERE ARE THE POINTS OF IRRATIONALITY IN THE STRUCTURE?

Within the stated definition of the Talmud, these composites form large-scale exceptions to the rule that the Talmud forms a sustained commentary upon the Mishnah: I.E; F, G; XIX.B, E; XXIII.D; XXX.B; XLI.B, F; XLIII.C; XLVI.D.

### POINTS OF SYSTEM

1. DOES THE BABYLONIAN TALMUD-TRACTATE SUKKAH SERVE ONLY AS A REPRESENTATION OF THE MISHNAH-TRACTATE OF THE SAME NAME?

The answer is negative for two reasons, first, because the Talmud's framers address most, though not all, sentences and paragraphs of the Mishnah-tractate, and also because some large-scale composites are set forth that have no bearing on the Mishnah-tractate.

2. How do the topical composites fit into the Talmud-tractate Sukkah and what do they contribute that the Mishnah-tractate of the same name would lack without them?

I.E, F, and G: I find here rules that express principles not illustrated or adumbrated by the Mishnah's statement but necessary for a full account of matters. The positioning is very sensible, since the opening Mishnah-paragraph provides basic rules governing the dimensions of the sukkah as well as its design ("shade must be greater than the light"), with the result that these further governing principles — it must be permanent, not temporary; it must be within a limited circumference, it is valid even though the intent in building it is irrelevant to the religious requirement for which it is built (use by gentiles, women, cattle, Samaritans). So while these compositions do not serve as Mishnah-commentary, they amplify the Mishnah-paragraph's rule and help achieve its purpose. What is surprising is not how many such composites we find in the Talmud, but how few.

XIX.B: Once we have been told that those engaged in a religious duty are exempt from having to dwell in a sukkah, we are given at XIX.B a list of others who fall into the same category, ending at B.3 with interstitial classes, e.g., liable at one point but not at some other. None of this wanders very far from the Mishnah's own allegations.

XIX.E: The introduction of the notion of eating and drinking outside of the sukkah on a random basis introduces not taking a snooze outside of the sukkah, and that yields a separate and independent discussion of the random nap. As before, all we have here is a secondary development of a theme introduced by the Mishnah, not a sustained effort at broadening the program of the Mishnah, on the one side, or introducing facts or conceptions that greatly revise the sense of the Mishnah's rule or even the context in which its topic is represented.

XXIII.D: This item on omens in general functions as those at XIX.B and E, that is, once a topic has been introduced, it is discussed more or less in its own terms. Here the fact that it rains during the Festival is taken to represent a bad omen, and, it follows other omens will be defined. Not only so, but the venue of much of the material in the Tosefta and other Tannaite sources suggests that the Mishnah's first exegetes among the Tannaite authorities supplied the amplified topical program to the Mishnah; the framers of the Talmud, coming at the end, here worked within a received exegetical program, commencing, it is clear, with the Mishnah's own statements.

## Chapter Six. The Structure of Babylonian Talmud Sukkah 41

XXX.B: This entry is introduced for formal reasons; it in no way serves as first-order Mishnah-exegesis for our tractate.

XLI.B: This is a little set-piece unit on the general theme of Isaiah's reference to the salvific standing of drawing water, inserted because of the citation at XLI.A of Is. 12:3.

XLI:F: The exegesis of Song 7:2 in terms of the beauty of Israel when it comes for the pilgrim festival, in fact is a topical appendix XLI.E.2, nothing more.

XLIII.C: Here we deal with a genuinely important composite, and one that moves considerably beyond the limits of the Mishnah's program. Specifically, the Mishnah has invited some comments on the "evil inclination," which in this context refers to libido in particular. Then we have at XLIII.C a rather substantial discussion of sexuality. But a second look shows us that the composite concerns not sexual misbehavior or desire therefor, so much as the Messiah-theme. And that theme is not invited by the Mishnah's formulation o matters. The Messiah son of Joseph was killed because of the evil inclination; the Messiah son of David will be saved by God; the evil inclination then is made the counterweight to the Messiah and a threat to his survival. It is overcome, however, by study of the Torah. The composite is hardly coherent in detail, but its thematic program — Torah, Messiah, in the context of the Festival of Tabernacles — imposes upon the topic of the Mishnah-paragraph a quite different perspective from that set forth in the Mishnah itself.

XLVI.D: Like I.E, F, and G, we find here valuable information, though the context is not that of Mishnah-commentary. But I see no way in which the topic of the Festival is vastly recast.

3. CAN WE STATE WHAT THE COMPILERS OF THIS DOCUMENT PROPOSE TO ACCOMPLISH IN PRODUCING THIS COMPLETE, ORGANIZED PIECE OF WRITING?

All but one of the Talmud's important, free-standing composites provide appendices to the Mishnah's own topics. With one important exception, examining the composites that do not serve as Mishnah-commentary pure and simple hardly yields a very strong case that the framers of the Talmud, in their commentary to the Mishnah, have vastly redefined the topic of the Mishnah, imparted to it dimensions not clearly contained within the Mishnah's own presentation, or otherwise given to the Mishnah's topic a character different from that defined by the Mishnah itself. That exception is an important one, and it occupies a prominent position in context. To understand the importance of XLIII.C, not only in size but in substance, we have to glance at XLIII.G. Here we have an invitation greatly to enrich the Mishnah's topic — the saints' and sages' conduct in song and dance at the bonfire. But apart from the enigmatic but clearly celebratory saying attributed to Hillel, I see nothing that strays outside of the Mishnah's own framework. By contrast, XLIII.B explains why the men were located below, the women above, and, when C forthwith introduces the matter of the Messiah, the issue of improper sexual desires falls away almost at once. At that point we are given a huge and complex composite on the evil impulse, the coming of the Messiah, and the power of Torah to overcome that evil impulse. For none of these propositions has the Mishnah prepared us.

A rapid recapitulation of the propositions in the large composite tells us what the Talmud has added to the Mishnah's topic, which is, the Festival of Tabernacles. None of them has any bearing at all on the topic at hand, but by introducing the set of propositions into the present context, the topic before us is recast:

1. God created the impulse to do evil but regrets it: there are four things that the Holy One, blessed be he, regrets he created, and these are they: Exile, the Chaldeans, the Ishmaelites, and the inclination to do evil.

2. The impulse to do evil is weak at the outset but powerful when it becomes habitual. The inclination to do evil to begin with is like a spider's thread and in the end like cart ropes. In the beginning one calls the evil inclination a passer-by, then a guest, and finally, a man of the household. The impulse to do evil affects one's status in the world to come.

3. The Messiah was killed on account of the impulse to do evil. That is why the Messiah, son of David, asked God to spare his life and not allow him to be killed the way the Messiah son of Joseph was killed.

4. The impulse to do evil is stronger for sages than for others. But they possess the antidote in the Torah: "For it has done great things" (Joel 2:20): "And against disciples of sages more than against all the others." A man's inclination [to do evil] overcomes him every day. A man's inclination to do evil prevails over him every day and seeks to kill him. If that vile one meets you, drag it to the house of study. If it is a stone, it will dissolve. If it is iron, it will be pulverized.

Now, if we did not know that the Festival of Tabernacles was associated with an autumnal celebration of the advent of rain and the fructifying of the fields, on the one side, and also identified as the occasion for the coming of the Messiah, on the other, then on the strength of this extrinsic composite, we should have formed the theory that those two protean conceptions governed. As is common in Rabbinic sources, we treat in one and the same setting private life and public affairs, this world and its concerns and the world to come as well. The private life — the role of the sexual impulse in one's persona affairs and fate — and the destiny of Israel in the world to come and the Messianic future correspond. God governs in both dimensions, the personal and the political. And sages then represent the realm of affairs: suffering more than others from the desires to sin, but better able than others to resist those desires.

The upshot of the one really substantial composite that the Talmud contributes to the re-presentation of the Mishnah-tractate introduces the great themes of the Talmud's system — Messiah, Torah, sage; this world and the world to come;

## Chapter Six. The Structure of Babylonian Talmud Sukkah

the life of the private person and its correspondence with the destiny of Israel the holy people. The Mishnah's topic, the Festival of Tabernacles, then is situated in that much larger systemic framework of meaning that our sages of blessed memory in the Talmud composed. Knowing the topic of the Mishnah-tractate, we could never have predicted the point at which the Talmud's compositors would vastly reshape matters. Knowing the character of the Rabbinic system, we have no difficult at all in making sense of what is before us. The Festival of Tabernacles is absorbed into the Rabbinic system through the anomalous elements in the Talmud's structure — as is to be expected.

# VII

## The Structure of Babylonian Talmud Besah

### Points of Structure

1. Does Babylonian Talmud-tractate Besah follow a coherent outline governed by a consistent rules?

The Talmud adheres closely to a simple program of Mishnah-exegesis, enhanced by a tendency to ask theoretical questions, transcending the cases at hand, as well. The principal focus, however, is on the kind of analytical question that allows the Mishnah's statements to emerge with still greater force and clarity. We want to know about the reasoning behind controverted positions, the deeper theory behind rulings, the sense of wordings, and the like. The reasons behind rulings, glosses of statements — these form the principal points of the Talmud's exegetical structure.

2. What are the salient traits of its structure?

The tractate stays so close to the Mishnah's and other Tannaite compilations' statements that a simple statement is possible. The structure of the Talmud's discussion derives from the order of the Mishnah's statements — and from no other source.

3. What is the Rationality of the structure?

"To what case does a ruling apply?" "What is at issue in the dispute" — these and comparable questions leave no doubt that, to the framers of the Talmud, the Mishnah defines an orderly and reasoned statement of rules, and together with its Tannaite complement, the Mishnah can be shown to be accessible, reasonable, and internally coherent and harmonious. Why a statement makes sense, how it is necessary to articulate a given rule, and illustrative cases define the main frame of inquiry.

4. Where are the points of irrationality in the structure?

These entries present other than Mishnah-exegesis: XIII.B; XIII.D; and XXIV.B. All other entries take shape around the tasks of Mishnah-exegesis or secondary development of compositions aimed at Mishnah-exegesis.

### POINTS OF SYSTEM

1. DOES THE BABYLONIAN TALMUD-TRACTATE BESAH SERVE ONLY AS A REPRESENTATION OF THE MISHNAH-TRACTATE OF THE SAME NAME?

Since nearly the whole of the Mishnah-tractate is covered but, except in a subsidiary or desultory way, little else, the answer is affirmative.

2. HOW DO THE TOPICAL COMPOSITES FIT INTO THE TALMUD-TRACTATE BESAH AND WHAT DO THEY CONTRIBUTE THAT THE MISHNAH-TRACTATE OF THE SAME NAME WOULD LACK WITHOUT THEM?

I identify only three sizable topical composites, as follows:

XIII.B: The proper observance of the festival day is set forth in the setting of rules on cooking in advance of the festival; then other actions appropriate to the festival day are reviewed — eating and drinking, as against Torah-study. The focus is upon the joy and holiness of festival days. In context, the unit simply amplifies the topic of the Mishnah and places the matter of cooking on the festival into a broader setting of theological and moral appreciation.

XIII.D: The setting is the fusion of the Sabbath and festival, e.g., through a fictive meal that links both distinct spells of sanctification. At issue now are rules that govern when the Sabbath and the festival day coincide, benedictions that are recited, and special problems in connection with the coincidence of two sources of sanctification of time. This enriches and broadens the topic of the Mishnah, but does not materially change its main point.

XXIV.B: This strikes me as an unimportant appendix, adding other rules of proper conduct to the Mishnah's main point.

These three topical appendices do not materially affect the Bavli's treatment of the Mishnah-tractate's main theme and its repertoire of problems. I do not see how the Bavli's framers have in any important way reframed the Mishnah-tractate or cast its topical program into a fresh perspective. To the contrary, the three composites simply broaden matters, but in no way change their basic point.

3. CAN WE STATE WHAT THE COMPILERS OF THIS DOCUMENT PROPOSE TO ACCOMPLISH IN PRODUCING THIS COMPLETE, ORGANIZED PIECE OF WRITING?

Let us classify the point of entry of a Talmud-composition devoted to Mishnah-analysis, and ask the results to tell us the purpose of the Talmud's Mishnah-exegetes:

1. with what circumstances do we deal; the limitations of a dispute's extent; secondary extension of the Mishnah's rule or clarification of how it applies I.A.1, VI.A.1; IX.A.1, X.A.1, XV.A.1, XVIII.A.1, XXII.C.1, XXV.A.1, XXIX.A.1, XXXIX.C.1, XL.A.1, XLII.B.1

## Chapter Seven. The Structure of Babylonian Talmud Besah

2. what is the reasoning behind a position taken in the Mishnah; other cases that express the same principle or reasoning
I.B.1, III.A.1, IV.C.1, XII.B.1, XII.D.1, XIV.A.1, XVII.C.1, XXI.A.1, XXXVII.A.1, XXXVIII.C.1, XXXIX.A.1, XXXIX.E.1, XL.C.1, XL.D.1, XLIII.A.1, XLIII.B.1, XLIII.C.1, XLIII.D.1, XLIII.H.1, XLIV.B.1, XLVI.B.1 secondary dispute clarifying the basic principle in hand, XLVII.1.A, XLVIII.A.1

3. the implications of the phrasing of a rule for the law to be derived from said rule
I.C.1, II.B.1, IV.D.1, VII.A.1, XIII.F.1, XXI.B.1, XXIII.A.1, XXIII.B.1, XXXV.A.1, XXXVI.B.1, XXXIX.B.1, XXXIX.D.1

4. the context in which a Mishnah-rule applies
I.D.1, II.A.1, XIII.C.1, XVII.A.1

5. criticism of the language of the Mishnah or explanation of its meaning or intent, inclusive of contradictions between one Mishnah-teaching and another
I.E.1, III.B.1, IV.A.1, IV.B.1, IV.E.1, XII.A.1, XII.C.1, XIV.B.1, XIX.A.1, XIX.B.1, XXII.A.1, XXVII.A.1, XXVIII.A.1, XXXI.A.1, XXXI.B.1, XXXIII.A.1, XXXIII.A.1, XXXIII.B.1, XXXIV.A.1, XXXV.B.1, XXXVI.A.1, XXXVIII.B.1, XLII.A.1 (wording), XLIII.E.1, XLIII.F.1, XLIII.G.1, XLIII.I.1 this is obvious, XLIII.J.1, XLIV.C.1, XLIV.D.1, XLIV.E.1, XLIV.F.1, XLV.B.1, XLVI.A.1

6. Tannaite gloss or complement
V.A.1, V.B.1, XI.A.1, XIV.C.1, XVII.D.1, XX.A.1, XXIV.C.1, XXXII.A.1, XL.B.1, XLII.C.1, XLV.A.1, XLVIII.B.1

7. who is or is not the authority behind a given rule of the Mishnah, and the implications of such an attribution
VIII.A.1, XIII.E.1, XVI.A.1, XXVI.A.1, XXXVIII.A.1, XLIV.A.1

8. the practical rule on a given matter of law
XII.E.1, XVIII.B.1, XXII.B.1

9. the foundation in Scripture for a rule of the Mishnah
XIII.A.1

These several categories may now be reframed in groups that undertake a fundamentally uniform inquiry; now I lay matters out in terms of the orderly arrangement by a logic that places earlier a simpler inquiry, later a more subtle one, with the latter relying upon the results (explicit or otherwise) of the former

A. Clarification of facts concerning a Mishnah-paragraph
who is or is not the authority behind a given rule of the Mishnah, and the implications of such an attribution
the foundation in Scripture for a rule of the Mishnah
criticism of the language of the Mishnah or explanation of its meaning or

intent, inclusive of contradictions between one Mishnah-teaching and another

with what circumstances do we deal; the limitations of a dispute's extent; secondary extension of the Mishnah's rule or clarification of how it applies

Tannaite gloss or complement (sometimes: further information to complement the Mishnah's law with other cases of the same law)

B.     Specification of the deeper implications of a rule given by the Mishnah; secondary expansion of a Mishnah-rule, showing deeper implications, underlying principles

the implications of the phrasing of a rule for the law to be derived from said rule

what is the reasoning behind a position taken in the Mishnah; other cases that express the same principle or reasoning

Tannaite gloss or complement (commonly: further applications of the same principle to new problems or cases)

the context in which a Mishnah-rule applies

the practical rule on a given matter of law

The various categories that accommodate nearly all of the Talmud's initiatives in Mishnah-commentary and analysis leave no doubt whatsoever concerning the character and program of the Talmud. The document has a single purpose, which is to open up the Mishnah and uncover its meaning and profound layers of principles. While rich in secondary clarification of its primary statements, the primary purpose always governs. That is shown by a single, simple fact. Nearly every principal unit of our outline commences with Mishnah-commentary, and nearly all of them proceed to a secondary expansion of that commentary. No rubric in our Talmud, except for the handful of anomalous entries, follows a program other than that dictated by the requirements of Mishnah-commentary (of a very particular, well-defined character). Indeed, the strikingly uniform program of the Talmud is shown most clearly when we compare the 98% of the units that commence with Mishnah-commentary with the negligible representation of the units that do not; the former follow a uniform program, choosing out of a limited repertoire one or another of the handful of analytical initiatives that the evidence before us indicates were available; the anomalous groups follow no cogent program we are able to discern.

This Talmud-tractate presents a commentary to the Mishnah, nothing less, nothing more. The document makes one remarkable statement: the Mishnah takes priority over all documents and traditions, except for Scripture; the Mishnah is a document bearing profound layers of meaning, reaching from cases deep into principles that in their abstraction govern in a wide variety of concrete instances of diverse character; the Mishnah is a perfect document, sustaining rigorous critical analysis, and the laws that comprise the document are wholly harmonious. The

Talmud before us forms a sustained hymn in celebration of the Mishnah, an exercise in applied reason and practical logic aimed at showing how the cases of the Mishnah yield principles that overspread the entirety of the workaday life. When we wish to find out what is talmudic about the Talmud, we shall seek our answer elsewhere. This tractate offers no answer at all: it is the Talmud as Mishnah-commentary and little more than that.

# VIII

## The Structure of Babylonian Talmud Rosh Hashanah

### POINTS OF STRUCTURE

1. DOES BABYLONIAN TALMUD-TRACTATE ROSH HASHANAH FOLLOW A COHERENT OUTLINE GOVERNED BY A CONSISTENT RULES?

This brief tractate shows in bold relief how the Mishnah defines the organization and structure of the Talmud. No large-scale composite stands entirely remote from the Mishnah's topical program, and most composites begin with systematic exegesis of the Mishnah's words, phrases, rules, or other salient traits.

2. WHAT ARE THE SALIENT TRAITS OF ITS STRUCTURE?

The Talmud is formed to spell out the sense of the Mishnah's rules, to draw out its implications, to articulate its inferences, and, in general, to amplify what the Mishnah says or to supply necessary information to clarify what the Mishnah means.

3. WHAT IS THE RATIONALITY OF THE STRUCTURE?

It follows that order, how things are juxtaposed and deemed self-evidently to relate — these traits of rationality that are critical to the character of the Talmud derive from the task of Mishnah-exegesis, that alone.

4. WHERE ARE THE POINTS OF IRRATIONALITY IN THE STRUCTURE?

Then by appeal to that definition of rationality, what points of irrationality have we identified, that is, large-scale composites that in one way or another accomplish a task other than that of mere Mishnah-commentary and amplification? I identify these items: I.C [The Special Problem of Improperly Postponing the Fulfillment of Vows beyond the Passage of the Year in which They Are Taken]; i.J [What Does TISHRÉ Commemorate?]; ii.b [Judgment at the New Year of TISHRÉ. The Character of Divine Judgment and Mercy]; III.D [Calculating the New Moon through Sightings and Otherwise: A Topical Composite]; X.C [Miscellany on Verses of Isaiah, including a Reference to Acacia-Wood]; XIX.D [Does the performance of religious obligations require intention?]; XXX.C [Composite on the Shofar Blasts and the Scriptural Bases Therefor].

### POINTS OF SYSTEM

1. DOES THE BABYLONIAN TALMUD-TRACTATE ROSH HASHANAH SERVE ONLY AS A RE-PRESENTATION OF THE MISHNAH-TRACTATE OF THE SAME NAME?

The answer is a qualified affirmative. Nearly the whole of the Mishnah-tractate of Rosh Hashanah is covered by the Talmud, and as to the lines that are omitted, I identify no distinctive and definitive traits that characterize them all. These seem to me random. But, as we have noted, some important composites do more than accomplish Mishnah-exegesis.

2. HOW DO THE TOPICAL COMPOSITES FIT INTO THE TALMUD-TRACTATE ROSH HASHANAH AND WHAT DO THEY CONTRIBUTE THAT THE MISHNAH-TRACTATE OF THE SAME NAME WOULD LACK WITHOUT THEM?

I divide into three parts the composites that set forth propositions or information outside of the framework of Mishnah-commentary. At the left hand margin are the important composites, which introduce topics and propositions that Mishnah-exegesis does not require. In the center are those composites that simply add valuable information to topics introduced by the Mishnah. At the right I ordinarily set those composites that in no way relate to the Mishnah-passages before us; there is none for our tractate.

I.C The Special Problem of Improperly Postponing the Fulfillment of Vows beyond the Passage of the Year in which They Are Taken
I.J What Does Tishré Commemorate?
II.B Judgment at the New Year of Tishré. The Character of Divine Judgment and Mercy
   III.D Calculating the New Moon
      through Sightings and Otherwise: A Topical Composite
X.C Miscellany on Verses of Isaiah, including a Reference to Acacia-Wood
XIX.D Does the performance of religious obligations require intention?
   XXX.C Composite on the Shofar Blasts
      and the Scriptural Bases Therefor

3. CAN WE STATE WHAT THE COMPILERS OF THIS DOCUMENT PROPOSE TO ACCOMPLISH IN PRODUCING THIS COMPLETE, ORGANIZED PIECE OF WRITING?

Now, when the compilers of the Bavli address the Mishnah, they define for themselves three tasks. First and paramount, they identify what they deemed to be the Mishnah's problematic, that is, what the Mishnah states that they deem to require amplification. So they clarify the Mishnah's words and phrases; they find Scriptural bases for the Mishnah's rules; they ask about the authority behind an anonymous ruling and make an effort to show that rulings belonging to a given authority may be accepted even by those who oppose his position on a parallel matter. Second, they add some sizable complexes of materials that address a topic

## Chapter Eight. The Structure of Babylonian Talmud Rosh Hashanah

of the Mishnah, rather than the problematic thereof, and as we now have seen, they organize sizable compositions into composites that supplement the Mishnah's inclusion of a topic with more information about that topic. And, third, as we now have seen, the Bavli's framers make us see the Mishnah's topic in a very different way from the way that we would understand that topic absent their work. This they do at critical points in the tractate, and they accomplish their task through a shift in emphasis, rather than through introducing altogether new considerations.

The important entries introduce into the consideration of the tractate a stress that draws the entire tractate off-center and focuses it upon a single matter. The Mishnah's framers announce their perspective and intention in their opening statement: there are four New Years, each for its purpose. But most of the points at which the Talmud's framers have added large-scale composites that stand outside of the framework of Mishnah-exegesis focus upon only one of these four New Years, and that is, the new year that is the first day of Tishré, that is, New Year (Rosh Hashanah) par excellence. So a tractate that wishes to deal with four new years is now made to address only one of them. But there is more: the Mishnah announces that that new year is the new year for the reckoning of years, for Sabbatical years, and for Jubilees. But the Talmud treats the new year marked by the new moon of Tishré commemorates the judgment of the world, and the framers go on to lay heavy emphasis on the theological questions bound up with divine judgment: justice vs. mercy, repentance and atonement. In that same context two special problems find a place. The first concerns postponing vows, a matter of intentionality and fulfillment thereof. The passage of the new year that pertains without fulfilling a vow taken in the prior year will mark a transgression, a breach of faith between man and God. The second involves the role of intentionality in the fulfillment of religious duties, again, the character of the good faith that is required in relating to God.

So the four genuinely fresh entries come together to make one fundamental point, which is, at the New Year — the first of Tishré in particular — we are judged by God, and God pays special intention to breaches of faith, on the one hand, and good-faith fulfillment of the commandments, on the other. Would these points of emphasis have surprised the framers of the Mishnah? Yes and no. M. 1:2 both articulates the character of the first of Tishré as judgment day and also treats that occasion as generic and not particular, when it states in so many words: "At four seasons of the year the world is judged: at Passover through grain; at Pentecost through fruit of the tree; at the New Year all who enter the world pass before Him like troops, since it is said at Ps. 33:15: 'He who fashions the hearts of them and who considers all their works;' and on the Festival of Tabernacles they are judged through water." But the Talmud concerns itself with only one kind of judgment, and that is, the moral judgment of the human being. What in the Mishnah is a repertoire of occasions of divine judgment in the Talmud is a crisis in the condition of humanity in particular. For the Mishnah, judgment pertains to nature and humanity, and, while not choosing to differ (why should they?), the framers of the Talmud have accorded priority to the judgment of humanity — and, within that divine scrutiny, they find heavy attention paid to matters of good faith and intentionality.

Our sages' reading of Mishnah-tractate Rosh Hashanah proves coherent with their reading of Mishnah-tractate Yoma. We recall (Chapter Five, above) that what mattered to the compilers of Leviticus and the Mishnah alike was the timeless rite of atonement through the bloody rites of the Temple What captured the attention of the framers of the Bavli-tractate, by contrast, was the personal discipline of atonement through repentance on the Day of Atonement and a life of virtue and Torah-learning on the rest of the days of the year. They took out of the Holy of Holies and brought into the homes and streets of the holy people that very mysterious rite of atonement that the Day of Atonement called forth. When the compilers of our Talmud moved beyond the limits of the Mishnah-tractate, they transformed the presentation the day and its meaning, transcending its cultic limits. And it was their vision, and not the vision of Leviticus Sixteen and the Mishnah's tractate, that would prove definitive. And so, we now see, is the case with Rosh Hashanah, transformed from generic to particular. The year, with its four beginnings, matters at only one of them, and that is, the point at which God and humanity face one another, at the sounding of the Shofar.

To generalize, the Mishnah sets forth a structure and a system for the holy community in its corporate life. The Talmud in reading some Mishnah-tractates places that holy community into the context of history — Israel's sacred history, the unfolding and manifestation of God's will for God's particular people — and, also, into the setting of the lives of ordinary persons. To claim that the Talmud has transformed the new year, which is various, into The New Year, the Day of Judgment, overstates the case, but not by much; to claim that the Talmud likewise recasts the Temple rite of the Day of Atonement into the occasion for the repentance of the private, introspective conscience of individual Israelites likewise ignores that deep roots in both Scripture and the Mishnah of the Talmud's convictions. But the upshot remains the same: what is perhaps present in potentiality is fully realized; what is a possibility is transformed into an actuality; what is a choice among choices is now accorded priority. The result is one and the same: the Judaic system of the Talmud reshapes the Mishnah's materials and imparts to them the structure that the Talmud's, not the Mishnah's, framers wish them to have.

# The Structure of Babylonian Talmud Taanit

### Points of Structure

1. Does Babylonian Talmud-tractate Taanit follow a coherent outline governed by a consistent rules?

The sequence of statements of Mishnah-tractate Taanit dictates the structure and order of the Talmud-tractate, beginning to end.

2. What are the salient traits of its structure?

The topical program follows that of the Mishnah-tractate, and each composite commences its work with the Mishnah-paragraph and only when that paragraph has been fully explored (within the limits of the Talmud-compilers' plan) will materials of an other-than-Mishnah-exegetical character find a place.

3. What is the Rationality of the structure?

It follows that coherence and cogency derive from the Mishnah, not from materials assembled or even written for some purpose other than Mishnah-commentary.

4. Where are the points of irrationality in the structure?

Within that theory of the logical cogency of the document, the irrational composites are those that are formed around a focus other than that defined by the task of Mishnah-exegesis or secondary expansion of the same. They are listed below. Most take up topics presented by the Mishnah, so while they do not explain specific statements made by the Mishnah, they do address topics supplied thereby. Some are formed around names of authorities, and a few introduce into the consideration of the Mishnah's topics other considerations, which expand our sense of the meaning of the Mishnah's rules or the dimensions of its topics.

### Points of System

1. Does the Babylonian Talmud-tractate Taanit serve only as a re-presentation of the Mishnah-tractate of the same name?

The Bavli-tractate does not take up every statement that the Mishnah makes, and it also contains large composites that do not address the Mishnah's statements. The upshot is that while the tractate forms around its Mishnah-counterpart, it cannot be regarded as solely a commentary to the Mishnah.

2. How do the topical composites fit into the Talmud-tractate Taanit and what do they contribute that the Mishnah-tractate of the same name would lack without them?

I present the account in three sections. On the left hand margin are important propositional composites that do not address the Mishnah's propositions but do affect them. Identifying these items and distinguishing them from those on the right hand margin involve a measure of subjectivity, and for that reason, I have tried to impose the most rigorous and narrowest possible definition of what is both free-standing and also affective of the rest. In the center I give those utterly anomalous composites that ignore the principle of propositional or at least topical cogency altogether. At the right are the composites that complement the Mishnah's statements with topically relevant amplifications or that carry forward the Mishnah's principle to new data. Finally, I underline and also position in the center column large composites that strike me as entirely out of phase with the Mishnah, lacking all point of contact, whether topical or in principle or even theme, broadly construed.

|  | II.B: Composite of Sayings with the Attributive, Said R. Nahman to R. Isaac |  |
| --- | --- | --- |
|  |  | II.D: Topical Composite on Rainfall |
| II.E: Comparison of Rain and Teachings of the Torah |  |  |
|  |  | II.F: Topical Composite on Rainfall |
|  |  | II:G: Collection of sayings of Isaac on Rain |
|  |  | II:H: Collection of Sayings of Yohanan on Rain |
|  |  | II:I: Further Topical Appendix on Rain |
|  |  | IV:B: Topical Appendix on the Individuals |
|  |  | IV:C: Proper Conduct in Times of Trouble |
|  |  | V:G: Composite of Statements by Eleazar on the Matter of Conduct in Fasting |
| VII:F: The Public Virtues of Various Sages |  |  |

Chapter Nine. The Structure of Babylonian Talmud Taanit    57

VII:H: The Public Virtues of Sages:
How Various Noteworthy Figures
attained Special Status
in Heaven through Acts of
Uncoerced Grace Performed
on Earth
VII:R: Others Who Prayed for Rain
or Performed Other Miracles
VII:S: Stories about Honi,
his Wife, Daughter,
Neighbors, Goats, and the Like
VII:T: Still Others Who Prayed for Rain
or Performed Other Miracles

3. CAN WE STATE WHAT THE COMPILERS OF THIS DOCUMENT PROPOSE TO ACCOMPLISH IN PRODUCING THIS COMPLETE, ORGANIZED PIECE OF WRITING?

The compilers of the Talmud clearly wished to accomplish three goals. First and foremost, they wished to explain the Mishnah's words, phrases, sources, and broader implications, inclusive of the coherence and harmony of the Mishnah's rules with those found in other places but deriving from the same standard of authority. Second, where they could, they wished to read into the Mishnah's topic the considerations of the Torah as sages themselves embodied the Torah: the relationship of Torah-learning to the topic at hand, the virtues of the sage as comparable to the virtues of those adepts at the matter at hand. In particular they showed how great sages could pray for rain and linked that power to knowledge of the Torah, on the one side, and to virtue, on the other. Third, they provided a sizable number of topical appendices, collecting more statements on the topics introduced by the Mishnah. These appendices supplement the Mishnah's topics, but do not change the sense of the Mishnah's treatment of those topics.

I cannot point to a single instance in which the Talmud vastly recasts the Mishnah's topic, let alone revises its propositions, other than in the specified manner, that is, through the introduction of considerations of the Torah into the topic of the miracle of rain. If, as some suppose, the sages meant to impose upon the charisma of figures such as Honi the routine of a well-regulated law, our tractate affords very little evidence of that fact. To the contrary, the representation of sages as miracle-workers is the one, but very important, point at which the Talmud makes its comment, its own, distinctive comment, upon the supernatural world set forth by the Mishnah. And that comment contradicts the Mishnah's judgment of Honi's power, since the Talmud affirms the power of great sages to do what Honi did (or expects that they should have such power) and attributes to Torah-learning the origin of supernatural power.

# X

# The Structure of Babylonian Talmud Megillah

### Points of Structure

1. Does Babylonian Talmud-tractate Megillah follow a coherent outline governed by a consistent rules?

Two coherent outlines govern, one for most of the tractate, the other, as indicated, for a considerable part of Chapter One. The former is the outline dictated by our Mishnah-tractate, the latter, a partial presentation of the book of Esther, following more or less the main lines of the biblical narrative. That some MSS omit the sizable composite underscores the anomalous character of what is before us. But what we have is, at any rate, a quite different presentation from the counterpart in Esther Rabbah I, as the appendix that follows indicates quite clearly. It follows that, overall, our tractate follows the sequence of the Mishnah, and no major composite except the indicated one diverges from that plan.

2. What are the salient traits of its structure?

As throughout the Bavli, the main traits of structure are dictated by the requirement of Mishnah-commentary; a great deal of clarification is contributed, much attention is paid to concrete rules and normative practices. But in the end, what we have is a well-constructed work of Mishnah-exegesis, taking account of some rich amplification here and there.

3. What is the Rationality of the structure?

The Mishnah follows a suitable order and structure so that all further discussion of the topic of the Mishnah can and should organize itself around the Mishnah's discussion. There is no need to recast matters or to reshape the discussion of the topic in such a way as to treat the Mishnah-tractate as a mere source of information. Quite to the contrary, the basic presentation of the topic by the Mishnah-tractate is now re-presented here.

4. Where are the points of irrationality in the structure?

These are the designated composites that form considerable statements on their own, without reference to the proposition or even the topic of the Mishnah.

In my discussion, below, I differentiate those composites that stand on their own from the ones that are carried in the wake of a statement that is required for the purpose of Mishnah-exegesis, with the former at the left, the latter at the right-hand margin; there is none. Omitting reference to the exegesis of the book of Esther, these are the items that require attention: I.C GLOSSING B.2. AND FOUR TEACHINGS OF RABBI YERMIAH OR RABBI HIYYA BAR ABBA; I.E GLOSSING B. 2. AND FURTHER TEACHINGS OF RABBI JOSHUA BEN LEVI ON MATTERS RELATED TO PURIM; XLII.C TOPICAL APPENDIX: ACCOUNTING FOR LONG LIFETIMES, INCLUSIVE OF AN ITEM PERTINENT TO THE FOREGOING; XLIII.B TOPICAL APPENDIX ON THE SYNAGOGUES OF BABYLONIA.

## POINTS OF SYSTEM

1. DOES THE BABYLONIAN TALMUD-TRACTATE MEGILLAH SERVE ONLY AS A RE-PRESENTATION OF THE MISHNAH-TRACTATE OF THE SAME NAME?

If we regard the huge Scripture-exegetical unit as integral to our tractate, then the answer is negative. This is the only Bavli-tractate that subjects to sustained exegetical work of a fundamental importance to the structure of the tractate a document other than Scripture. As to the treatment of the Mishnah, most, though not all, sentences of the Mishnah are supplied with an ample explanation.

2. HOW DO THE TOPICAL COMPOSITES FIT INTO THE TALMUD-TRACTATE AND WHAT DO THEY CONTRIBUTE THAT THE MISHNAH-TRACTATE OF THE SAME NAME WOULD LACK WITHOUT THEM?

I.C Glossing B.2.
And Four Teachings of Rabbi Yermiah or Rabbi Hiyya bar Abba
I.E Glossing B. 2.
And Further Teachings of Rabbi Joshua ben Levi on Matters Related to Purim
XLII.C Topical Appendix: Accounting for Long Lifetimes, inclusive of an item pertinent to the foregoing
XLIII.B Topical Appendix on the Synagogues of Babylonia.

3. CAN WE STATE WHAT THE COMPILERS OF THIS DOCUMENT PROPOSE TO ACCOMPLISH IN PRODUCING THIS COMPLETE, ORGANIZED PIECE OF WRITING?

Two large-scale composites supply to the tractate a perspective other than the Mishnah's. One stresses the special value of the synagogues in Babylonia, the particular affection that God shows to Babylonian Jews, and the Presence of God in that locale. Given the topic of the book of Esther, which Babylonian Jews regarded as an account of their own immediate past (as the Dura Europos synagogue paintings show, with their ample illustration of the book of Esther), we can hardly find that fact surprising. What impact does the other topical appendix make? With its stress on the life-nourishing power of rabbinical virtue — restraint, respect, self-abnegation, dignity — that excellent composite makes the point that people can do much, through proper conduct, to secure for themselves the desired longevity. But it is not clear to me that the composite has found its place here because of the Talmud's compilers' desire to make some further, oblique observation about the book of Esther. Since they stress Mordecai's virtues and present Esther as wholly virtuous, it seems to me unjustified to suggest that that may be so. We are therefore left with the fairly obvious and unsurprising observation that what the Bavli's compilers add is a composite pleasing to local self-esteem. Our sages in forming the Talmud to Mishnah-tractate Megillah seem to me to have remained well within the framework of the Mishnah's perspectives and to have added nothing surprising or jarring or, therefore, consequential for the history of Judaism except in one aspect. Keeping things the same also makes a difference.

# XI

## The Structure of Babylonian Talmud Tractate Moed Qatan

### Points of Structure

1. Does Babylonian Talmud-tractate Moed Qatan follow a coherent outline governed by a consistent rules?

The outline I have proposed answers this question. The Talmud-tractate follows a coherent outline; at remarkably few points were we unable to account for the position and purpose of a complete composition, one with a beginning, middle, and end. I can identify few, if any, such compositions that do not relate to the composite of which they form a part, and I can point to not a single composites without a clear purpose in the tractate's large-scale constructions. The outline I was able to construct followed a simple order: topic sentence, ordinarily a sentence of the Mishnah-tractate, at some points a subject or proposition not supplied by it; analytical discussion of the topic-sentence; propositions generated by the topic-sentences. Where the compilers wish to provide both analysis and illustrative cases, the order is, first, analysis, then illustration.

2. What are the salient traits of its structure?

The outline of the Talmud-tractate follows the outline of the Mishnah-tractate, but extends beyond the Mishnah-tractate in two ways. First, important statements of the Mishnah-tractate are not analyzed at all. Second, important propositions not set forth in the Mishnah-tractate are examined, and significant topical composites are inserted without regard to the Mishnah-tractate's program but in addition to it. The rules that the outline reveals present no surprises. In examining any sentence of the Mishnah or of a comparable Tannaite document, [1] the compilers first discuss the formulation, authorities, or scriptural foundations for the Mishnah's or other Tannaite document's statement. Then [2] secondary augmentation will begin, whether through an extension of the rule to other cases, or an investigation of the implicit principle of the rule and its intersection with other types of cases altogether. Following comes [3] the consideration of Tannaite formulations of rules that pertain in theme or problem or principle, and these will be subjected to the same sequence and type of analytical questions that have already been brought to bear upon the Mishnah.

3. WHAT IS THE RATIONALITY OF THE STRUCTURE?

We proceed from the particular — the Mishnah's rule — to the general. We first deal with the details of the particular, then we move outward to theoretical considerations. We deal with rules accorded Tannaite origin or sponsorship, first found in the Mishnah, then found in the Tosefta (not so firm a rule), and finally given a signal of Tannaite but not found in a compilation of Tannaite statements now in our hands (e. g., Tenno rabbanon, Tanné and the like).

4. WHERE ARE THE POINTS OF IRRATIONALITY IN THE STRUCTURE?

The foregoing account of the orderly structure of the Talmud-tractate Moed Qatan contains no explanation of the introduce of large-scale composites that we find as principle subdivisions of the divisions of the outline, I-XXI. With only the Mishnah-tractate in hand, we should have no basis for predicting the topics of the composites that provide other than Mishnah-exegesis, augmentation, and extension. Only when we ask why a given topical composite, extrinsic to the Mishnah-tractate, has been positioned where it is, and whether or not said composite can have occupied a position elsewhere in the Talmud-tractate or have been omitted with a significant loss of meaning, which we do at Points of System No. 2, will the topical composites be shown to participate in the rationality of the Talmud-tractate.

## POINTS OF SYSTEM

1. DOES THE BABYLONIAN TALMUD-TRACTATE MOED QATAN SERVE ONLY AS A RE-PRESENTATION OF THE MISHNAH-TRACTATE OF THE SAME NAME?

For negative and positive reasons, the answer to this question is one-sidedly negative. The negative reason is that Talmud-tractate does not re-present Mishnah-tractate Moed Qatan, because it omits consideration of sizable passages of the Mishnah-tractate. I can conceive of no way to predict what the Talmud-tractate's framers will omit; I see no pattern, nor can I explain why, in the same set of sentences, a given sentence will attract extensive consideration and another will not. But it suffices to say that the Talmud-tractate in no way pretends to cover every clause of the Mishnah. I further have formed the subjective impression that at no point do the framers of compositions concerning clauses of the Mishnah strain to find something to fill up space where they have nothing to say. I cannot point to a passage that strikes me as extraneous or fabricated for the occasion. That subjective impression gains a measure of objective standing when we observe that the same types of discussion accorded to a given Mishnah-clause recur throughout. A coherent and cogent program of Mishnah-exegesis governs everywhere. That seems to me to bear the implication that the framers of the Talmud-tractate do not acknowledge the task of filling up space by making statements where they have nothing interesting to say. My tentative hypothesis is that where a sentence of the Mishnah attracts no analytical inquiry, it is because it contains nothing that the framers of our Talmud-tractate found problematic; where they say nothing, it is because they have nothing to say. But to test that hypothesis we should have to pursue the question of the sources of the Talmud-tractate, that is, the resources upon which the compilers of composites drew, or the authors of compositions devoted to Mishnah-exegesis wrote up. That is not a question that concerns me here, since the answer tells us nothing about structure and system, explaining what we do not have, not what we do.

The positive reason is that the Talmud-tractate Moed Qatan includes presentation of topics and principles and propositions that the Mishnah-tractate does not present. Because of the inclusion of large-scale topical composites at I.B, IIB, VII.B, C, IV.B, C, X.B, C, XV.C, D E, XVIII.B, C, D, E, F, G, I, XIX.B, C, D, F, XX.C, E, F, XXI. B, C. The proportion of the tractate represented by the freestanding topical composites is accurately estimated only by a word count, that is, the number of words in the listed composites as against the number of words in the tractate as a whole. Without making such a word-count, I believe readers will concur in the simple judgment that the important topical composites extrinsic to Mishnah-exegesis and yet primary in the Talmud-tractate form a substantial component of the whole. These extrinsic composites and compositions take shape around their own subjects or propositions or problems, and they do not respond to those of the Mishnah-tractate. But, as we shall now see, they do change the re-presentation of the Mishnah-tractate in important ways, to which we now turn.

2. How do the topical composites fit into the Talmud-tractate Moed Qatan and what do they contribute that the Mishnah-tractate of the same name would lack without them?

    I.B:    The comparison of the Sabbatical Year's rules with those governing the intermediate days of the festival: this composite imposes the study of the relationship between two species of the single genus, occasions on which, by reason of a lesser degree of sanctification, limitations less drastic than those governing the Sabbath or the festival day are placed on acts of labor. The Mishnah has introduced the comparison of the two occasions, the Sabbatical Year and the intermediate days of the festival, and the Talmud-composite has taken up that comparison in its own terms, not for the purpose of Mishnah-exegesis, as an examination of I.B shows. This composite could not have made sense anywhere else in the tractate and had to be situated exactly where it is. It is therefore intrinsic to the exposition of the Mishnah, and what it does is redefine our perspective upon the Mishnah by insisting on a broader, comparative framework for reflection on the law.

II.B: This composite simply pursues the Mishnah's topic. It can have been introduced only here.

VII.B, C: What this freestanding composition and its appended composite contributes is the theme, taking leave of the master. The Mishnah-rule covers taking wives and the conduct of a woman on the occasion of a wedding. I see no direct connection to the Mishnah-topic. Introducing disciples' relationships with the master and their coming and going calls to mind the comparability of the familial relationship (here: marriage) and the supernatural relationship of master-disciple. I cannot point to any other appropriate setting in our tractate for this topic. What is contributed is the consideration of that other relationship, the supernatural one. But how the occasion — intermediate days of the festival — plays a role I cannot say. Since the composite continues the theme introduced in VII.A.1.c.2, I am inclined to think the reason for introducing it derives from the needs of expounding the composite to which it is attached, rather than the tractate into which the whole is inserted.

IX.B, C: The general theme of the composite is the conduct of workers, using workers to do work that Israelites may at the same span of time not carry out, contracting for work to be done on the intermediate days of the festival and the like. The composite serves very well in context and cannot have found a comfortable location any where else in the tractate. It expands the case of the Mishnah into the consideration of the principle of contracting — whether with gentile or with Israelite workers — to perform various acts of labor. The net effect is vastly to expand the scope of the Mishnah, transforming the case into a rule, the rule into a broad and ubiquitously relevant principle.

X.B: Here we compare two sets of laws that have in common the same status, namely, laws that apply to interstitial cases. The intermediate days of the festival are not the festival, but also not secular; the Samaritan is not an Israelite, but is also not a gentile. Once more, if we look back at the Mishnah-rule, X.A, we find ourselves in a comparable situation, namely, an interstitial case, involving a situation that has come about by accident and that can cause great loss, and how we contend with it; the way we deal with a middle-range situation — two rules in conflict — frames the problem throughout. Then the net effect again is to recast the Mishnah-rule in a much broader framework and to highlight the deeper conflict at hand.

## Chapter Eleven. The Structure of Babylonian Talmud Moed Qatan

X.C: The issue here is limits on labor performed on the intermediate days of the festival in connection with observance of the festival — another kind of interstitiality. Now, there are limits, just as pertain in general to the intermediate days of the festival. But there also is a reason to extend those limits, since the acts of labor now pertain to the festival itself. Once more, the composite cannot serve elsewhere in the tractate, and it makes a formidable contribution to the examination of the Mishnah in a broader context than suggested by the Mishnah-rule itself.

XV.C, D, E: Here is the point at which the framers of the Talmud have made a statement that is entirely their own, reshaping the topic of the Mishnah in ways that the Mishnah-tractate cannot have led us to anticipate in any way. The set of composites takes up the rules governing the mourner on the intermediate days of the festival, and this shades over into a systematic presentation of the rules of mourning in their own terms. Then, E, others who are comparable to the mourner in their status — not permitted to conduct themselves in ordinary society in accord with the rules that otherwise govern uniformly — are introduced. The net effect is to transform the re-presentation of the Mishnah-tractate by introducing a topic that the Mishnah-tractate scarcely touches.

XVIII.B, C, D, E, F, G, I: The topic of mourning is once more treated in its own terms, out of all relationship to the Mishnah-tractates interest in it. Here again, we have what amounts to a small tractate on mourning, a range of general rules, special problems, and then the inevitable case of the sage produced in this context as in many others now carrying us far beyond the limits of the Mishnah-tractate.

XIX.B, C, D, F: The topic of mourning for sages, the death of sages, and the like, along with further comments on mourning rites, predominates once more. Here again, the Mishnah-tractate in a tangential way has introduced a topic in the contest of the Mishnah-tractate's program. Then the Talmud-composite treats the topic in terms not to be predicted out of the way in which the Mishnah-tractate has introduced said topic. Now the topic takes on a life of its own.

XX.C, E, F: Forms of lamentation take over, and the matter of the intermediate days of the festival falls by the way. Once more the result is the same. The essay shades over from mourning to death: dying suddenly, the angel of death, and the angel of death and sages.

XXI. B, C, D: Not surprisingly, the freestanding composite pursues its own interest, which is [1] rules of mourning with [2] special interest in sages. It is hardly surprising that D ends with the condition of sages in the world to come, that is, after death.

The topical composites fit in in two distinct ways. First, some of them — represented by I.B, IX.B, C, and X. B (a very subtle entry indeed) — greatly expand the scope of the Mishnah-rule, introducing a level of abstraction that Mishnah-exegesis does not require. Mishnah-exegesis is made to set the stage for a much broader consideration of principles that transcend cases and recast rules into representations of underlying conceptions of a high order of generalization. In this first type of topical composite, the Mishnah's rule is re-presented as an indicator of a deeper, compelling problem of thought, often of a philosophical, rather than a narrowly-legal character.

Second, and more strikingly, the larger number of the topical composites — represented by the composites from XV.C-E to the end! — change the face of the Mishnah-tractate by raising to prominence subjects treated by the Mishnah only incidentally and in a subordinate status. A tractate on conduct on the intermediate days of the festival has been turned into one on that subject and on another as well.

3. CAN WE STATE WHAT THE COMPILERS OF THIS DOCUMENT PROPOSE TO ACCOMPLISH IN PRODUCING THIS COMPLETE, ORGANIZED PIECE OF WRITING?

The answer to this question lies in explaining the connection between rites of mourning and the rules governing conduct on the intermediate days of the festival. What made sages conceive that the latter should find a comfortable and capacious place amid the former — even to the extent of extensively and promiscuously interspersing rules of mourning in expositions of intermediate days of the festival? True, the Mishnah-tractate introduces the mourner, along with other classes of persons in a special situation on the intermediate days of the festival. But the Talmud has not then given us large-scale discussions of the person released from prison or others who appear on the same lists as the mourner. So the formal explanation — the topic is introduced by the Mishnah, so it is discussed in its own terms in the Talmud — begs the question.

Rather, a substantive explanation is required, and it is contained in the answer to a simple question. Precisely what has death to do with the intermediate days of the festival? The principal mode of thought of the Mishnah is that of comparison and contrast. Something is like something else, therefore follows its rule; or unlike, therefore follows the opposite of the rule governing the something else. So as a matter of hypothesis, let us assume that the framers of Talmud-tractate Moed Qatan found self-evidently valid the modes of thought that they learned from the Mishnah and so made connections between things that were alike, on the one side, or things that were opposite, on the other. How do death and

## Chapter Eleven. The Structure of Babylonian Talmud Moed Qatan

mourning compare to the intermediate days of the festival? The point of opposition — the contrastive part of the equation — then proves blatant. Death is the opposite of the celebration of the festival. The one brings mourning, the other, joy. And the Mishnah's inclusion of the mourner on its list of those whose special situation must be taken into account then precipitates thought about the item on the list — the mourner — that most clearly embodies the special circumstance of all items on the list.

But if the contrast proves obvious, the point of comparison — how are these things similar, and what rule pertains to both — emerges with equal facility. Extremes of emotion — mourning, rejoicing — come together in the normal cycle of life and the passage of time. Each takes its place on a continuum with the other, whether from the perspective of the passage of time in nature or the passage of life, also in nature; whether from the perspective of the sacred or from the standpoint of uncleanness. The natural rhythm of the year brings Passover and Tabernacles, the celebration of the first full moon after the vernal and autumnal equinoxes, respectively. The natural rhythm of life brings its moments of intense emotion too. But death and the festival also form moments of a single continuum, one of uncleanness yielding to its polar opposite, sanctification, sanctification yielding to uncleanness. Death, we must not forget, also serves as a principal source of uncleanness, the festival, the occasion for sanctification beginning with the removal of cultic uncleanness and the entry into a state of cultic cleanness. These opposites also take their place on a single continuum of being.

So in establishing the connection, through treating the categories as equivalent and counterpart to one another, between death and the festival's intermediate days, what have our sages in Talmud-tractate Moed Qatan said in their own behalf, not about the Mishnah but through their re-presentation of the Mishnah? They make the connection between the one and the other — death and the festival's intermediate days — so as to yield a conclusion concerning the everyday and the here and now. These are neither permanently sanctified nor definitively unclean, neither wholly the occasion for rejoicing without restriction as to acts of labor nor entirely the occasion of common ventures without restriction as to attitudes of exaltation. The days between festivals, like ordinary life, after birth but before death — these are to be seen as sanctified but not wholly so, just as life forms the realm of the angel of death, but only for a while. The festival comes — and so does the resurrection of the dead and the life of the world to come, of which the festival, like the Sabbath, gives us a foretaste.

# XII

# The Structure of Babylonian Talmud Tractate Hagigah

### POINTS OF STRUCTURE

1. DOES BABYLONIAN TALMUD-TRACTATE HAGIGAH FOLLOW A COHERENT OUTLINE GOVERNED BY A CONSISTENT RULES?

The fact that we may outline the document in a consistent manner and explain the inclusion of each composition and composite and the location thereof — here, not somewhere else, in this particular context, not in some other — proves that the compilers of the tractate do follow a coherent outline. That outline is supplied by the Mishnah, and most of the compositions and composites in the tractate have been made up or chosen because of their usefulness in amplifying the Mishnah-tractate that is subject to discussion.

2. WHAT ARE THE SALIENT TRAITS OF ITS STRUCTURE?

The tractate does contain some striking and massive topical or thematic composites, but while the tractate looks to be padded by their inclusion, in fact, every one of the large-scale composites has been selected because it expounds a topic introduced by the Mishnah. With only a few important exceptions, treated presently, we can account for the inclusion of every massive miscellany simply by referring to the Mishnah-tractate. That fact emerges most strikingly in Chapter Two, where one of the most remarkable composites in the entire Talmud — the exquisite presentation of the Outsider, with its moving portrait of the heretic-master and the loyal, orthodox disciple — turns out to fit in quite naturally to a larger exegetical program. The character of the tractate as a Mishnah-commentary is seen in page after page, and most of the units of the foregoing outline amply instantiate the fact that the Bavli is a commentary to the Mishnah, and whatever message its compilers wished to set forth beyond that of the Mishnah, whatever means they chose to use to recast or revise the meaning of the Mishnah — all emerge in a single mode.

3. WHAT IS THE RATIONALITY OF THE STRUCTURE?

It suffices to state simply that what makes sense derives its rationality from the statements of the Mishnah, and its logic from the sequence in which those statements are made in the Mishnah.

4. WHERE ARE THE POINTS OF IRRATIONALITY IN THE STRUCTURE?

The following are the exceptions to the rule that our outline has highlighted: I:F, G, H;VI.D (with attention to E), F, G, H, I, J; IX:C. These are not minor exceptions; they form an important component of the volume of the tractate as a whole. Remove them, and the tractate loses approximately a fourth of its sheer volume.

## POINTS OF SYSTEM

1. DOES THE BABYLONIAN TALMUD-TRACTATE HAGIGAH SERVE ONLY AS A RE-PRESENTATION OF THE MISHNAH-TRACTATE OF THE SAME NAME?

For the reasons given above, the answer is a qualified positive. But we note that the Bavli's compilers have not found it necessary to say something about everything. Interesting omissions are at III.B, IV.C, VIII.A, an important omission; IX.A, B, X.E, XII.B. It may be of interest to observe that all omitted clauses and sentences form integral parts of statements that are subjected to principled analysis. It would be difficult to make a case that the specified items are completely bypassed. But the line by line or statement by statement pattern that governs throughout does not apply to these items.

2. HOW DO THE TOPICAL COMPOSITES FIT INTO THE TALMUD-TRACTATE HAGIGAH AND WHAT DO THEY CONTRIBUTE THAT THE MISHNAH-TRACTATE OF THE SAME NAME WOULD LACK WITHOUT THEM?

The tractate's two massive miscellanies, serving Chapters One and Two, respectively, impart to the topic a profound, theological dimension. First of all, they identify the deeper religious experience inherent in the topic; then they point to the religious message to be drawn therefrom. We deal with a truly amazing transformation of a Mishnah-tractate by the Talmud-tractate that re-presents it. To understand what is to come, we have to keep in mind that the hagigah- or festal-offering, and the appearance-offering, bring Israel into the Temple for a pilgrimage to see God, as Scripture says in so many words. So the topic of the Mishnah-tractate, the rules governing these offerings, as Chapter One lays out the topic, carries in its aftermath the profound issue, what does it mean to see God? That accounts, in the Mishnah-tractate itself, for the inclusion of Chapter Two, with its disruptive statements at M. 2:1-2 about the Chariot and the Works of Creation, the Torah that pertains to them, and the rules governing who may or may not be taught those topics. These represent the counterpart to the appearance-offering, that is to say, this is where, in the Torah, Israel sees God, just as much as, in the Temple, in the rites, Israel sees God. Now our sages in the Talmud take up the two topics —

## Chapter Twelve. The Structure of Babylonian Talmud Hagigah 73

the festal and appearance offering, the counterpart to appearing before God in the study of the Torah — and spell out dimensions of those topics that the Mishnah-tractate simply does not explore. Whatever place the Mishnah-tractate assumes for itself in the system of the Mishnah, in the Talmud's recasting of that system, the tractate is given a massive position in the center of the religious statement that the Talmud's framers mean to make. This is in two parts, as we shall now see: Israel's historical condition, taken up in Chapter One, and Israel's encounter with God through the person of our sages of blessed memory, taken up in Chapter Two. The former makes the point that God weeps for Israel's present circumstance, missing Israel and yearning to see Israel in the Temple once more. The second makes the point that it is through Torah-study that our sages now meet God, as once, and once more in time to come, meeting God took place and will take place in the Temple. Now to the specifics of this remarkable transformation of a rather dry and technical tractate of the Mishnah.

I.F: To this point, the Talmud has given a discussion of the rules of the appearance offering, with special attention to whom need not present one. The vast insertion, F-H, then adds a stunning and jarring point, deriving from the present of the compilers of the Talmud. Israel as a whole cannot now present the appearance offering, since making an appearance in Jerusalem at the Temple is rendered moot by the destruction of the Temple. So added to the list of those who do not make the pilgrimage is the entire people of Israel. Not only the lame, blind, sick, and old, but all Israel are now exempt — and what an exemption! The inclusion of the composite, formed around the theme of sages' weeping upon encountering various verses of Scripture, is accomplished in a simple way. A proof-text vital for the exposition of a Mishnah-rule is now treated in its own context, which is a formal one. But the formal construction turns out remarkably, since this and the other verses that provoked tears make the same point, which is, Israel is estranged from God and cannot make the pilgrimage to greet him. This is spelled out in so many words. Women, slaves, the lame, and so on, are excluded from the pilgrimage; then the slave is made to stand for Israel: a slave whose master yearns to see him is estranged from him." The profound irony of the sentence cannot be missed: the master owns the slave and the slave possesses no independent power of will for that reason. Yet the master yearns for the slave but is estranged from him. Beyond that one scarcely need to go. The inclusion of the entire formal set imparts to the tractate a depth that, on its own, the Mishnah-tractate simply lacks; the Mishnah's rule for an aspect of the pilgrimage festival now are recast into that one context that in the Mishnah's presentation the topic lacks, which is, the historical one. The Mishnah's framers of the tractate on the pilgrimage simply ignore the context in which the tractate is set forth; the Talmud's commentators' intrusion of the proposition at hand, at this very point, imparts to the Mishnah's presentation an irony and a message of tragedy but also hope — God yearns for a reconciliation, the study of the pilgrim offering then underscoring the coming reward for penitence — that the Mishnah-tractate simply lacks.

I.G: Without the intrusion of I.G, the statement of I.F lacks symmetry. Sages weep at Israel's condition. But so does God. The message of I.F, the tragedy of estrangement, now finds its completion: God weeps too. The juxtaposition of VI:34 and VI:35 is jarring, since the one speaks of the domestic condition of Israel, which is measured by study of the Torah and the character of the community's leadership, and the public condition of Israel, signaled by the book of Lamentations. It would be difficult to miss the point expressed through that juxtaposition of otherwise unrelated compositions. And for reasons of a shared hero, Rabbi, VI:36 is tightly linked to the foregoing, yielding a message that transcends the formal point of intersection. That is to bring us back to the topic of our tractate, the pilgrimage to see and by seen by God. Nor can VI:37 be dismissed as tacked on, since the analogy is then drawn between Temple and Torah-study, and that analogy is specific and not merely generic: one goes to the Temple for a day, makes the offering, and goes home; one may do the same, making a pilgrimage for three months to an academy, spending a day, and going home.

I.H: The foregoing remark shows that this composite is integral to the message of I.F, G.

The massive miscellanies of Chapter Two are all grouped together and organized in a coherent program. They expand upon the theme of the Mishnah, first, the works of Creation, then the vision of the Chariot. The several units flow naturally from one to the next. There is nothing miscellaneous about the compositions, nothing disorganized about the composite.

VI.D: To understand what is at stake in VI.D-J, we recall the point of intersection between Chapters One and Two of the Mishnah-tractate, which is, the appearance offering, the being seen by, and seeing, God. At that point, the matters of the works of creation and of the chariot enter in; these are, in the Torah, the specific statements that concern God's presence in the world: through creation, the Creator is made known; through the vision of the Chariot, Ezekiel recorded seeing God. So the topic is natural to the deeper concern of the Mishnah-tractate. This unit treats the works of creation.

Chapter Twelve. *The Structure of Babylonian Talmud Hagigah* 75

VI.E: The Mishnah's next topic, and this composite, as much as the ones fore and aft, serves the purpose of Mishnah-commentary. But the commentary takes a very particular form. The Mishnah refers to a topic. The topic then takes over and a vast collection on Ezekiel and his vision follows; some of the compositions form subunits, e.g., exegeses of Ez. Chapter One; some then trail off into discussions of angels and other subtopics.

VI.F: I am somewhat puzzled by the inclusion of this miscellany on Is. 3:5-7. Perhaps because Isaiah had a vision of God, he came to mind when Ezekiel's vision was presented. That seems a somewhat flimsy reason for IV:25-28. But I can think of nothing more substantial.

VI.G: There can be no doubt about why this item is included, since it reverts to Ezekiel's vision (and makes all the more difficult to explain the appearance of VI.F). From this point to the end, the presentation flows inexorably. First we have the presentation of a scene involving the work of the chariot, and VI.G, and this is a prologue to VI.H. G-H certainly form a continuous statement, and the whole form an admirable fit with the exposition of Ezekiel's Chariot-vision.

VI.H: The four who "entered paradise" are those who have taken up the study of Heavenly mysteries. Here we see an exposition of what happens to those who pursue that subject. The principal figures are Ben Zoma, who went mad, and the Outsider, or Elisha b. Abbuyah.

VI.I: This wonderful composite forms a striking counterpart to Chapter One's exposition of the sage as counterpart to God. Sages weep, God weeps, at Israel's condition. So mastery of the Torah produces a human being in God's model. But learning in the mysteries discussed here, which falls into the category of Torah-study, may also have a different result: an apostate-sage, not only a sage gone mad. The Outsider then forms in Chapter Two the mirror-image of the sage who weeps like God at Israel's estrangement from God. The arrangement of the items in VI.I is logical and orderly, from beginnings with Meir to end, the sad and lonely death.

VI.J: The fact that the several items are carefully compiled to make a single point emerges when we consider the Aqiba-collection. Given the huge number of stories at hand, we must regard the selection as careful and deliberate. Aqiba is introduced for a purpose, and both of the operative items serve that purpose.

IX.C: This exposition is coherent with the foregoing and simply expands in more abstract terms on precisely the issues of its context.

3. CAN WE STATE WHAT THE COMPILERS OF THIS DOCUMENT PROPOSE TO ACCOMPLISH IN PRODUCING THIS COMPLETE, ORGANIZED PIECE OF WRITING?

Mishnah-tractate Hagigah Chapter One deals with the festal and appearance offerings. The Talmud imparts to those offerings a profound message:

they signal the character of Israel's relationship with God. When Israel can make the pilgrimage to see and be seen by God, as the offering's very name indicates, that is a mark of Israel's relationship with God. That Israel cannot make the pilgrimage at this time evokes weeping not only among sages but also in God; the condition of Israel, the slave whose master yearns for him, is marked by the tragic flaw of estrangement. Study of the rules of who makes the pilgrimage then is made into an occasion for reflection upon the condition of Israel and what is required to correct that condition, which is, study of the Torah under the guidance of the sages. Sages' weeping for Israel, like God's, marks the point of commensurability; sages' mastery and teaching of the Torah form the measure of Israel's hope; and God's weeping for Israel's condition brings assurance that the estrangement is only for the moment, but reconciliation will be forever. That is the theological depth to which reflection on the rather dry topic of our tractate has drawn our sages of blessed memory in their composition of Chapter One of this tractate.

The expansion of Chapter Two centers upon two accounts of studying the works of creation and the chariot, Yohanan ben Zakkai's disciple, and the four famous sages. The warning of the Mishnah-rule is amply instantiated. But the power of including the sages' encounter with the mysteries is such as to change the face of the tractate once again. What happens when sages glimpse Paradise? Two play minor roles, Ben Azzai and Aqiba. The principal players are Ben Zoma, who went out of his mind, and the Outsider, who left the holy community of Israel. They represent what we may call an anti-pilgrimage, that is, a journey made for sacred purposes but with a bad end. Ben Zoma ended up insane. The Outsider is introduced to show that the wrong kind of Torah-study, in the present context, leads to the oblivion of apostasy; mastery of the Torah by itself does not save the Outsider. His own disciple, who has mastered his Torah but done so in a proper manner, attests to the tragedy involved in improper utilization of Torah-learning. So the free-standing exposition, which turns from what is studied to what happens to those who undertake the particular topics of Torah-learning, makes its own point.

The tractate in the Mishnah's version tells about the pilgrimage in three aspects: the trip to Jerusalem, who goes and who need not; seeing God and being seen by God, not now in the context of the sanctuary but in the setting of the Torah, therefore in creation and in the chariot; and the rites of purification involved in the pilgrimage. The tractate in the Talmud adds two further topics to the presentation: Israel's condition of estrangement, the end for the time being of pilgrimage to see God; and seeing God in the Torah, with the apostate-sage the complement to the now-estranged Israel. Just as Israel is estranged from God, so the sage has become estranged from the Torah. Wrong learning, for the latter, like wrong attitudes and actions, for the former, account for the end of the occasion for seeing and being seen by God. Then right learning in the Torah form the goal of today's pilgrimage, so that tomorrow's may once more be a journey to see God in the Temple, not alone in the Torah.

# XIII

## The Structure of Babylonian Talmud Yebamot

### Points of Structure

1. Does Babylonian Talmud-tractate Yebamot follow a coherent outline governed by a consistent rules?

The tractate is organized as a commentary to the Mishnah-tractate of the same name. While some compositions are formed around interests other than those dictated by the work of Mishnah-exegesis, few large-scale composites are put together for a purpose other than that of Mishnah-exegesis, or the amplification of said exegesis.

2. What are the salient traits of its structure?

The tractate's framers rarely wander far from the program of the Mishnah. Once they have worked out the explanation of its words and phrases, the identification of the authorities behind anonymous statements, and the provision of scriptural foundations for some of the Mishnah's rules, they turn to the second-layer study of the law. This may involve an inquiry into the premises of the detailed rules, or it may concern how a given principle of law in general is illuminated by the particular rule at hand. But when engaged in Mishnah-exegesis, the framers of the overall structure of the Talmud-tractate have not brought a large-scale and systematic set of such abstract principles; these occur episodically and rarely systematically for more than two or three Mishnah-rules at a time.

3. What is the Rationality of the structure?

In light of what has been said, little needs to be added concerning the principles of order and reason that govern the layout of the tractate and the selection of the compositions and even composites that comprise its contents. However fragmentary a piece of writing may appear to be, it finds its natural place within a given composition; and however truncated a composition may seem, it discovers its natural locus within a composite; and nearly all composites relate to one another through the sentences or paragraphs of the Mishnah; that alone is what holds them together.

## 4. WHERE ARE THE POINTS OF IRRATIONALITY IN THE STRUCTURE?

What is irrational then is what does not relate to the work of Mishnah-exegesis, either directly or indirectly.

### POINTS OF SYSTEM

1. DOES THE BABYLONIAN TALMUD-TRACTATE YEBAMOT SERVE ONLY AS A RE-PRESENTATION OF THE MISHNAH-TRACTATE OF THE SAME NAME?

As we have found in the tractates that have already been examined, so in the case of Yebamot, passages of the Mishnah receive no comment. These follow no pattern, and no theory of how framers of the Talmud selected for exegesis a given passage but determined that another should be neglected comes to mind. In addition, some few composites ignore the Mishnah altogether. These we now address.

2. HOW DO THE TOPICAL COMPOSITES FIT INTO THE TALMUD-TRACTATE AND WHAT DO THEY CONTRIBUTE THAT THE MISHNAH-TRACTATE OF THE SAME NAME WOULD LACK WITHOUT THEM?

I present the account in three sections. On the left hand margin are important propositional composites that do not address the Mishnah's propositions but do affect them. At the right are the composites that complement the Mishnah's statements with topically relevant amplifications or that carry forward the Mishnah's principle to new data. Finally, I underline and also position in the center column large composites that strike me as entirely out of phase with the Mishnah, lacking all point of contact, whether topical or in principle or even theme, broadly construed. Identifying these items and distinguishing them from those on the right hand margin involve a measure of subjectivity, and for that reason, I have tried to impose the most rigorous and narrowest possible definition of what is both free-standing and also affective of the rest. In the center I give those utterly anomalous composites that ignore the principle of propositional or at least topical cogency altogether.

XXXII.B: Composite on the
Marriage-Rules Governing A Slave
XXXII:C: Composite on
Conversion in General
XLI:C, E: Topical Appendix
on Wives and Marriage
XLI:D: Composite of Further
Teachings Attributed to Eleazar
LV:B:Topical Appendix on
he Disposition of the Tithes
LXIII:C.Riddles of Consanguinity

## Chapter Thirteen. The Structure of Babylonian Talmud Yebamot

### LXVII:B: Independent Proposition, Analysis of Which Utilizes the Mishnah-Materials at Hand

The two items of XXXII extend the coverage of the Mishnah's rule, the former by taking account of the fact that slaves are part of the marriage-system, and latter by introducing the further fact that slaves are converted to Judaism as part of the process of acquisition. The Mishnah has not attended to these classes of persons, and the Talmud has insisted that they too come under consideration. The number, all the more so, the proportion, of free-standing composites prove negligible. Apart from a handful of topical appendices, and two odd composites of a quite familiar type — rare in any tractate — the entirety of Bavli Yebamot takes shape around the Mishnah or around secondary expansion of Mishnah-commentary and amplification.

3. CAN WE STATE WHAT THE COMPILERS OF THIS DOCUMENT PROPOSE TO ACCOMPLISH IN PRODUCING THIS COMPLETE, ORGANIZED PIECE OF WRITING?

This large and in many ways profound and rich Talmud-tractate, full of important intellectual initiatives, serves in only a single way, and that is, as a commentary to the Mishnah-tractate of the same name. It has no other purpose, and that one purpose governs throughout. A search for an account of the other-than-Mishnaic components of the Rabbinic structure and system could well bypass this tractate, since, in its form and its program, it bears the character of a recapitulation of the Mishnah's ideas, within the Mishnah's framework. And yet — the fact that the entire Talmud imposes upon the Mishnah its rhetoric, its logic, and its program, one that hardly accepts the programmatic limitations of the Mishnah's program contradicts this now-established fact and raises a profound issue of its own. The law of the Mishnah has been given more than a reprise; the framers have not merely clarified but have reshaped and deepened the received law of treated in the three components of the Mishnah-tractate. So, while everything appears to be the same, in fact, much has changed, as we move from the Mishnah into the writing that purports to do little more than, assigning the Mishnah a privileged standing, recapitulates the Mishnah's own statements in a clearer way than in the original.

If, as one major tractate after another informs us, the Talmud is a commentary to the Mishnah and little more than that, then how do we account for the character of not the parts but the whole: the fact that, in the aftermath of the Talmud, the Mishnah would never be the same and would utterly loses its distinctive and independent voice within the natural sounds of the Talmud's own melody.

# XIV

## The Structure of Babylonian Talmud Ketubot

### Points of Structure

1. Does Babylonian Talmud-tractate Ketubot follow a coherent outline governed by a consistent rules?

The outline of the Talmud-tractate is the same as that of the Mishnah-tractate, because the former follows the latter. We can account for the presence of all composites that do not serve the purpose of Mishnah-commentary. These are compiled in their own terms and are then inserted for purposes deemed appropriate by the compositors of the Talmud as a whole, as the foregoing outline has shown in rich detail.

2. What are the salient traits of its structure?

Most of the sentences of the Mishnah-tractate are amplified, and the program of exegesis is limited and disciplined. The language, then the rules, then the principles of the Mishnah's statements are systematically expounded. Then secondary materials may be added, inclusive of cases, various sorts of obiter dicta, and the like.

3. What is the Rationality of the structure?

It follows that the principle of cohesion and juxtaposition derives from the structure of the Mishnah-tractate, and outside of the framework of Mishnah-exegesis, the Talmud has no independent medium for explaining what comes first and what must follow, on the one side, or what logically coheres to what else, on the other side. But the process of formation yields the inclusion, also, of compositions and even sizable composites that are put together by other principles than those governing Mishnah-exegesis. Once framed in their own terms, these will be attached, for reasons that, to the framers of the Talmud-tractate, appeared quite rational and orderly. In general these additional composites, outside the framework of Mishnah-exegesis, form topical appendices to subjects important in Mishnah-exegesis. The exceptions to that rule are few and inconsequential.

4. Where are the points of irrationality in the structure?

These are compiled in the setting of the discussion of the topical composites, given presently.

### POINTS OF SYSTEM

1. DOES THE BABYLONIAN TALMUD-TRACTATE KETUBOT SERVE ONLY AS A REPRESENTATION OF THE MISHNAH-TRACTATE OF THE SAME NAME?

Some sentences of the Mishnah-tractate are not discussed at all, and even a few of the Mishnah's illustrative cases. But the Talmud-tractate exhibits no other sustained or even meaningful principle of conglomeration than that of Mishnah-commentary, pure and simple.

2. HOW DO THE TOPICAL COMPOSITES FIT INTO THE TALMUD-TRACTATE AND WHAT DO THEY CONTRIBUTE THAT THE MISHNAH-TRACTATE OF THE SAME NAME WOULD LACK WITHOUT THEM?

I present the account in three sections. On the left hand margin are important propositional composites that do not address the Mishnah's propositions but do affect them. At the right are the composites that complement the Mishnah's statements with topically relevant amplifications or that carry forward the Mishnah's principle to new data or in some other, material way pertain to the Mishnah's statements. Finally, I underline and also position in the center column large composites that strike me as entirely out of phase with the Mishnah, lacking all point of contact, whether topical or in principle or even theme, broadly construed. Identifying these items and distinguishing them from those on the right hand margin involve a measure of subjectivity, and for that reason, I have tried to impose the most rigorous and narrowest possible definition of what is both free-standing and also affective of the rest. In the center I give those utterly anomalous composites that ignore the principle of propositional or at least topical cogency altogether.

<u>I:C: Miscellany of Sayings
in the Name of Bar Qappara</u>
      XI.B: Celebrating the Bride:
      A Thematic Composite
    XII:B: Other Rules on the Validation
      of Documents by Witnesses
    XXIX:B. Free-Standing Analysis,
    Inserted because of the Utilization of
      Simeon's Statement in the
      Present Mishnah-Paragraph
    XXXI.C: Topical Composite on Modes
      of Execution of a Betrothed Girl
    XXXIV.B: Further Rules Ordained in Usha

## Chapter Fourteen. The Structure of Babylonian Talmud Ketubot

XL.G: Topical Composite on the Provisions Made for the Waiter at a Meal. From what the wife does for the husband, we move to what the waiter does for the sages; what is owing to the waiter, and similar topics. This item cannot be divorced from its context — acts of personal service — but it also changes the frame of reference from the family to the master-disciple circle. That is why I regard it as a recasting of the Mishnah's topic, a re-presentation of that topic in a different, distinctively Talmudic, context.

XLVII:B: Topical Composite on Marrying Off Orphans. Support of the Poor

LVI:D: Stories of Deaths of Various Sages and how their Mastery of the Torah Afforded Them Special Standing after Death. Why this massive composite is tacked on is scarcely self-evident. My best guess is that the Mishnah's reference to the death of the tanner and the right of the wife to reject the levir triggered the association with the deaths of sages. The positioning of the composite also is odd, since it interrupts the exposition of III.4.

LXXXIV:B. Judges Who Take Bribes:
Topical Composite
LXXXIV:C: Proper Payment for Services
Rendered in the Context of Sanctification
XCIV:D: The Messianic Age, the Age to Come,
in the Context of Residence in the Land of Israel
XCIV:E: The Remarkable
Productivity of the Land of Israel

We note also that a sizable composite is located after M. 11:1 but belongs after M. 11:2. But the composite exhibits close ties to the Mishnah-paragraph the theme of which it explores.

3. CAN WE STATE WHAT THE COMPILERS OF THIS DOCUMENT PROPOSE TO ACCOMPLISH IN PRODUCING THIS COMPLETE, ORGANIZED PIECE OF WRITING?

Where a composite has no bearing upon the Mishnah's statement but at the same time may claim to make a coherent and intelligible statement in the Talmud's context if not the Mishnah's (thus excluding the items in the center-list), the point that is made concerns two matters: sages special, supernatural situation and the age to come and the advent of the Messiah. This latter topic, for the present tractate, falls within the natural range of the Mishnah's interest; that is, once we speak of the priority of residence in the Holy Land, the reversion of all Israel to the Holy Land in the world to come or the Messiah's day represents a natural next step. The only significant composites that impart a dimension on a topic introduced by the Mishnah but not required thereby then add sages' perspective on matters.

# XV

# The Structure of Babylonian Talmud Nedarim

### Points of Structure

1. Does Babylonian Talmud-tractate Nedarim follow a coherent outline governed by a consistent rules?

By examining the statements of the Mishnah we can explain the location of every composite and most compositions. Nearly all are situated where they are because of the requirements of Mishnah-exegesis, or because of an interest in a secondary amplification of a problem of Mishnah-exegesis. The tractate is no different from any other in its coherent program, which is dictated solely by the Mishnah's counterpart.

2. What are the salient traits of its structure?

The order and program of all primary composites — those attached to a Mishnah-paragraph — derive from the sequence of statements made by the Mishnah-tractate. There is no other source of order, nor does any agenda other than that of the Mishnah play a role.

3. What is the Rationality of the structure?

It follows that compositions and composites that themselves bear no affinity for one another hold together because of their reference-point in common to the Mishnah.

4. Where are the points of irrationality in the structure?

These are indicated in the catalogue given below.

### Points of System

1. Does the Babylonian Talmud-tractate Nedarim serve only as a re-presentation of the Mishnah-tractate of the same name?

Because of the omission of discussion for a sizable number of Mishnah-pericopes, the Talmud-tractate does not adequately serve as a re-presentation if the Mishnah-tractate. But it serves no other purpose. So while it may be distinguished from other tractates by reason of the paucity of sustained discussions and secondary developments of primary exegetical initiatives, such as are common elsewhere, still the tractate falls well within the parameters of all others in its basic structural qualities.

2. How do the topical composites fit into the Talmud-tractate and what do they contribute that the Mishnah-tractate of the same name would lack without them?

I present the account in three sections. On the left hand margin are important propositional composites that do not address the Mishnah's propositions but do affect them. At the right are the composites that complement the Mishnah's statements with topically relevant amplifications or that carry forward the Mishnah's principle to new data. Finally, I underline and also position in the center column large composites that strike me as entirely out of phase with the Mishnah, lacking all point of contact, whether topical or in principle or even theme, broadly construed. Identifying these items and distinguishing them from those on the right hand margin involve a measure of subjectivity, and for that reason, I have tried to impose the most rigorous and narrowest possible definition of what is both free-standing and also affective of the rest. In the center I give those utterly anomalous composites that ignore the principle of propositional or at least topical cogency altogether.

I:D: Composite of Sayings<br>
by R. Giddal-Rab on the General Theme<br>
of Personal Acts of Piety

XIV:C: Topical Appendix in<br>
the Matter of Adultery

XV:B: Topical Composite on
Losing One's Temper,
Deemed the Basis for Taking Vows

XXX:B: Topical Composite<br>
on Abraham<br>
XXXIV:D: Topical Appendix on<br>
the Correct Way of<br>
Writing and Reading Scripture<br>
XXXVI:B: Topical Composite on<br>
the Matter of Korach and His Sect<br>
XLV:D: Topical Composite Concerning<br>
Eating Various Types of Food<br>
XLV:F: Miscellany Concerning<br>
Food: Marks of Poverty or Wealth

LX:A: Free-Standing Problem,<br>
to which the Foregoing<br>
Makes a Factual Contribution

*Chapter Fifteen. The Structure of Babylonian Talmud Nedarim* 87

LXII:C: Not Utilizing the Torah and
Commandments for
an Inappropriate Purpose

Two points of interest capture our attention, first, the extended statement on how losing one's temper causes vow-taking, surely implicit in the Mishnah-tractate itself but nicely articulated; and, second, the insertion of a free-standing demonstration of a proposition with no bearing on our tractate but utilizing facts thereof for its own purpose, a kind of composition or composite we find here and there. Otherwise all we have before us is a set of topical appendices, which provide information deemed useful, if not essential, in the exposition of the tractate's topical program.

3. CAN WE STATE WHAT THE COMPILERS OF THIS DOCUMENT PROPOSE TO ACCOMPLISH IN PRODUCING THIS COMPLETE, ORGANIZED PIECE OF WRITING?

The compilers put together a fairly systematic exegesis of most, though not all, of the Mishnah-tractate's statements, and that is all. They have not changed our reading of its topic, with the stated exception, and their topical appendices do not enrich our appreciation of the tractate's larger context of meaning. The tractate compared to others is somewhat anomalous, covering less of the Mishnah-tractate than we ordinarily anticipate will be dealt with; but the presentation of the Mishnah-tractate by the Talmud follows the ordinary lines of order and takes up the familiar issues, beginning to end. It is quite clear that a single, and simple, program of exegesis guided the compilation of Talmud-tractates.

# XVI

## The Structure of Babylonian Talmud Nazir

POINTS OF STRUCTURE

My preliminary outline — pending completing of the academic commentary expected from Professor Paul V. McM. Flesher, suffices only to establish that the structure of Bavli-tractate Nazir rests upon the Mishnah-tractate of the same name, and that nearly all of the principal composites depend for coherence, cogency, and even order upon the structure of the Mishnah-tractate. However, further judgments on the secondary and tertiary problems of structural analysis must await the systematic and fully analyzed translation that is to appear in due course.

# XVII

## The Structure of Babylonian Talmud Tractate Sotah

### POINTS OF STRUCTURE

The outline before us leaves no doubt on the program of the Talmud's compilers. They intended to produce a commentary to the Mishnah, and nearly everything before us has been organized to serve that purpose, even though a formidable part of the raw materials that the compilers used was originally formulated for a purpose other than Mishnah-commentary. A study of the state of writing among the sages prior to the work of Talmud-compilation would benefit from an analysis of the compositions and large-scale composites that have been recast for the purposes of making this Talmud. But that is not what defines the present task. Since we want to know about the Talmud, and not the history of the formation of the materials that ultimately were selected for use by the framers of the Talmud, identifying materials that were made up in the labor of "the talmud before the Talmud" suffices for the present task and has been done through the various signals of the translation and outline. From those signals, readers may reconstruct the state of writing among sages during that indeterminate, but probably quite protracted, age prior to the decision to make the Mishnah the centerpiece of composition. During that time other kinds of writing went forward, even though the results did not encompass the formation of large-scale documents comparable to this one. Our question is not what might have been but what was, which is, the statement in a single coherent writing of the law and theology that "our sages of blessed memory" set forth as the Torah, and that we call Judaism.

1. DOES BABYLONIAN TALMUD-TRACTATE SOTAH FOLLOW A COHERENT OUTLINE GOVERNED BY A CONSISTENT RULES?

From beginning to end, Babylonian-Talmud-tractate Sotah is organized as a commentary to the Mishnah, and no composition or composite finds its way into the document other than in the setting of Mishnah-commentary, even though some composites and many compositions were originally written down in other contexts than Mishnah-commentary. The character of the document as Mishnah-commentary is signalled even at I.A, which commences by telling us why one tractate of the Talmud is situated in proximity to some other, fore and aft.

2. WHAT ARE THE SALIENT TRAITS OF ITS STRUCTURE?

The order of Mishnah-commentary is [1] study of problems of language, formulation, and reading; [2] exposition of the source, in the written Torah, of rules of the Mishnah; [3] authorities behind anonymous, therefore authoritative rules of the Mishnah, with attention to conflicting opinion, principles and premises that underlie the case at hand, possibilities of contradiction among premises and principles held by authorities behind anonymous rulings, and the harmonization of such apparently disharmonious premises and principles (a process that I view as single and unitary). At no point does any other inquiry besides that marked by those three points take priority over that formal structure.

3. WHAT IS THE RATIONALITY OF THE STRUCTURE?

We attend to the Mishnah, phrase by phrase, and then we expand upon themes that the Mishnah treats, or theories of law that the Mishnah's rule calls to mind. The Mishnah's sequence defines the order of discourse and sets the problems for analysis. It follows that the rationality of the structure of the Talmud consists in its focus upon the Mishnah's statements and exegesis thereof. By "irrationality" in this context I mean, compositions that prove asymmetrical with the task of Mishnah-commentary and amplification.

4. WHERE ARE THE POINTS OF IRRATIONALITY IN THE STRUCTURE?

In this setting, "irrational" compositions and composites are those that stand out of phase with the words and phrases of the Mishnah. These are I.A, E, F, H, I; II, VI.E, IX.B, XI.A, XIII.A,, XV.A, B, L, XVIII.C, L, XIX.B, C, D, XXI.F, XXVII.H, I, J, K.

## POINTS OF SYSTEM

1. DOES THE BABYLONIAN TALMUD-TRACTATE SOTAH SERVE ONLY AS A REPRESENTATION OF THE MISHNAH-TRACTATE OF THE SAME NAME?

The answer is a qualified affirmative. The compilers of the tractate find it possible to make noteworthy comment upon much of Mishnah-tractate Sotah, but by no means on every paragraph, sentence, or phrase. Noteworthy omissions are XIV.A. We note here that the comments are brief and the entire unit is cogent, that is, systematic provision of a scriptural basis for the Mishnah's rule (XIV:B-M). What this seems to me to mean is that we have here a cogent piece of writing, produced by authorities for the passage at hand, who had in mind a brief and formally disciplined statement of scriptural bases for sequential rules. Whether other kinds of talmud besides this one could have been written hardly needs to be considered; the evidence in the affirmative lies spread out before us. When we find large-scale and formally and substantively cogent treatments of a Mishnah-paragraph such as this one — and our tractate has very many of them — all we know is what we have,

## Chapter Seventeen. The Structure of Babylonian Talmud Sotah

not what the framers did not have or did not choose to fabricate for themselves. Since Mishnah-commentary takes many forms, we can say only what those forms were, but I see no basis for speculation on a policy of selection or omission, on the one side, or on what the framers might have chosen from an available heritage and repertoire of compositions and composites of Mishnah-commentary. Nor is there any way of assigning priority or posteriority to one kind of writing over some other. The upshot is very simple: a process of selection has governed the kind of Mishnah-commentary that would emerge, but we cannot describe it; a principle of identification of what required commentary and what did not require commentary operated, but we cannot imagine what that principle might have been; and, it goes without saying, a received corpus of Mishnah-commentary laid out before the compilers of the document a variety of writings, of which only part has been utilized, but it would waste much time and effort to try to invent writings made up in the model of the kinds we have, on the one side, or to manufacture writings for the purpose of Mishnah-commentary of some other kind that the kinds we have. That sort of speculation will not materially change the answer to our question, which is, the Babylonian Talmud tractate certainly does far more than recapitulate the Mishnah-commentary. It also does far less. Now we turn to the question of where the Babylonian Talmud tractate has made a difference.

2. HOW DO THE TOPICAL COMPOSITES FIT INTO THE TALMUD-TRACTATE SOTAH AND WHAT DO THEY CONTRIBUTE THAT THE MISHNAH-TRACTATE OF THE SAME NAME WOULD LACK WITHOUT THEM?

The topical composites or massive miscellanies, introduced into the Talmud even though they do not constitute Mishnah-commentary, form that anomaly that requires attention. We need not speculate in any way about the character of the other-than-Mishnah-exegetical compositions and composites. We have to explain what difference their presence makes in the formulation of the Talmud's treatment of the topic of the Mishnah-tractate. We turn forthwith to a survey of the passages that have been identified as irrational, within the definition operative here.

I.A: The explanation of the sequence of topics of Mishnah-tractates remains wholly within the limits of Mishnah-commentary; the arena for exegesis broadens.

I.E: The exposition of the themes of faithfulness; the power of sin; the effects of a single action puts into perspective the topic of the tractate, which is, the accusation of adultery. Faithfulness is the opposite; the power of sin explains the act; and the result of a single action is then underscore. The composite then draws that moral conclusion that the legal exercise requires, placing the whole into a higher plane than merely legal formalities would suggest.

I.F: continuous with the foregoing.

I.H: The treatment of adultery in more general terms picks up the immediately adjacent Mishnah-rule. The general theme of I.H is not well-constructed, but I.I leaves no doubt about the point of the whole. It is that sin is a result of arrogance, and right deed is a result of humility. The power of the whole, then, is to underscore the governing virtues and vices of the Torah, which are one set of matched opposites: humility vs. arrogance. Then the topic of the tractate is situated in that larger theological and moral framework that holds together a wide variety of specific sins and concrete virtues. What we have here is an explanation of why adultery takes place — which is the same explanation as serves for most other sins.

VI:B: The introduction of Judah and Tamar alongside the story of Samson and Delilah derives from a merely formal connection, as is made explicit. But the comparison is substantive, since the exposition makes the point that Judah was humble, Samson, arrogant.

VI:E: This massive composite underscores the arrogance of Pharaoh and the faithfulness of Israel — a proposition Scripture itself introduces into its narrative. I cannot claim that the purpose of the composite is exhausted by that one proposition, but it certainly forms a dominant motif.

IX.B: Zekhut is attained through acts of self-abnegation, e.g., Abraham says he is dirt, the children gain zekhut through the use of dirt. The relevance here is the dirt used for the accused wife.

XI.A: I do not see the relevance of this exposition to the commentary on the Mishnah, though information therein is utilized for an exegesis of the paragraph at hand.

XIII.A: The composite here contributes to the exposition of the theme of the Mishnah. The observation that God is so humble as to permit his name to be blotted out to restore amity between husband and wife plays no role here.

XV.A and B: here we have a large theoretical essay on whether the woman requires a warning if she is to be deprived by her action of payment of her marriage-settlement. The deeper questions concern whether the outcome depends on the husband's objection to the wife's conduct, or whether we impute to the husband an attitude that he does not necessarily express. How much power does the husband have in the outcome of the transaction? This is a systematic essay in legal theory on the husband's rights and power.

XV:L: This composition fits into the context of marriage to a woman who stands in a prohibited relationship to the man; the issue is subordinate to its context.

XVIII.C: One should speak in a low voice and not in a loud voice when it comes to claiming credit or announcing failure, respectively; a subset on the theme of arrogance.

*Chapter Seventeen. The Structure of Babylonian Talmud Sotah* 95

XVIII:L: The theme of the spies and the land of Canaan is introduced in the setting of Israel's successful crossing into the land, because these form the contrasting events, the former, the result of lack of faith, the latter, the consequence of an act of faith. The contrast is necessary to make the point that the Talmud's framers wish to make, which is, the crossing into the land, to which the Mishnah makes reference, forms a great act of faith and faithfulness, and this is shown by the systematic contrast to the conduct of the spies in the generation of the wilderness.

XIX.B, C, D: The topical miscellany belongs in the setting in which the Mishnah takes up the theme; Joshua b. Levi's sayings on the subject then form a subset of the former, and his sayings on generosity were joined to his other sayings before the whole was introduced. That accounts for the agglutination of D to C and the introduction of C-D along with B; and B's exposition is entirely within the rationality of Mishnah-commentary.

XXI.F: The theme of flattery is invited by the contents of the Mishnah, which refer to sages' flattering Agrippa.

XXVII.H, I, J, K: The theme of providing an escort is required by the topic of the Mishnah, the neglected corpse. The reason that the man was murdered is that those responsible for him did not provide an escort. Then providing an escort for travellers is taken up as a free-standing theme, with H, I, as systematic expositions of verses and the general theme; then J, a specific case, with K, a subset of the specific case. The principle of composite-formation and agglutination is self-evident, and there in no irrationality here.

3. CAN WE STATE WHAT THE COMPILERS OF THIS DOCUMENT PROPOSE TO ACCOMPLISH IN PRODUCING THIS COMPLETE, ORGANIZED PIECE OF WRITING?

We identify large-scale composites formulated and included in our tractate for a purpose other than Mishnah-commentary. These in general take shape around a problem, such as the husband's role in the rite, or a theme, as in the cases of Judah and Tamar, Pharaoh, Zekhut, the spies' conduct in Israel's first entry into the land, generosity, flattery, providing an escort, and the like. Two principles explain the selection of such massive miscellaneous composites. One is, to pursue a theme that the Mishnah and its exposition have required, and that explains the matter of Judah and Tamar, the spies' conduct, the matter of flattery, and the like. These composites then form a secondary but quite reasonable expansion on the exposition of the Mishnah's contents.

The second principle is the more interesting one, since the face of the Mishnah-tractate has been transformed by the materials that have been inserted in compliance with this other principle. It is, to introduce into the topic of the Mishnah-tractate a dimension of interpretation that deepens and reshapes matters. In our tractate the Talmud introduces this question: why does adultery take place, and what is the basis for jealousy? The answer is, adultery is an expression of arrogance, and so too is jealousy. A larger theory of sin and virtue then takes over this topic, among many others: sin is an expression of arrogance, and virtue, of humility. The marital bond expresses that same faithfulness that is required of Israel in relationship to God. Sin contrasts with faithfulness, since the opposite of faithfulness is arrogance, the opposite of sin, humility. A single action suffices. Judah contrasts with Samson. Pharaoh forms the very model of arrogance. Zekhut — the heritage of acts of humility performed by one's ancestors or oneself — opposes arrogance, self-abnegation, self-aggrandizement. God is humble, Pharaoh is arrogant. A low voice is used to record one's virtue, a loud voice, one's failure. The faithfulness of Israel in crossing the Jordan (and the Sea) is contrasted with the faithlessness of the spies. Flattery is a form of manipulation of the other, thus arrogance; accepting flattery is a form of self-praise.

It follows that composites that do not relate to Mishnah-exegesis, extending to the topics touched upon by the Mishnah, impose upon the theme of the Mishnah-tractate a proposition that the Mishnah-tractate lacks but invites. It is the proposition that the opposite of the vice of adultery and jealousy, imputed to the wife and the husband, respectively, is faithfulness and humility. Then the Mishnah-tractate, concerning the private affairs of home and family, is here transformed into a statement on the public condition of Israel, the people. What the framers of the Talmud say in their own behalf, and not in the setting of Mishnah-commentary, is that Israel's humility defines that virtue that God prizes, and that humility takes the form of faithfulness. Hosea could not have said it better.

# XVIII

## The Structure of Babylonian Talmud Gittin

### Points of Structure

1. Does Babylonian Talmud-tractate Gittin follow a coherent outline governed by a consistent rules?

The tractate takes form around Mishnah-tractate Gittin, and the intent of the compilers is to provide a systematic commentary to most of the statements of the Mishnah-tractate. Not only so, but the character of this commentary is cogent and coherent, with a limited program of issues brought to bear upon the elucidation of the Mishnah-tractate.

2. What are the salient traits of its structure?

Simple questions of amplification are worked out, then more complex issues of theoretical law; rules pertinent to those in the Mishnah and formulated in accord with the formal and linguistic rules governing the formulation of the Mishnah-rules are brought into juxtaposition with the Mishnah-rules and systematically compared and contrasted, with the result that the corpus of law provided by the Mishnah is enriched and shown harmonious with a variety of further official statements. The principles of the law are then tested against interstitial cases.

3. What is the Rationality of the structure?

The principle of cogency derives from the Mishnah's sequence and propositional program; there is no other principle of cogency that unites large composites to one another, though within those composites, secondary accretions do abound.

4. Where are the points of irrationality in the structure?

These are listed presently.

### Points of System

1. Does the Babylonian Talmud-tractate Gittin serve only as a re-presentation of the Mishnah-tractate of the same name?

Not all passages of the Mishnah are systematically investigated, and there are sustained inquiries into passages that presently occur in the Tosefta or in other compilations of authoritative rules. So the Talmud-tractate serves not only as a re-presentation of the Mishnah-tractate of the same name, but the principal basis for the compilation of the tractate is the Mishnah-tractate, and no other composition or composite competes in importance or intellectual focus with the Mishnah-tractate.

2. How do the topical composites fit into the Talmud-tractate and what do they contribute that the Mishnah-tractate of the same name would lack without them?

In compiling the relevant data for the other tractates, I present the account in three sections. On the left hand margin are important propositional composites that do not address the Mishnah's propositions but do affect them. At the right are the composites that complement the Mishnah's statements with topically relevant amplifications or that carry forward the Mishnah's principle to new data. Finally, I underline and also position in the center column large composites that strike me as entirely out of phase with the Mishnah, lacking all point of contact, whether topical or in principle or even theme, broadly construed. Identifying these items and distinguishing them from those on the right hand margin involve a measure of subjectivity, and for that reason, I have tried to impose the most rigorous and narrowest possible definition of what is both free-standing and also affective of the rest. In the center I give those utterly anomalous composites that ignore the principle of propositional or at least topical cogency altogether. Here, as we now see, the results are so paltry and one-sided that the analytical presentation required elsewhere proves simply irrelevant.

> I.B. Miscellaneous Rulings
> on Proper Conduct
> I.E: The Status of Syria
> VII.D. Other Cases in Which We
> Take Account of Halves
> XXII.D. Topical Appendix
> on the Winds
> XXVI.B. Topical Appendix
> on Freeing Slaves
> XLI.B. Topical Appendix
> on the Wars against Rome
> LV.B. Various Remedies for
> Maladies. Demonology

The paltry result is striking. The handful of composites that find cogency in a problem other than one defined by the labor of Mishnah-exegesis all serve a single purpose. That purpose is to complement the Mishnah with a topical composite

## Chapter Eighteen. The Structure of Babylonian Talmud Gittin

relevant in some way or another either to the understanding of the Mishnah, as at I.E, XXVI.B, and XLI.B, or to extend and supplement a passage that, for its own reasons, is introduced as part of Mishnah-exegesis, as in the remaining entries. The anomalous composites in no way reshape our understanding of the Mishnah-tractate. They do not introduce perspectives that make us see the Mishnah's propositions or even its topical program in some fresh way; all merely convey information; none attempts a re-presentation let alone a reformation of the matter at hand.

3. CAN WE STATE WHAT THE COMPILERS OF THIS DOCUMENT PROPOSE TO ACCOMPLISH IN PRODUCING THIS COMPLETE, ORGANIZED PIECE OF WRITING?

Before us is a large tractate, rich in powerful ideas and principles, vastly deepening our grasp of the laws and principles of Mishnah-tractate Gittin. The framers of the Talmud-tractate made one decision that would dictate the character of their work, which was, to privilege the Mishnah-tractate as the medium for organizing and presenting the topic of that tractate, the matter of divorce. The result is a well-disciplined, carefully-organized, and entirely coherent and systematic account of not the topic, divorce, but the Mishnah-tractate on that topic. Among numerous tractates that accomplish the systematic re-presentation of Mishnah-tractates and in no material way reshape those tractates or diverge from their program, I can find no better evidence to refute the false notion that the Talmud is in any way disorderly, random, or disorganized.

Let us conclude by reverting to the contrary opinion set forth by Adin Steinsaltz, "One of the principal difficulties in studying the Talmud is that it is not written in a systematic fashion; it does not move from simple to weighty material, from the definition of terms to their use. In almost every passage of the Talmud, discussion is based on ideas that have been discussed elsewhere, and on terms that are not necessarily defined on the page where they appear."[1] He further states, "Viewed superficially, the Talmud seems to lack inner order. ...The arrangement of the Talmud is not systematic, nor does it follow familiar didactic principles. It does not proceed from the simple to the complex, or from the general to the particular...It has no formal external order, but is bound by a strong inner connection between its many diverse subjects. The structure of the Talmud is associative. The

---

[1] Adin Steinsaltz, *The Talmud. The Steinsaltz Edition. A Reference Guide* (N. Y., 1989: Random House), p. vii. The more I study Steinsaltz's conception of the Talmud as set forth in his general introductions to his "edition," the more I am persuaded that he does not have a clear grasp of the character of the document at all, though his re-presentation of matters, in the tradition of the Romm edition of the Bavli, certainly has much to recommend it. But his strength lies in the explanation of words and phrases, not in the characterization of the document or in the grasp of its structure and coherence. Whether his explanation of words and phrases bears the marks of more than paraphrastic erudition is for specialists in philology and exegesis to indicate; my impression is that it does not.

material of the Talmud was memorized and transmitted orally for centuries, its ideas are joined to each other by inner links, and the order often reflects the needs of memorization. Talmudic discourse shifts from one subject to a related subject, or to a second that brings the first to mind in an associative way."[2] What Steinsaltz proves in these statements is that he does not grasp the structure, order, or purpose of the Bavli. In the outline before us, we find ample refutation of every single allegation at hand.

Specifically, we have seen in this outline, as in the outline of every other tractate, these facts: [1] The Talmud exhibits a well-crafted inner order. [2] The arrangement of the Talmud is systematic and assuredly does follow familiar didactic principles. [3] It does proceed from the simple to the complex, from the general to the particular...[4] It has a ubiquitous and blatant formal external order. [5] The structure of the Talmud is not associative but systematic, referring at every point to the exegesis of a passage of the Mishnah or the secondary development of such an exegesis. [6] The order of discourse reflects not the needs of memorization but the requirement of systematic, logical exposition of, first the Mishnah's text, then the Mishnah's law. [7] The Talmudic discourse therefore does not shift from one subject to a related subject, or to a second that brings the first to mind in an associative way, because the authors of compositions and compilers of composites intended to set forth a clear, well-articulated, propositional document, and that is precisely what they have accomplished. These are the facts that this academic commentary has laid out in detail for Bavli-tractate Gittin; these are the irrefutable results of the outline at hand. The contrary view rests upon mere impressions and guess-work and has been refuted in these pages.

---

[2] ibid., p. 7.

# XIX

# The Structure of Babylonian Talmud Qiddushin

### POINTS OF STRUCTURE

1. DOES BABYLONIAN TALMUD-TRACTATE QIDDUSHIN FOLLOW A COHERENT OUTLINE GOVERNED BY A CONSISTENT RULES?

As this outline shows time and again, the Mishnah enjoys the privileged, indeed, the sole paramount position, dictating the flow of discussion, the order, the issues, the entire problematic.

2. WHAT ARE THE SALIENT TRAITS OF ITS STRUCTURE?

Once the Mishnah-passage is discussed — if such discussion of the Mishnah takes place at all — we turn to the Tosefta's or other Tannaite formulations of rules on the subject the Mishnah has introduced. Then other, subordinate issues will come under analysis. Few sizable composites diverge from the Mishnah's primary program or from the Tosefta's secondary one. The sequence and program of the Talmud originate in the Mishnah.

3. WHAT IS THE RATIONALITY OF THE STRUCTURE?

What holds the whole together is solely the common point of reference and source of context and coherence, which is, the Mishnah, pure and simple.

4. WHERE ARE THE POINTS OF IRRATIONALITY IN THE STRUCTURE?

These are catalogued below.

### POINTS OF SYSTEM

1. DOES THE BABYLONIAN TALMUD-TRACTATE QIDDUSHIN SERVE ONLY AS A RE-PRESENTATION OF THE MISHNAH-TRACTATE OF THE SAME NAME?

The tractate attends to nearly every line of the Mishnah, and, by indirection, to every word thereof. No other document contributes a comparable proportion of the document, though passages of the Tosefta and of Sifra that occur in the Talmud are given talmuds of their own, as is indicated in this outline.

2. How do the topical composites fit into the Talmud-tractate and what do they contribute that the Mishnah-tractate of the same name would lack without them?

In general, though not for this tractate, I present the account in three sections. On the left hand margin are important propositional composites that do not address the Mishnah's propositions but do affect them. For this tractate I discern not one. At the right are the composites that complement the Mishnah's statements with topically relevant amplifications or that carry forward the Mishnah's principle to new data. Finally, I underline and also position in the center column large composites that strike me as entirely out of phase with the Mishnah, lacking all point of contact, whether topical or in principle or even theme, broadly construed. In the center I give those utterly anomalous composites that ignore the principle of propositional or at least topical cogency altogether. Bavli Qiddushin contains not one of these.

II.G: Topical Appendix
Concerning Severance Pay
II.K:Topical Appendix on the Marriage
to the Captive Woman of Goodly Form
VIII.C: Miscellany on
the Honor of Mother and Father
VIII.E: Topical Composite
on Rising before One's Master
XXXVIII.F: Topical Appendix on the Mamzer
and the Result of Other Inappropriate Unions
XXXVIII.G: Topical Appendix on the
Status of Various Territories in the Iranian Empire
XLV.C: Topical Appendix on Ridiculing Sinners,
Attached to Supplement a Detail in the Foregoing

All the sizable composites that serve a purpose other than that of Mishnah-amplification are appended because they contain substantial supplements on topics introduced in the process of Mishnah-amplification or secondary development thereof. From the perspective of the compilers of the document, none of these items is miscellaneous, and all would find a place in a well-crafted book that promised information of a supplementary character, that is, in any standard and complete work of scholarship.

3. Can we state what the compilers of this document propose to accomplish in producing this complete, organized piece of writing?

These conclusions emerge not only from this tractate's outline, but from all the other chapters of this volume and from the other three of the *Complete Outline* as well.

## Chapter Nineteen. The Structure of Babylonian Talmud Qiddushin

The Talmud of Babylonia is carefully organized in large-scale, recurrent structures and guided by a program that we may call systematic. This piece of writing presents not ad hoc or random information but a program, a philosophically and aesthetically cogent statement about how things should be. The document exhibits structure and sets forth a system, it is accessible to questions of rationality. Structure and systematic inquiry yield both propositions, arguments, viewpoints and an encompassing thesis on the character and message of the Mishnah overall as well as on the contents — the law — initially set forth in the Mishnah. We now know, in complete detail, precisely what is principal and what subordinate, and how each unit — composition formed into composites, composites formed into a complete statement — holds together and also fits with other units, fore and aft. Viewed whole, this Talmud contains no gibberish but only completed units of thought, sentences formed into intelligible thought and self-contained in that we require no further information to understand those sentences, beginning to end. As to those composites that do not undertake Mishnah-commentary or further analysis of the law of the Mishnah, these appendices or footnotes do belong and serve the compilers' purpose.

# The Structure of Babylonian Talmud Baba Qamma

### POINTS OF STRUCTURE

1. DOES THIS BABYLONIAN TALMUD-TRACTATE FOLLOW A COHERENT OUTLINE GOVERNED BY A CONSISTENT RULES?

The compilers of Bavli-tractate Baba Qamma drew upon a variety of compositions and composites. These they organized around the exegesis and amplification of the Mishnah. While some compositions and even large-scale composites go in their own direction, all of them find their place in the Talmud only in relationship to the Mishnah, or to a secondary amplification of a principle that the Mishnah's law sets forth in terms of its own distinctive cases. The sizable composites that have nothing to do with the Mishnah invariably have much to do with a detail of a composition or composite that to begin with is inserted for the purpose of Mishnah-exegesis, as just now defined: if not the case, then the principle. Not only so, but a consistent rule of editing is that what pertains to the Mishnah comes first; no secondary expansion ever makes its statement prior to the amplification of the Mishnah, and the Mishnah's clauses or phrases are never treated as secondary in interest to matters of principle. When it comes to Mishnah-exegesis, if words or phrases require amplification, that ordinarily comes first; if scriptural foundations are to be uncovered, that exercise takes priority; only after one or the other of these two exegetical procedures has been accomplished will any other issues come to the fore.

2. WHAT ARE THE SALIENT TRAITS OF ITS STRUCTURE?

As just now noted, first comes the Mishnah's statements and the Mishnah's principles, then will come secondary and subordinated amplification of those matters, and, finally, attention to items tangential in even that secondary and subordinated statement. That simple fact stands behind the character of this outline — and the very possibility of making an outline of the Bavli-tractate that consistently subordinates (in the formal outline before us, indents) what comes later in an exposition. That is, the later a composition, the more remote from the Mishnah's own statement — and the outline before us, with its systematic indentation, shows what is at issue. Readers will have noted, to be sure, that within a composition devoted to the Mishnah or to an exposition of an abstract principle or other analytical exercise will be indented items, which I have treated as insertions or secondary glosses within the primary structure at hand. But that does not change the clear picture of a composite that follows a simple and orderly structure.

3. WHAT IS THE RATIONALITY OF THE STRUCTURE?

First comes what is primary, defined by what is in the Mishnah; then comes what is secondary, defined by the primary exposition; then comes additional materials of one or two kinds: [1] footnotes to the primary or secondary exposition; [2] topical composites formulated in their own terms, around their own point of interest, and inserted here as an appendix; these topical composites serve neither Mishnah-exegesis nor the secondary amplification or theoretical or analytical inquiry precipitated by Mishnah-exegesis. In that sense they mark the boundary between the structural rationality of our Talmud and the aspects of irrationality.

4. WHERE ARE THE POINTS OF IRRATIONALITY IN THE STRUCTURE?

These are the relevant points of irrationality: I.B, II.D, V.B, XII.C, XXVII.C, D, XLI.I, XLV.B, C, L.C, D, LV.D, LVI.B, LXI.B, C, LXIII.D, LXVI.E, G, H, LXVIII.B, LXIX.C, LXX.C, LXXIX.C. It is noteworthy that none of the composites formulated in terms other than those of Mishnah-commentary or amplification comes at the head of its Mishnah-unit; all of them are subordinated to sizable composites that clarify the sense or implications of the Mishnah's statements.

## POINTS OF SYSTEM

1. DOES THE BABYLONIAN TALMUD-TRACTATE SERVE ONLY AS A RE-PRESENTATION OF THE MISHNAH-TRACTATE OF THE SAME NAME?

The answer is a qualified affirmative. Not every Mishnah-phrase or clause is supplied with a comment, but the omissions prove episodic and random. I cannot offer a theory that would permit us to predict which types of Mishnah-statements will be given talmuds, which not; or for that matter, which types of Tosefta-statements will carry their own talmudic amplification, and which not. If the data are other than random, I am unable to discern any pattern at all. So the structure of the tractate — Mishnah-commentary, then Mishnah-amplification (inclusive of amplification of the Mishnah's implicit principles) — prevails in detail.

2. HOW DO THE TOPICAL COMPOSITES FIT INTO THE TALMUD-TRACTATE AND WHAT DO THEY CONTRIBUTE THAT THE MISHNAH-TRACTATE OF THE SAME NAME WOULD LACK WITHOUT THEM?

Here I distinguish between appendices that demand a position in a commentary on the Mishnah, even though the character of their contribution diverges from the narrowly exegetical or topical, and composites that stand wholly

*Chapter Twenty. The Structure of Babylonian Talmud Baba Qamma* *107*

autonomous from the Mishnah and from the secondary amplification of its statements. The former are indented, the latter not. Further, I underline those appendices that contain no proposition at all or that address no common theme but take shape around some other than a topical program.

        I.B: The scriptural foundations for the definition of the generative classifications of causes are spelled out in their own terms. The subsets are defined. While this composite is enormous, it also borders on Mishnah-exegesis and in no way can be identified as free-standing or as a mere appendix. I state very simply that the reading of our Mishnah-paragraph is inconceivable absent this magnificent composite.

II.D: <u>This composite is formed around the citation-formula Ulla-Eleazar; there is no one topic that prevails, and I discern no order for the whole. Clearly, a principle of organizing composites involved collecting sayings around set-piece names. Nothing in the composite, other than the opening item, has any bearing upon the larger discussion, and the composite as a whole makes no impact upon its context, either upon our grasp of the principles at hand or even upon our perception of what may be introduced into the exposition of the topic itself.</u>

V.B: <u>The composite on Hezekiah and on Jeremiah set here in particular strikes me as random, out of relationship to the larger context. As in the foregoing, from within the rationality of the Mishnah and the Talmud, this item is to be classified as irrational — or as expressing a different rationality of coherence and cogency.</u>

        XII.C: A man has got the right to take the law into his own hands where there will be a loss — introduced here because our Mishnah-paragraph contributes to the analytical exercise.

        XXVII.C. The appendix on gentiles and their carrying out religious duties is inserted because the Mishnah has referred to the property rights of gentiles in torts involving Israelites.

        XXVII:D: The special case of the Samaritan follows suit.

        XLI.I: The composite on hybridization responds as a secondary amplification to the exegesis of the Mishnah-passage at hand, which calls for a reference to that topic.

XLV.B: Composite on how punishment and misfortune come into the world: here we really do have an important insertion, since the cited verse refers to a misfortune that is caused by the action of a person, who therefore is responsible for what he has done. Then the issue of culpability and punishment, responsibility and unavoidable accident, is introduced and framed in the anticipated, theological framework. Misfortune takes place because there are wicked people in the world, and the righteous suffer first of all. That insertion, at just this point, reframes the issue of the Mishnah: "he who causes fire to break out..." then is responsible, and innocent people suffer for his action. That stands at the head of a large and important composite on the stated theme.

XLV.C: Once we have introduced the larger theological issue of culpability and penalty, we immediately raise the subject of that other fire — the fire that destroyed the Temple — and speak of responsibility for what has happened: It is my obligation to pay for the fire which I kindled. "I was the one who kindled a fire in Zion."

    l.C: Composite on the Exegetical Rules of Amplification and Extension as against Those of Generalization, Particularization, and Generalization. This expands on the foundations in Scripture for the rule that is given in explanation of the Mishnah's law's origin.

    L:D: How compensation is assessed: this introduces the more abstract issue, implicit in the Mishnah, of the affect upon title of a change in the character of an object: a change in the character of an object effects a transfer of title.

    LV.D: The difference between the thief and the robber forms part of the exegetical premise of the Mishnah-amplification before us. It is not a free-standing intrusion and it does not effect a drastic revision in our reading of the larger context.

    LVI.B: Rules on Correct Management of the Land of Israel: Here we have a large, free-standing composite, which has not been assembled for the amplification of our Mishnah-rule. But the theme of the Mishnah-rule — general principles governing utilization of the land, the protection of the environment, and the common rights accorded to all — that theme certainly encompasses the Mishnah's own rule. So the composite is topical and inserting it here is quite rational: it is a standard thematic appendix.

LXI:B: Sayings attributed to Raba before Rabbah bar Mari. How on the basis of Scripture do we know...

LXI:C: Reverting to the Topic of Abimelech, Abram and Sarai.

    LXIII.D: Composite of Rulings by Rabbah on Exemptions for Destroying Other Peoples' Property. This composite falls well within the thematic and even the logical framework of Mishnah-exegesis.

LXVI.E: Raba's Refinements of the Theory of Restitution: Theoretical Problems. As above.

<u>LXVI.G: Composite of R. Hiyya bar Abba in the Name of R. Yohanan</u>

LXVI:H: Theoretical problems, in line with LXVI.E.

LXVIII.B: Three Theoretical Questions Raised by Raba. These problems fall well within the framework of the Mishnah's topical program.

LXIX.C: Composite on Accepting Testimony even though the other party is not present. As above.

LXX.C: The Legal Status of Gentiles and their Property. As above.

LXXIX.C: Composite on Dealing with Thieves and Robbers. As above.

3. CAN WE STATE WHAT THE COMPILERS OF THIS DOCUMENT PROPOSE TO ACCOMPLISH IN PRODUCING THIS COMPLETE, ORGANIZED PIECE OF WRITING?

Clearly, my definition of the asymmetrical composites proves too generous, since a sizable proportion of the ones identified here turn out to supplement the Mishnah's own topic or propositional principle. I have treated as falling outside of the Talmud's principles of rationality a sizable number of composites that pursue a legal problem quite coherent with that of the Mishnah-paragraph into the discussion of which they are inserted. These cohere fully with the rationality of Mishnah-commentary, broadly defined. On the other extreme come the non-propositional composites. Specifically, several of the composites are formed around quite asymptotic principles — a given authority's name.

That leaves only a few items introduce quite fresh dimensions to the consideration of the Mishnah's program. Specifically, XLV.B, C require attention. These two, rather lonely items introduce a theological dimension into the consideration of the Mishnah's program: why do these things happen at all? What, in God's plan, accommodates misfortunes. At the end, with Baba Batra, we shall see a more systematic study of that profound issue; and when the problem of evil — in the setting of torts — intervenes, it will be read in the dimensions of Israel's catastrophe in particular. But we must conclude that our Talmud-tractate has presented the Mishnah-tractate in a faithful way, clarifying, amplifying, explaining — but rarely contributing a fundamentally fresh perspective on the topic of the Mishnah.

# XXI

## The Structure and System of Babylonian Talmud Baba Mesia

### Points of Structure

1. Does Babylonian Talmud-tractate Baba Mesia follow a coherent outline governed by a consistent rules?

The Mishnah's statements read one-by-one and in sequence define the structure of the Talmud. Even where the Talmud introduces compositions and composites organized around problems not defined by the Mishnah, these extraneous entries are inserted into position in relationship to some point of relevance to the Mishnah, however tangential. There is no large-scale legal problem that is considered wholly on its own and not in conjunction with the Mishnah. Large-scale non-legal composites, e.g., the set of stories involving Eleazar b. R. Simeon, are parachuted down as appendages to secondary or tertiary discussions of problems relevant to the Mishnah.

2. What are the salient traits of its structure?

As usual, first comes Mishnah-exegesis in a narrow sense: [1] meanings of words and phrases; [2] the foundations in Scripture for statements in the Mishnah; [3] the named authority behind an anonymous and therefore authoritative statement of the Mishnah. Then comes analysis of legal theory encompassing the case of the Mishnah or exemplified in the law of the Mishnah. Finally, in orderly sequence, will come topical exercises that deal with the theme of the Mishnah's law, but in some fresh way.

3. What is the Rationality of the structure?

All considerations of order, sequence, and appropriate juxtaposition ("why this, not that?" and "what has this to do with that?") derive to begin with from the program of the Mishnah. Where that is not the case, a secondary expansion may be introduced as the amplification of a tangential point that is made in a composition devoted to Mishnah-exegesis; but that amplification may then go its own way and bear in its wake a massive construction, a composite of its own. One recurring example of that phenomenon is the sustained inquiry into the relationship of law to Scripture, that is, how Scripture generates law, with special attention to conflicting positions that the same verse of Scripture sustains, and the conflicting principles of exegesis or hermeneutics that generate the conflict in positions. So what we have is Mishnah-exegesis, then amplification — not much more.

### 4. Where are the points of irrationality in the structure?

The composites that violate the prevailing norms of rationality are to be divided into two parts: [1] composites that fall within the circle of the Mishnah's theme, or even its legal principles, or even the details of its case; [2] composites that take shape entirely independent of anything we now find in the Mishnah, e.g., amplification of Scripture, the names of the same authority and tradent(s). Among the latter, we have also to distinguish among free-standing composites that by inference or implication affect the character of the Mishnah-exposition that the Talmud provides and those that in no way intersect with, let alone affect, our grasp of the Mishnah's themes and their implications. For some tractates, the free-standing composite takes over and changes perspective on the Mishnah's topic, the Talmud's amplification of that topic, or our very grasp of what is at stake in the law. For others, such as this one, the inserted, large-scale and autonomous ("miscellaneous') composites in no way affect the character of the larger context in which they make their appearance. For the three Babas, the one important point at which the Talmud has included enormous and affective composites, those that materially recast our perspective upon the very topic of the Mishnah and its talmudic extension, is Baba Batra. There, only in the third of the three tractates of civil law, as we shall see, are introduced themes and even specific propositions that require us to see in a quite fresh perspective the Mishnah's entire program.

In this tractate, that "more" to which I referred at the end of the penultimate paragraph is found in the following composites, which, in my outline, seem to me to stand on their own and not in relationship to a clause or sentence in the Mishnah. Those described here prove to provide a secondary expansion or augmentation of the Mishnah's own topic, on the one side, or of a tangential point in the Talmud's amplification of the Mishnah, on the other. In the unit below, I deal with the composites that stand on their own in my outline and that also do not relate to Mishnah-exegesis in any way.

The free-standing units that turn out to expand the Mishnah's topic are as follows: III.B, a further saying inserted by reason of a shared attributive formula; VI.B, a composite of statements assigned to the same authority as is cited in VI.A and addressed to the same legal problem; XIX.D, a composite of cases illustrated the same exegetical procedure as predominates at XIX.C, that is, a topical appendix; XXI.C, dealt with below; XXV.C: This is a secondary refinement of the statement of the Mishnah, explicitly alluding to that point of connection, From the position stated here in the view of Rabban Simeon b. Gamaliel we may infer that a relative

## Chapter Twenty-one. The Structure of Babylonian Talmud Baba Mesia

may dispose of the property of a captive, while from the position of rabbis we may infer that a relative may dispose of the property of a captive, though the composite then goes its own way; XXXVI:E: the composite on the added fifth takes shape round its own theme and then is parachuted down as a thematic appendix, joined to the context of Mishnah-commentary and amplification because of a tangential reference in the immediately-prior composition; XXXIX.C: the same is to be said of XXXIX.C — Other Matters to which the Law of Overreaching Does Not Apply; XL.B: discussed below; XLVIII.B: this is a special problem that flows from the generic problem subject to discussion in Mishnah-commentary; XLIX.B: the point that one may take usury from, or pay usury to, gentiles is introduced because the Mishnah itself has spoken about allowing in relationship to gentiles contractual arrangements that cannot be set with Jews. So while the passage takes shape around its own, vital question, it still remains well within the topical program of Mishnah-commentary; LX. B, C, D, E, I: dealt with below; LXI. B: this is a thematic extension of the Mishnah's topic; LXI:C: here we have a comment not on the Mishnah but on its general proposition; LXI:D: dealt with below; LXXX.B: here we have a well-formed and cogent composite: sayings by a single authority on a single theme, which, moreover, intersects with that of the Mishnah; LXXXII.B: all we have here is more definitions of the kind that is required for Mishnah-exegesis, a topical appendix; LXXXV.C: this is a composite of sayings assigned to a single authority, tacked on but free-standing in program and consequence; LXXXV.D: this is an add-on to the foregoing; LXXXV.E: discussed below.

There are two other points to notice. The first is a very strange one: LXIX.B, a beautifully composed talmud-composite, entirely focused upon a Mishnah-composition — but not for our tractate's Mishnah. The composite is standard in its order and interests: what is the Scripture source? how explain the Mishnah's formulation? the logic behind a Mishnah-rule, and the like. If this composite were situation in Mishnah-tractate Shebuot, we should have classified it as standard Mishnah-commentary and amplification. But located here, the composite stands out and demands an explanation. But for my part, even though the topical program of our Mishnah-tractate at this very passage invites the theme and its exposition that are before us, still, I cannot account for the inclusion here of another tractate's Mishnah-paragraph together with its Talmud. It would carry us far afield now to compare the two Talmuds that the same Mishnah-paragraph, M. Shebu. 8:1ff., has been given. Work on the history of the materials now set forth in our Talmud, on the other hand, will be considerably advanced in due course by comparative Talmud-studies: how the same passage is treated in various contexts. That work will have to commence with this strange passage. At this stage in my outline of the Talmud (with *A Complete Outline* III to appear first in the sequence), I cannot point to another example of the same strange phenomenon.

Second, I find one genuinely disruptive item, which is LXXXV.E. This item in a very general way intersects with the Mishnah's theme, though none of its propositions that are before us. Here is an item that is genuinely miscellaneous in both character and location. The people who compiled these important sayings and those who inserted the set here did so in accord with principles — whether of form, whether of a substantive character — I cannot discern. My explanation of both form and substance is general and does not eliminate the paramount possibility that a program of legal exposition and of large-scale formation of such expositions different from the one guiding the Mishnah-commentary that dictates the character of most of the Talmud and the majority of its constituent components guided work quite different from that before us.

### POINTS OF SYSTEM

1. DOES THE BABYLONIAN TALMUD-TRACTATE SERVE ONLY AS A RE-PRESENTATION OF THE MISHNAH-TRACTATE OF THE SAME NAME?

The answer is, not only but mainly. And that answer is validated by our examination of the free-standing composites. Most of these connect to the Mishnah or to the Talmud's composites of Mishnah-amplification, as we have now seen.

2. HOW DO THE TOPICAL COMPOSITES FIT INTO THE TALMUD-TRACTATE AND WHAT DO THEY CONTRIBUTE THAT THE MISHNAH-TRACTATE OF THE SAME NAME WOULD LACK WITHOUT THEM?

For this tractate, as we shall now observe, the free-standing units that in no way contribute to the amplification of the Mishnah's topics or propositions make no impact upon the Talmud's on-going discussion of those topics and propositions; they in no way change our perspective on matters, e.g., by introducing a subject that places into a different context the very rules and problems on which we concentrate here. That is to say, in my view, every topical composite before us is introduced for formal, and not for substantive, considerations. The upshot is that the miscellaneous items make no impact upon the presentation of the Mishnah's statement that the Talmud effects with such remarkable power.

XXI.C: Since the Mishnah speaks of the contrast between the sage and the father, the former enjoying supernatural standing, a further issue is raised: the differentiation among sages in accord with their specialties: Those who are occupied with study of Scripture — it is a meritorious quality that is not all that meritorious. ...with the Mishnah — it is a meritorious quality on account of which reward is gained. ...with the Gemara — you have no greater meritorious action than that. This does not vastly change the character of the larger context in which it is located. Rather, it represents a secondary refinement of the point of differentiation introduced in the Mishnah and clarified in the prior segments of the Talmud.

XL.B: The Wife's Prayer: All gates are locked, except for the gates that receive complaints against overreaching. That theme, which XL.A introduces,

Chapter Twenty-one. The Structure of Babylonian Talmud Baba Mesia    115

accounts for the insertion of the vast complex on Eliezer b. Hyrcanus, his excommunication, and the like. I see no important point in that important composite that has any bearing on the reading of the Mishnah-passage at hand, on the one side, or on the Talmud immediately preceding, on the other. Here is a case in which the inserted composite is included for formal reasons, that is, as an exemplification of a point already made, and not for any supererogatory purpose that I can discern. The insertion impedes rather than advances the on-going discussion. It does not shed a new light on what is the primary issue at hand. It does not vastly change our perception even of the issues of the law that are before us. Proof of the essentially-inert character of this enormous insertion lies in XL.C, which follows: the passage simply reverts to the prior discussion, as though nothing intervened.

LX.B, C, D, E: The massive composite on Eleazar b. R. Simeon + Yohanan is parachuted down because it commences with an exegesis of Ps. 104:20, which plays a role in the immediately preceding composition. On that basis, this enormous complex of materials is entered. It has no bearing upon anything in context, and its insertion makes no impact upon that larger context. The one point that can have made its impact upon our Mishnah-tractate and its exposition is E, the genealogy of learning; but that passage, which would have been welcome earlier when we contrasted the father and the Torah-teacher, here is a mere appendage, tacked on for obvious reasons, self-evident at the immediately-receding item.

LX.I: The meals of Abraham and associated items, a systematic amplification of Gen. 18:7 and surrounding materials, is inserted because of the reference in the Mishnah to the children of Abraham, on the one side, and the obligation to provide appropriate meals for them, on the other. So in topic if not in form the insertion qualifies as Mishnah-amplification. An available set of compositions is situated precisely where it should be for the purpose of clarifying what is at stake in the Mishnah.

LXI:D: This is a mere topical appendix, nothing more;

3. CAN WE STATE WHAT THE COMPILERS OF THIS DOCUMENT PROPOSE TO ACCOMPLISH IN PRODUCING THIS COMPLETE, ORGANIZED PIECE OF WRITING?

The compilers of Bavli Baba Mesia have accomplished a vast, systematic, and orderly exposition of the Mishnah-tractate that they have selected for their work. They have re-presented its law in a vast and encompassing context, in that way transforming law into jurisprudence, and, at some points, jurisprudence into philosophy, on the one side, or theology, on the other. Theirs was the work of commentary — but commentary that vastly enhanced the text subject to the commentary. Learning the lessons of intellect, mastering the rules of analysis, applied reason and practical logic, that the Talmud's sages here have exemplified, future lawyers of Judaism would govern holy Israel's everyday and practical life in accord with a law that was animated by philosophy and motivated by theology: the Torah's, as our sages of blessed memory formulated both.

# XXII

## The Structure of Babylonian Talmud Baba Batra

### POINTS OF STRUCTURE

1. DOES THIS BABYLONIAN TALMUD-TRACTATE FOLLOW A COHERENT OUTLINE GOVERNED BY A CONSISTENT RULES?

Mishnah-tractate Baba Batra's Talmud is enormous, and that fact makes all the more impressive the uniformity that governs throughout. While enriched with sizable composites not addressed to Mishnah-exegesis, the tractate in the aggregate is organized around a systematic commentary to the Mishnah. That is why the Talmud-tractate follows a coherent outline; at remarkably few points were we unable to account for the position and purpose of a complete composition, one with a beginning, middle, and end. I can identify few, if any, such compositions that do not relate to the composite of which they form a part, and I can point to not a single composites without a clear purpose in the tractate's large-scale constructions. The outline I was able to construct followed a simple order: topic sentence, ordinarily a sentence of the Mishnah-tractate, at some points a subject or proposition not supplied by it; analytical discussion of the topic-sentence; propositions generated by the topic-sentences. Where the compilers wish to provide both analysis and illustrative cases, the order is, first, analysis, then illustration.

2. WHAT ARE THE SALIENT TRAITS OF ITS STRUCTURE?

The outline of the Talmud-tractate follows the outline of the Mishnah-tractate, but parts company from the Mishnah-tractate in two ways. First, important statements of the Mishnah-tractate are not analyzed at all. These prove few, perhaps proportionately less consequential than in other tractates, though I have not systematically assessed that matter. Second, important propositions not set forth in the Mishnah-tractate are examined, and significant topical composites are inserted without regard to the Mishnah-tractate's program but in addition to it. The rules that the outline reveals present no surprises. In examining any sentence of the Mishnah or of a comparable Tannaite document, [1] the compilers first discuss the formulation, authorities, or scriptural foundations for the Mishnah's or other Tannaite document's statement. Then [2] secondary augmentation will begin, whether through an extension of the rule to other cases, or an investigation of the implicit principle of the rule and its intersection with other types of cases altogether. Following comes [3] the consideration of Tannaite formulations of rules that pertain in theme or problem or principle, and these will be subjected to the same sequence and type of analytical questions that have already been brought to bear upon the Mishnah.

3. WHAT IS THE RATIONALITY OF THE STRUCTURE?

We proceed from the particular — the Mishnah's rule — to the general. We first deal with the details of the particular, then we move outward to theoretical considerations. We deal with rules accorded Tannaite origin or sponsorship, first found in the Mishnah, then found in the Tosefta (not so firm a rule), and finally given a signal of Tannaite but not found in a compilation of Tannaite statements now in our hands (e. g., Tenno rabbanon, Tanné and the like). That we deal with a clearcut and consistent principle of compilation derive proof from a variety of striking facts. The first is, no composition or composition devoted to other-than-Mishnah-exegesis stands at the head of a large-scale composite devoted to a Mishnah-paragraph. The second is still more remarkable. All extraneous compositions and composites that the compilers have introduced take positions that are subordinated to the labor of Mishnah-exegesis, and, one way or another, link to passages that serve for the clarification or amplification of the Mishnah. As we shall see, we take up a considerable corpus of writings that were formulated for a purpose other than Mishnah-exegesis, but none of these is parachuted down, lacking all relationship to materials fore or aft, ordinarily the former. Third, the systematic order of types of compositions and composites does not vary and always takes as its task the coherent amplification of the Mishnah and its law.

4. WHERE ARE THE POINTS OF IRRATIONALITY IN THE STRUCTURE?

These are the compositions and composites that do not take up the task of Mishnah-commentary: III.C, IV.D, IV.F, V.C, V.D, V.G, V.H, V.I, V.J, V, IV.G, VIII.B, XV.B, XX.B, XXV.B, XXX.E, XXXI.C, XL.E, XL.F, XL.G, XL.H, XL.I, XL.J, XL.K, L.C, L.E, L.F, L.G, L.H, L.I, LII.C, LIV.E, LXII.B, LXIV.B, LXIV.H, LXV.C, LXVI.C, LXVI.D, LXVII.C, LXVII.D, LXVIII.B, LXVIII.C, LXVIII.D, LXXIII.D, LXXVII.C, LXXVIII.D, LXXX.C, LXXXII.B, LXXXII.E, LXXXII.F, LXXXVIII.C.

### POINTS OF SYSTEM

1. DOES THE BABYLONIAN TALMUD BABA BATRA SERVE ONLY AS A RE-PRESENTATION OF THE MISHNAH-TRACTATE OF THE SAME NAME?

The answer is a qualified negative. Most of the tractate is devoted to the twin-tasks of Mishnah-exegesis and the amplification of principles of law implicit in the Mishnah's cases or rules. But some Mishnah-statements are bypassed. And,

Chapter Twenty-two. The Structure of Babylonian Talmud Baba Batra       *119*

as indicated just now, we do have a variety of free-standing compositions and even composites that have not been formulated in response to the work of Mishnah-commentary, on the one side, or exposition of law, on the other. To these we now turn.

2. How do the topical composites fit into the Talmud-tractate and what do they contribute that the Mishnah-tractate of the same name would lack without them?

In the following I indent the entries that carry forward in large-scale composites the theme or problem or proposition of the Mishnah, and I focus upon those composites that treat topics not relevant to the Mishnah; further, I underline items that fall into neither category.

I.D:  The sizable composite about dismantling synagogue buildings, shading over into the distinct composite on the Temple of Herod. The discussion of dismantling synagogue buildings is fully articulated; it has no relationship I can discern to the context defined by the Mishnah.

I.E:  The Temple that Herod Built.

    III.C:  The introduction at the Mishnah, III.B, of the consideration of assumptions as to facts where we cannot prove the facts leads to a secondary exercise on the presumptive rights signified by established usage. The composite, while autonomous, is situated in a relevant context.

    IV.D:  Once we deal with forcing neighbors to contribute to the common defense, the special rules that pertain to sages are worked out; sages represent an exception to the Mishnah's rule.

    IV.F:  Philanthropic obligations that apply to residents of a town, shading over into a discussion of how the funds are collected and distributed, remains well within the established framework of the exposition of common obligations of citizens of a community. This is a massive composite with its own interests, but viewed whole, it remains within the classification of a secondary topical supplement to an exposition of the Mishnah. Its insertion here is not jarring, though its dimensions and full articulation certainly are not to have been predicted on the basis of comparable insertions.

V.C:  The composite on prophecy and sagacity is inserted whole because of the casual reference at V.B.II.3 to the status of a statement of a prophet as having no legal standing. Then the exposition takes up the subject in its own terms; but the six items are scarcely more than a long footnote.

    V.D: Special problems here do not vastly change the face of the Mishnah-exposition.

V.G:  Dividing up Sacred Scriptures, V.F, to which the Mishnah makes reference, draws in its wake an enormous exposition about the rules of joining, and dividing, Sacred Scriptures. This carries us forward to the correct order of the books of Scripture, and that continues with

V.H:    who wrote various books of Scripture.

V.I:    The composite on Job is added because V.I invites further discussion of that subject. So the first three items of this composite pursue the systematic exposition of the theme, and the penultimate one is an add-on,

V.J:    as is the final item, the theme of Abraham, often compared to Job and treated as Job's counterpart. This continues the foregoing, these latter two items being footnotes to the foundation-set.

    VI.G:   This is inserted because it intersects with the interests of the Mishnah to the exposition of this it is attached.

    VIII.B: The discussion of the rights and rules of shop-keeping invites the secondary exposition of rules governing limitation on competition. The connection is at the opening item, which is in detail an appropriate amplification of the Mishnah's principle, but the exposition of which shades over into the larger issue treated here.

    XV.B:   The basic theme here is the four winds and what each brings, and that surely forms a valid amplification of the Mishnah's interest in keeping noxious odors out of town. The ubiquity of God's presence certainly is not a topic introduced by an explanation of how we must keep carrion, graves, and tanneries away from a town. We can readily see how the gloss of the opening item, which does amplify the Mishnah's rule, yields a secondary point on the meaning of "constant," and once we are told that only God's Presence is "constant," the rest follows.

    XX.B:   This is a massive compilation of cases that illustrate the general principles of the Mishnah on settling conflicting claims.

XXV.B:  The set on Benaah is introduced because it glosses a detail of the prior composite; but it is free-standing. It makes a variety of points, and the whole holds together only around the named authority.

XXX.E:  This important compilation is tacked on because it makes the point that, in mourning for the Temple, one does not fully stucco his house but leaves a bare spot, which intersects with a detail of the foregoing. But the composite stands on its own and in no way serves to amplify a detail let alone a principle pertinent to the Mishnah.

    XXXI.C: The meaning of the language used in selling real estate carries forward the Mishnah's interest in interpreting the language that describes commercial transactions of sale.

XL.E:   The composite of sailors' and other travellers' tales begins with those of Rabbah bar bar Hannah, moving on to

Chapter Twenty-two. The Structure of Babylonian Talmud Baba Batra    121

XL.F:   other travellers' tales, yielding an interest in
XL.G:   sea monsters in general, and Leviathan in particular,
XL.H:   bearing a brief insertion on the character and sources of the waters of the sea,
XL.I:   then reverting to the theme of Leviathan again.
XL.J:   Since Leviathan serves as the meal for the Messianic banquet, the theme of the coming of the Messianic age once more intrudes.
    XL.K:   This item reverts to the Mishnah's topic and problematic.
    L.C:    Interest in just weights and measures shades over into an exposition of the penalty for falsifying weights and measures.
    L.E:    The same theme as above is worked out here.
    L.F:    The same theme as above is worked out here.
    L.G:    From one form of unjust market practices, we move on to the next, which is, price manipulation and hoarding.
L.H:    Once the theme of market crises enters, we turn to the correct response to shortages, which is not migration from the Land of Israel. That introduces the case of Ruth's family, which migrated because of famine.
L.I:    From famine we move on to plenty.
    LII.C:  The theme of the Mishnah invites a free-standing complement of important information.
    LIV.E:  As above, this item simply provides information invited by the Mishnah's own topic.
    LXII.B: The problem of the Mishnah's rule is here extended by introducing some further details.
    LXIV.B: As above.
    LXIV.H: As above.
    LXV.C:  The theme of the Mishnah, how others inherit the estate of someone who does not have sons, explains the introduction of the composite on dying without sons and what it means. It is a sign of divine wrath.
    LXVI.C: The fact that on the fifteenth of Ab, the tribes were permitted to intermarry, which forms the background for the problem of the Mishnah's case, accounts for this and the next entry.
    LXVI.D: As above.
    LXVII.C: The general theme of the Mishnah, the disposition of the birthright, the division of an estate among the sons, is amplified by the case of Jacob and his sons.
    LXVII.D: As above: the special claim of the firstborn of a priest and other special cases of inheritance.
    LXVIII.B: A secondary problem, how we deal with special problems of inheritance, explains the intrusion of this small st.
    LXVIII.C: Here is another special problem on inheritance, namely, the father's right to deprive the firstborn of his special portion.

LXVIII.D: This is a formal intrusion, based on a shared formula, and I see no substantive reason for inserting the entire composite except the one that accounts for its intersection with the immediately preceding item — a substantive intersection, bearing in its wake a formal intrusion.

LXXIII.D: This composite does not amplify the particular law of the Mishnah but it does pursue its main theme and interests.

LXXVII.C: The Mishnah's own interests invites the addition of this autonomous composite.

LXXVII.D: As above.

LXXX.C: This brief appendix does not greatly affect the context in which it is introduced; it is nothing more than a secondary exposition of a tangential theme.

LXXXII.B: The Mishnah's own interests invites the addition of this autonomous composite.

LXXXII.E: Once we deal with gifts of real estate and movables, we turn to the question of the status of a slave: how is he classified?

LXXXII.F: The matter of gifts shades over into a discussion of the form of gifts, with special attention to gifts that are made in writing.

LXXXVIII.C: The Mishnah's principle is illustrated by a distinct case.

3. CAN WE STATE WHAT THE COMPILERS OF THIS DOCUMENT PROPOSE TO ACCOMPLISH IN PRODUCING THIS COMPLETE, ORGANIZED PIECE OF WRITING?

When we examine the program of our Mishnah-tractate and compare it with the topics of the composites that the compilers introduced on their own, not in response to the task of Mishnah-exegesis, we can readily reconstruct their reading of the Mishnah. Eliminating the numerous free-standing composites that serve to amplify the Mishnah's own propositions or introduce principles to reshape the Mishnah's topics, what topics do we find our Talmud's framers have added on their own? The single most obvious insertion is their attention to the special rights and status of the sages themselves. But that is only the starting pint Beyond lie the items on the familiar list of historical-Messianic and transcendent themes: the Temple of Herod; prophecy in the present age; the dimensions of the various books of Scripture and their correct order and their authors; Job and Abraham; mourning for the Temple; travellers' tales, shading over into a large-scale composite on Leviathan and on the Messianic age; remaining in the Holy Land at all costs and famine and plenty.

Now with this simple and compelling result in hand, we have little difficulty in answering the question, what did the compilers of the Talmud find lacking in the Mishnah's repertoire of cases and principles? What they missed in the Mishnah was attention to precisely those issues that the Mishnah-tractate ignored, which is, the historical-Messianic context in which the everyday conflicts over inheritances and estates, property and land, and the conduct of the civil order took place. It is as though the compilers of the Talmud wished to remind those engaged in the secular and everyday matters on which this tractate centers that in the end God will resolve the mundane issues taken up here. History intrudes on the eternal present of home and family, inheritance and estates, the continuities of the private life. A public world intervenes, one for which the Temple on the one side, and Scripture on the other, form the media and provide the motive. So what makes our Mishnah-tractate insufficient — its very success in disposing of the everyday problems of property and conflict over property, cheating customers and overreaching in prices for example — forms the program of the compilers of the Talmud when they work on their own.

Their expansion of the Talmud's boundaries far beyond the limits of Mishnah-exegesis now proves purposive and turns out to make its own comment on the Mishnah, once that the Mishnah's exegetes in no way can have conceived. Specifically, the inclusion of a range of topics omitted by the Mishnah, the sometimes quite jarring introduction of themes entirely out of phase with what is being discussed — from stuccoing a house to leaving off stucco in memorial to the destruction of the Temple, for example! — leave no doubt in our minds concerning the compilers' perception of the Mishnah-tractate. And how they wished us to conceive the Mishnah-tractate's topics and concerns, the dimensions in which they wished to recast these matters, the perspective they proposed to introduce — these form the particular statement of the Talmud's compilers. What counts, what really counts in the perspective of eternity, is precisely what is omitted by the Mishnah's program, and, furthermore, demands its proper place in any consideration of what the Mishnah's framers have set forth as their principal message for the civil order.

# XXIII

## The Structure of Babylonian Talmud Sanhedrin

### POINTS OF STRUCTURE

1. DOES BABYLONIAN TALMUD-TRACTATE SANHEDRIN FOLLOW A COHERENT OUTLINE GOVERNED BY A CONSISTENT RULES?

The Talmud-tractate follows the program of the Mishnah-tractate of the same name and rarely diverges from it. Where we have a large composite that does not expound a topic or proposition set forth by the Mishnah-tractate, it complements one that does. This tractate more slavishly adheres to the program of the Mishnah than any other, and that is the fact despite the appearance of prolixity.

2. WHAT ARE THE SALIENT TRAITS OF ITS STRUCTURE?

For the first ten chapters, the Mishnah sets forth topics or propositions inviting analysis. For the eleventh chapter, the Mishnah defines a topical program, which the Talmud richly augments with collections of information.

3. WHAT IS THE RATIONALITY OF THE STRUCTURE?

The Mishnah defines what is orderly and what is not. There is no other organizing principle that governs throughout. What I have marked as secondary or derivative or complementary nearly everywhere carries forward what has begun as Mishnah-commentary. I see only very, very few entries — compositions, never composites — that are parachuted down on their own. All composites and nearly all compositions can be shown to stand in logical or at least topical relationship to the Mishnah's program: propositional or topical.

4. WHERE ARE THE POINTS OF IRRATIONALITY IN THE STRUCTURE?

I have identified a variety of composites that serve a purpose other than that of Mishnah-commentary. These are to be divided into three groups, only one of which requires further comment. The first group is made up of composites that do not directly comment upon a proposition of the Mishnah or deal with a topic introduced by the Mishnah. These I list below, in my discussion of topical composites that the Talmud contributes but that the Mishnah does not require on its own. The second group comprises composites that form appendices to the treatment of a Mishnah-topic or proposition, e.g., clarifying a subsidiary point or otherwise standing in subordinate relationship to the Mishnah. These I list below, indenting the items and so differentiating them from the ones that change the character of the Talmud's re-presentation of the Mishnah. The third set are items that have no clear relationship whatever to the work of Mishnah-commentary, e.g., formal composites, in which an extrinsic trait, not one intrinsic to what is said, accounts for the agglutination of compositions. These I indicate by underlining. Readers are referred to the treatment of topical composites in what follows.

### Points of System

1. Does the Babylonian Talmud-tractate Sanhedrin serve only as a re-presentation of the Mishnah-tractate of the same name?

Enough of the Mishnah is covered by the Talmud to require an affirmative response to this question. Certainly the net effect is to treat the Mishnah as principal and as privileged, and all composites are set into the Talmud in relationship to the Mishnah's requirements. I cannot find a single exception to that rule, and that is now an established fact. That the Talmud must be described as a commentary to the Mishnah and as nothing other than a commentary to the Mishnah is the outcome of this work to date.

2. How do the topical composites fit into the Talmud-tractate Sanhedrin and what do they contribute that the Mishnah-tractate of the same name would lack without them?

> I.C: The judgment of cases by fewer than three judges is simply a question invited by the law of the Mishnah.
> 
> I.D: Arbitration as an alternative to a legal contest falls into the same category as the foregoing.

I.E: In praise of justice and true judges: This entry is invited by the general theme and premise of the Mishnah-rule and does not vastly change our impression of the Mishnah's topic, which is, the judgment of cases and the fair conduct of trials.

> > VI.D Composite on the Writing and Revelation of the Torah: This is a thematic composite, inserted because of the discussion, by the Mishnah, of the King's writing out a scroll of the Torah and carrying it about with him. I do not see how this composite vastly changes our perception of the Mishnah's rule or its context.
> > 
> > VII.B The evils of divorce, particularly of an aging wife: This composite is inserted without any clear relationship to the Mishnah;'s rule. Including the set has probably been provoked by the story of Abishad and Bath Sheba.

## Chapter Twenty-three. The Structure of Babylonian Talmud Sanhedrin

XVI.F: The creation of man, the minim, debates with unbelievers, the emperor and the patriarch. This is a vast and important composite on a variety of topics. It is added as a complement to the Mishnah's statement that God put his mint-mark on everyone, yet not one is like another. While this passage moves in a variety of directions, it seems to me wholly complementary to the Mishnah's interests and statements and in no way does the composite (or, really, set of composites) reshape the setting or context in which we are to read the Mishnah's statements. To the contrary, what we have is a rich and dense extension of what the Mishnah clearly wishes to emphasize.

XVI.H: The exegesis of the story of Ahab's death illustrates the statement of the Mishnah immediately preceding, which is, "When the wicked perish there is rejoicing." This item then illustrates that point. But of course, the composite moves in its own direction, guided by the requirements of the theme that it pursues.

XVII.H: Topical appendix on reciting the blessing over the New Moon. The Mishnah's statement introduces this theme, which is then a compendium of useful information, nothing more.

XXIV.E: Burial as the preferred mode of disposition. This is a clear appendix to the statement that one may not leave the deceased to stay unburied overnight. The composite simply reenforces the Mishnah's premise.

XXXI.B: The religious obligations of the children of Noah: idolators and slaves. This composite begins with the statement that idolators as much as Israelites are admonished not to curse God, which is precisely the topic that the Mishnah has introduced. The composite goes off in its own direction, but blasphemy remains a principal consideration throughout, even though the governing topic is now not blasphemy but the obligations of non-Israelites.

XLI.B: The evils of wine: This is a topical composite added after a reference to the rebellious son's drinking a half-log of Italian wine. The Mishnah's general interests thus are advanced, and the premise of Scripture and the Mishnah, that drunkenness is evil, is reenforced.

XLIX.B: Marrying off one's children in the proper manner: This item forms a positive side to the Mishnah's negative, that is, those put to death for incest and similar sexual crimes. Now we are given the opposite: how matters should be carried on.

LVII.C: The zealotry of Phineas: This is a first-rate illustration of the Mishnah's interest in how zealots may enforce the law outside the normal framework of court procedures.

LXV.B: Topical Appendix on Gebiha and Alexander: This is added because of the reference in the foregoing to Gebiha's proof for the resurrection of the dead.

> LXV.C: Topical Appendix on Antoninus and Rabbi: My best guess is that this composite was joined to the foregoing as part of a set on sages and emperors; I see no point of topical, let alone propositional, intersection with our Mishnah.

LXV.D: The death of Death: Here we really do have a point of extension, beyond the limits of the Mishnah, so as to recast the Mishnah's topic and set forth a proposition that the exegesis of the Mishnah does not require and that greatly changes our sense of the Mishnah's meaning. The Mishnah's interest in the resurrection of the dead is now shown to be part of a larger proposition, which is, in time to come, death itself will die.

> LXV.E: How on the basis of the Torah do we know about the resurrection of the dead. This large composite carries forward the exegesis of the Mishnah, proving in various ways on the strength of Scripture the facticity of the Mishnah's claim.

> LXV.F: Topical appendix on Hananiah, Mishael, and Azariah: Here is an example of how death is overcome.

LXV.G: The Messiah. Pharaoh, Sennacherib, Hezekiah, and other Players in the Messianic drama. Here is the point in our tractate at which the Mishnah's program really comes under considerable revision. The Talmud treats as self-evident the link between the Messiah and the resurrection of the dead, but the Mishnah has not done so, indeed, has no introduced the Messiah-theme at all. The Talmud then wants to know how the Messiah's coming relates to the resurrection of the dead. Various salvific occasions are then introduced, Pharaoh and Moses; Sennacherib and Hezekiah. These form secondary expositions of the general theme of the Messiah.

LXV.H: When will the Messiah come? Here is yet another major revision in the presentation of the Mishnah, a systematic recasting of matters to link the resurrection to that other, and quite separate, issue. The upshot is that Israel's historical fate and its salvation at the end of time form a component in the exposition of the theme of the resurrection of the dead. Since this passage of the Mishnah does not introduce the Messiah-theme, the radical re-presentation of matters emerges with great force.

> LXV.R: Wicked monarchs who nonetheless merit a portion in the world to come: This is a clear extension of the Mishnah, since the point of interest is to form a catalogue of kings who, despite their evil, will inherit the world to come.

LXV.S: The special case of Hezekiah. The Exegesis of Lamentations. Since Hezekiah is designated as a player in the Messianic drama, and since the exegesis of Lamentations is introduced as if out of nowhere, it seems to me we should regard this composite, mostly devoted to Lamentations, as a further treatment of the Messiah-theme. Here is why Israel requires the Messiah: the city sits solitary.

LXV.T: Summary judgments. What we have here is yet another secondary amplification of the Mishnah's topic. The composite is situated where it belongs for the purpose of Mishnah-commentary, precisely at the end of the account of the kings who do not merit the world to come, and at the outset of the account of the commoners who likewise lose out.

LXV.W: After Doeg we deal with David, who is matched against Doeg. I am somewhat puzzled by the introduction of this composite, but it does seem to me continuous in its general proposition with the preceding one.

LXVIII.K: Jericho in Particular. Here we have a fine illustration of the one case in which a town really was treated in accord with the law of the Torah governing the apostate city.

3. CAN WE STATE WHAT THE COMPILERS OF THIS DOCUMENT PROPOSE TO ACCOMPLISH IN PRODUCING THIS COMPLETE, ORGANIZED PIECE OF WRITING?

The first ten chapters of the tractate conform to the general rules of sustained, analytical investigation that govern in the Talmud in general. Chapter Eleven contains much information, many well-crafted compositions and purposive composites, but it exhibits singular deficiencies in the analytical process to which we become accustomed. But the rules of large-scale conglomeration remain firm. When we take a second look at Chapter Eleven, we find a sustained effort at recasting the Mishnah's topic by introducing themes that the Mishnah either omits altogether or treats in a casual way. These emerge in unit LXV: the death of death; the coming of the Messiah — past time; the coming of the Messiah — future time; the special case of Hezekiah and the pertinence of the book of Lamentations. Here in a single set of composites we find introduced a set of propositions concerning the Messiah and Israel's history that the Mishnah has neglected. The Mishnah, after all, has focused upon private persons — specific kings and commoners who have lost the world to come. The Talmud, by contrast, introduces the dimension of the Israelite community seen whole. The Mishnah tells us how individuals lose out, e.g., by denying that the Torah itself teaches that the dead will be raised. The Talmud turns to the more profound question of the death of death, which itself then comes as the prologue to the advent of the Messiah. As though to underscore the main point — the issue is Israel the holy people, not merely individual players in Israelite life — the exegesis of Lamentations is inserted, whole and in no clear connection to what has preceded. The result of this analysis leaves no doubt that the framers of the Talmud have both commented upon the Mishnah in a rich and remarkably profound way but also recast the context in which the Mishnah is to be received and understood. The Talmud truly forms the re-presentation of the Mishnah. And what the Talmud's framers find self-evident in the exposition of the Mishnah's statements that the Mishnah's authors treated casually or not at all speaks for itself.

# XXIV

## The Structure of Babylonian Talmud Makkot

### Points of Structure

1. Does Babylonian Talmud-tractate Makkot follow a coherent outline governed by a consistent rules?

The outline given above serves for nearly the whole of the tractate. That is to say, if we start with the principles of a topical outline, with the conception that a topic-sentence governs what is to be said in the sequence of paragraphs that follow, then with the paragraphs laid out as secondary expositions and expansions of the topic or proposition, with a new topic-sentence signalling a new set of expositions and expansions relevant to that, and so on down, we can outline nearly every line of the tractate. The Mishnah's statements serve as the topic sentences in the outline I have worked out. The secondary expositions, bearing capital letters as their marks, then form a succession of close and logically-sequential expositions of the topic-sentences that the Mishnah has provided and the Talmud's framers have selected. These are the exceptions: III.A, B, IX D, XVI B, C, XVI F, G, H, XXII D, XXX C. It follows that Bavli-tractate Makkot does follow a coherent outline, and we may inductively define the rules that govern throughout.

2. What are the salient traits of its structure?

The of a Talmud-composite had in hand completed compositions deriving from an indeterminate past. What he then did was to follow a simple outline. He laid out the Mishnah-tractate, making a decision on which passages of the tractate he wished to expound. I have no clear theory of the criteria that instructed him on the matter, because a theory on why given paragraphs of the Mishnah were not treated must await the examination of a much larger sample than the three tractates (Moed Qatan, Keritot, Makkot) that at this moment are in hand. In any event we cannot show that the framer picked and chose among a large corpus of available Mishnah-comments; we cannot show that he included everything to which he had access; we cannot show that he made up pretty much everything he had to say; and we cannot show that he limited himself to the utilization of received materials.

What we cannot show, we do not know. So the first salient trait of the structure of the tractate is, the formulation of a systematic exegesis for (parts of) tractate Makkot.

A fixed order of exposition governed: [1] the scriptural foundations of, or links to, rules of the Mishnah; [2] the explanation of words or phrases in the Mishnah; [3] the introduction of Tannaite complements to the Mishnah, meaning, compositions (or even composites) bearing the marks of origin among the official, Tannaite memorizers.[1] Afterward, so far as exegesis of a given Mishnah-sentence or paragraph was underway, [4] theoretical problems would be introduced, refinements of the law, interstitial cases in which two principles intersected and produced unclarity, and the like. That order is not a matter of hypothesis, so far as this tractate is concerned, it is demonstrated beyond doubt, beginning to end. That is, if all four types of material are set forth in the exposition of a given Mishnah-sentence or paragraph, the specified order governs. The third or fourth types will appear first in order only when the first and second types are not introduced at all. That seems to me ample evidence that a well-defined structural program governed. Other components of the program, e.g., cases, tangential discussions, not to mention the free-standing composites that in no way bear upon Mishnah-exegesis, all are organized in a logical way as well, but have to be dealt with in their own terms.

### 3. What is the Rationality of the structure?

The rationality of Bavli-tractate Makkot may be defined very simply. The framers of the tractate undertook to examine and analyze Mishnah-tractate Makkot so as to clarify its contents, on the one side, and to show the logical coherence and cogency of the diverse rules of the tractate, on the other. The principles of cogency were two. First, the discrete rules of the Mishnah relate to the received, written Torah of Sinai, and they gain cogency not because they spin out a single logical proposition, or even because they work out in an orderly way the components of a topic and explain each component in its place. Rather, they gain cogency because all of the discrete statements derive from a single, prior source, which is, the written Torah. The first principle of rationality then concerns the coherence of discrete and free-standing statements, e.g., this Mishnah-paragraph, that Mishnah-rule, and coherence is imposed by a common derivation in the Torah. The first principle of cogency therefore is formal.

But a second principle of cogency plays an equally important role, and that concerns the substance of matters. The Mishnah-rules cohere not only because all of them derive from the same prior source, but because each of them takes up its

---

[1] We do not know when the Tannaite component of the corpus was formulated for transmission, whether in writing or orally (and the document time and again insists on the transmission through the memory of professional memorizers). That all compositions and composites bearing the signal of Tannaite authority originated in the period prior to the closure of the Mishnah is demonstrably impossible, and the Bavli contains ample evidence that throughout the period of the composition of its principal parts, Tannaite work was going on.

position in the exposition of a topic. The orderly presentation of the tractate, line by line, defines a rationality that insists upon the principle that subjects themselves exhibit an inner logic; hold together by reason of the fit of the parts thereof. That accounts for the principle of organization that lays out the tractate as a commentary to the Mishnah, itself a topical formulation of the law, rather than as a commentary to those passages of Scripture to which the Mishnah-rules relate. That that alternative rationality of structure can have governed hardly can be doubted, since we do have systematic expositions of topics in accord with their appearance in Scripture, not the Mishnah, in Mekhilta, Sifra, and the two Sifrés.

It follows that two principles of cogency intersect, the scriptural and the topical, and the topical takes pride of place. That is the meaning of the Bavli's presentation of its ideas in the form of a commentary to the Mishnah.

4. WHERE ARE THE POINTS OF IRRATIONALITY IN THE STRUCTURE?

If rationality derives from the interplay of form and substance, as just now spelled out, then rationality defines, also, its counterpart and opposite, irrationality. Where does Mishnah-exposition break down? There we find the points of irrationality. Then the answer is simple: at the listed passages, III.A, B, IX D, XVI B, C, XVI F, G, H, XXII D, XXX C, where Mishnah-exegesis does not define the focus of a composite, but where some other principle does. The point of irrationality on the surface is structural. But in that aspect, it also conflicts with both the scriptural and the topical principles of coherent discourse; neither Scripture's relevant passages nor the Mishnah's topical program governs, and at some interesting points in this tractate, a completely different theory of the composition of an exposition of the law, and not the Talmud's theory, takes over. Had this other theory prevailed, we should have law, but not the Talmud; and we should have exegesis, but not the Midrash-compilations as we know them.[2]

---

[2] I shall not expand upon that point in this project; it is something to be investigated in the context of Midrash-compilation: what other of the collection and arrangement of Midrash-compositions functions alongside the ones that the documents themselves take for granted? Just as we can contemplate the Bavli that might have been, and here begin the examination of the alternative to the Talmud as we know it that can have been produced, so in due course we must consider the Midrash-compilations that we might have had but do not have. In my *Making the Classics in Judaism: The Three Stages of Literary Formation.* Atlanta, 1990: Scholars Press for Brown Judaic Studies, I begin the work to which reference is made here. The classification of materials there called "compositions for no document we now can imagine" corresponds to what I have in mind here as the Midrash-counterpart to "points of irrationality" in the Talmud. These observations suffice for the moment.

## POINTS OF SYSTEM

1. DOES THE BABYLONIAN TALMUD-TRACTATE MAKKOT SERVE ONLY AS A RE-PRESENTATION OF THE MISHNAH-TRACTATE OF THE SAME NAME?

This Bavli-tractate serves mainly as a re-presentation of the Talmud-tractate of the same name, in that the structure of the document finds its definition therein. But, as we recognize, large tracts of Mishnah-tractate Makkot are ignored or given the most routine exposition. When we realize that a fair measure of the Mishnah-exposition follows a repeated formula over the discussion of several Mishnah-paragraphs, the routine character of the re-presentation becomes striking. But since the framers obviously picked and chose, we must say that their system rests only asymmetrically upon that of the Mishnah. But, I hasten to add, in this tractate as in most others, where the authors of a composition do expound the meaning of a sentence or paragraph of the Mishnah, I cannot point to a single passage in which, it seems to me, they have brought a program of their own such that they have recast the Mishnah-sentence or paragraph into a different framework of meaning from that defined by the Mishnah's authors or framers. That seems to me a consistent, and very important, result of our examination of this tractate.

2. HOW DO THE TOPICAL COMPOSITES FIT INTO THE TALMUD-TRACTATE MAKKOT AND WHAT DO THEY CONTRIBUTE THAT THE MISHNAH-TRACTATE OF THE SAME NAME WOULD LACK WITHOUT THEM?

An answer composed of generalizations contributes nothing. We turn directly to each specific item.

III.A and B: The entire composition goes its own way, and if this kind of composition predominated, we should have nothing resembling a talmud, such as the Talmuds that we know. The law of Judaism would have reached us in a completely different form from the form — the applied reason and practical logic given dynamism by dialectics — that we know. And the history of Judaism, so far as the intellectual life of the faith defines that history, would have taken a different course from the one that it took.

The composite at 1:1L-N, from beginning to end, shows a different theory of composite-making from the one that predominates in the Talmud overall. In this theory we collect statements attributed by a principal authority to a founder of the tradition in Babylonia, Rab or Samuel; these statements cover a variety of topics and express no single cogent principle; nor do they take up one problem in a variety of forms. And since the composite does not take shape around a problem of Mishnah-exegesis or of the analysis of a problem of law, exegesis of Scripture, or theology, it follows that the theory of composite-making is different from the theory that produced the Talmud's composites as we know them. Had the present theory prevailed, we should have no Talmud — systematic exposition of the Mishnah, with additions — but rather collections of sayings joined by the formality of common source in a given authority's school. These collections then will have yielded something other than a coherent statement of the law of the Mishnah, properly expanded. They will have given us the same law, but in very different form.

And yet, we notice, the character of the discussion of the components of the composite that sets forth the formulation of Judah in Samuel's or in Rab's name in no way differs from the character of the discussion of our conventional Talmud. I take that fact to mean people subjected to the same sort of sustained analytical discussion diverse types of composites, not only the types that yielded the Talmud as we know it. So in circulation were composites built on various principles, analyzed in a uniform manner. Then, it must follow, those who made the Talmud as we know it picked the kinds of materials they wanted for their Talmud and, in general, omitted such other kinds as did not serve their purpose. And one of the important other kinds is the one before us: compilations of masters' sayings, organized around other than topical-programmatic lines.

This composite does not change the face of our tractate, because it has no bearing upon the re-presentation of the tractate's topical program. The composite rather shows us a different face of the law, one that, had it predominated, would have ignored the structure of the Mishnah altogether and re-formed the law into a set of rulings assigned to this authority or that one, to this set of verses of Scripture or that one, to this formulary pattern or that one. Then the topical organization of the law would have given way to a mode of presentation bearing a different rationality altogether. The figure of the authority, the tradition of his school, would have predominated; the law would then have consisted of what the authority taught, and search for the rule in a given case or concerning a given problem would have involved finding which authority dealt with the topic. Along with the orderly presentation of topics, the analytical and dialectical discussion of them would never have gotten under way, since dialectics as we know them depend upon not personality or authority but reason and the governing, objective logic that inheres in a given topic. From our perspective, the one contribution this composite makes to our tractate is to show us how things might have been, and to underscore the reasons for admiring the way in which the framers of the Talmud laid matters out.

IX D: This item introduces the complication of the suitability of testimony of witnesses. It may be that the intent is to carry forward the introduction of the rules of testimony into the matter at hand, but that is not a compelling consideration.

XVI B: The introduction of the matter of relationships of disciples and masters — a general point, of enormous interest — into the rules governing going into exile reshapes the topic by adding a profound observation. It is that while someone may go into exile from his home town and family, the Torah never leaves him; if his master goes into exile, he goes along; if he goes into exile, his master goes along. The point then is that exile affects the natural relationships, but not supernatural ones. In a case of manslaughter, God knows that there has been no murder and does not inflict the penalty of separation from the Torah upon the surviving party to a tragic accident. The Torah legislates for this world, allowing for a penalty to manslaughter, since, after all, the victim has died; but the Torah also distinguishes this world's penalties, which are painful but can be endured, from those of Heaven. Exile from the Torah would be a penalty that cannot be endured and may not be inflicted. So XVI.B recasts the rules at hand into a very original point.

XVI C: In light of the foregoing, we cannot find surprising the explicit statement of what is implicit, which is, the Torah is the sole source of authentic, enduring wealth. This world's rewards are transient; Torah-study with a multitude of disciples forms the reward of eternity. So XVI.C forms an essential step in a carefully-wrought statement. Then the topic, exile, provides the occasion for making a statement that the framers of the Talmud wish to make, not only in its own terms, therefore abstractly, but also in terms of one topic after another, and so in a very concrete way.

XVI F: Since an "elder" is a sage, the addition here makes the same point once more: a city that lacks elders, or sages, is not a suitable city of refuge. This addition is now predictable: the dimension of Torah-learning, which is supernatural, completely recasts our perception of the topic, its issues, and its messages.

XVI G: While this composition does not expound a clause of the Mishnah, it fits into the context of those that do.

XVI H: This passage is built on the following structure:
> On the verse, "And Joshua wrote these words in the book of the Torah of God" (Josh. 24:26), *there was a difference of opinion between R. Judah and R. Nehemiah.*
>
> As to the suitability of a scroll of the Torah, the parchment skins of which are sewn together with thread of flax, *there was a difference of opinion between R. Judah and R. Meir.*

The principle of composition then is obvious: disputes between Judah and someone else; and the principle of inclusion is beyond comprehension within the rationality of our Talmud — and of the Mishnah.

## Chapter Twenty-four: The Structure of Babylonian Talmud Makkot

XXII D: The curse of a sage takes effect even when it is not justified. The passage to which this propositional composite is attached concerns the curse of the mother of the manslayer. Once more, therefore, we know why the passage has been included: it is to recast the topic in a new dimension, one in which the supernatural enters in. The mother's curse may not take effect; the sage's curse will.

XXX C: Here we find a systematic set of reflections on Israel's history, which make a striking point. A quick review of the reflections shows us what that point is. To restate the main propositions laid out in sequence: The statement maintains that [1] the sage succeeds to prophecy, because now the sage, through master of the Torah, can convey Heaven's statement to Israel; [2] the Holy Spirit appears to Israel, but the upshot is the same as that of Torah-learning; and Moses our rabbi made decrees, but sages annulled them. This last point yields the proposition that the sage is the master of prophecy, because the sages know how to read prophecy in the correct way.

3. CAN WE STATE WHAT THE COMPILERS OF THIS DOCUMENT PROPOSE TO ACCOMPLISH IN PRODUCING THIS COMPLETE, ORGANIZED PIECE OF WRITING?

With the sole exception of IX.D, we can account for the intruded compositions and composites in one of two ways. One set of materials portrays legal topics by organizing teachings of named masters. Then the named master, not the topic, forms the source of coherence. The other set of materials portrays the topic of our tractate in a quite fresh way, by introducing a dimension of all law that the Mishnah ordinarily does not portray, namely, how the intrusion of the sage imparts a supernatural character to the affairs of this world. [1] The Torah does not abandon a person, but accompanies the disciple into exile; that means the supernatural family of master and disciples forms a unit subject to the judgment of the law; the Torah is the sole enduring and reliable form of wealth; a city without "elders," that is, sages, cannot afford the refuge that the Torah has provided for the manslayer; the sage is the heir to prophecy, has direct access through his powers of analytical learning, to Heaven's wishes, and disposes of prophecy much as the prophets were able to dispose of even the teachings of Moses.

The Mishnah-tractate that concerns flogging and exile has been transformed into a statement about the glory of the Torah as represented by the sage, who may be subject to flogging and exile, but who always represents that transcendent reality that the Torah conveys in this world. The topic is now seen from a different perspective altogether, and though the Mishnah has been faithfully set forth, through the introduction of topics not required for Mishnah-exegesis, and through the juxtaposition of those topical presentations with the exposition of the Mishnah, all things have changed. It is probably extending matters beyond the limits to observe that in a tractate bearing such a message, the presentation of composites formed around the names of sages delivers the message of the priority of the sage over prophecy, as much as the power of the sage to transcend exile and the power of the Torah to secure a permanent endowment, that other intruded compositions and composites deliver as well. That observation about the appropriateness even of what is least coherent in the most definitive and formal traits must, for the moment, form a mere footnote. But the text and its message leave no grounds for doubt on how the Talmud-tractate has recast the Mishnah-tractate and made the Mishnah-tractate into a medium for the message that the Talmud's system, and not the Mishnah's, wishes to set forth.

# The Structure Babylonian Talmud Shebuot

### POINTS OF STRUCTURE

1. DOES BABYLONIAN TALMUD-TRACTATE SHEBUOT FOLLOW A COHERENT OUTLINE GOVERNED BY A CONSISTENT RULES?

While the Bavli to tractate Shebuot includes a few important essays that do not conduct word-for-word exegesis of the Mishnah, the Bavli overall comprises a systematic commentary to the Mishnah and little else. The tractate commences with some general observations that compare Mishnah-tractates, asking why two tractates are juxtaposed, this one ant Makkot. There are some further, broad-brush comparisons, e.g., with counterpart passages in Mishnah-tractate Shabbat and Negaim. But these rather engaging discussions focus our attention on our tractate in its own context and do not constitute Mishnah-criticism of a systematic order. So too at I.F, we find a systematic discussion of the Mishnah seen whole.

2. WHAT ARE THE SALIENT TRAITS OF ITS STRUCTURE?

The outline of the Talmud-tractate follows the outline of the Mishnah-tractate. We note that important statements of the Mishnah-tractate are not analyzed at all. There is no accounting for the omissions. But these do not materially change the picture of the Bavli-tractate as a commentary to the Mishnah-tractate to which it is attached. As we shall note, to be sure, important propositions not set forth in the Mishnah-tractate are examined. But these respond to the Mishnah-tractate's own program or to form secondary expansions of the Bavli's reading thereof. In examining any sentence of the Mishnah or of a comparable Tannaite document, [1] the compilers first discuss the formulation, authorities, or scriptural foundations for the Mishnah's or other Tannaite document's statement. Then [2] secondary augmentation will begin, whether through an extension of the rule to other cases, or an investigation of the implicit principle of the rule and its intersection with other types of cases altogether. Following comes [3] the consideration of Tannaite formulations of rules that pertain in theme or problem or principle, and these will be subjected to the same sequence and type of analytical questions that have already been brought to bear upon the Mishnah.

### 3. WHAT IS THE RATIONALITY OF THE STRUCTURE?

We proceed from the particular — the Mishnah's rule — to the general. We first deal with the details of the particular, then we move outward to theoretical considerations. We deal with rules accorded Tannaite origin or sponsorship, first found in the Mishnah, then found in the Tosefta (not so firm a rule), and finally given a signal of Tannaite but not found in a compilation of Tannaite statements now in our hands (e. g., Tenno rabbanon, Tanné and the like).

### 4. WHERE ARE THE POINTS OF IRRATIONALITY IN THE STRUCTURE?

Nearly every principal rubric of our outline finds its definition in the Mishnah's statements. By way of exceptions, I find the following items demanding attention: I.Q, II.L, X.B, XV.C, and XX.I.

## POINTS OF SYSTEM

### 1. DOES THE BABYLONIAN TALMUD-TRACTATE SHEBUOT SERVE ONLY AS A RE-PRESENTATION OF THE MISHNAH-TRACTATE OF THE SAME NAME?

Because of the omissions of various Mishnah-paragraphs, the answer must be negative. But because of the absence of large-scale miscellanies that materially change the proportions or shape of the Mishnah-tractate, the negative answer is reenforced.

### 2. HOW DO THE TOPICAL COMPOSITES FIT INTO THE TALMUD-TRACTATE SHEBUOT AND WHAT DO THEY CONTRIBUTE THAT THE MISHNAH-TRACTATE OF THE SAME NAME WOULD LACK WITHOUT THEM?

Unlike many other important tractates, I see no point at which the large-scale composites that form rubrics unto themselves and in no way serve as Mishnah-commentary redefine the shape and structure of the tractate. On the contrary, the rather negligible selection of free-standing composites fit well into the larger program of Mishnah-exegesis.

I.A: As noted earlier, the impressive composite that views our tractate whole in relationship to its neighbors, and that further compares our tractate's formulation of matters with the counterpart formulation of the same matters elsewhere, takes an integral place in the exposition of the Mishnah-tractate. The issues in no way introduce fresh subjects or perspectives into the topic at hand, as distinct from the Mishnah-tractate. All we have is a different kind of Mishnah-criticism, not the exegetical kind that predominates, but still, a form of exegesis.

I.Q: Since the premise of the discussion in context is the conception of a court-imposed stipulation that governs the conditions under which an individual may act, e.g., an individual's act of consecration is subject to the unarticulated stipulations that the court imposes, willy-nilly, upon all such actions, the extensive and excellent discussion of this principle in its own

## Chapter Twenty-five. The Structure of Babylonian Talmud Shebuot 141

terms flows directly from the work of Mishnah-exegesis. Indeed, this is articulated in so many words when I.Q.3 explicitly reverts to Simeon's position in the Mishnah itself. So while we take up the matter of mental stipulations and unstated conditions imposed by the court, in fact this excellent composite forms an integral chapter in the exegesis undertaken at I.P.

II.L: The systematic exposition of the topic at hand — not having sexual relations with a menstruating woman — is set forth because the immediately prior Mishnah-clause has referred to such an action. So the topical composite is tacked on essentially to develop the point, introduced by the Mishnah itself, that such sexual relations are forbidden. Not only is the face of the Mishnah not vastly changed, but the intention of the Mishnah's rule is reenforced.

X.B: The oath of testimony serves all parties to a court proceeding, and the secondary exposition on how court procedures must be scrupulously fair to all parties simply enriches the basic point with which the Mishnah-chapter is occupied. Once we say that all who have testimony to give are adjured to give it, we proceed quite naturally to other ways in which we attempt to insure a fair adjudication of conflicting claims. Distinctive to the Talmud, as expected, is the special problem of how the superior status of the sage and his disciple is taken into account; that forms a subdivision of the composite. If I had to specify a single composite that does materially deepen the consideration of the Mishnah-paragraph, it would be this one, since it makes articulate the premise of the Mishnah-chapter as a whole. But then all we have are more details pointing to the same generalization.

XV.C: The Mishnah-paragraph deals with euphemisms for the divine name, and the further discussion simply amplifies that subject; all we have is a topical appendix.

XX.I: A set of sayings in the name of a given authority is inserted whole, even though some contribute nothing to the problem at hand; this is typical of the Talmud's use of what clearly are received composites formulated along lines other than those that generally govern in the Talmud itself.

3. CAN WE STATE WHAT THE COMPILERS OF THIS DOCUMENT PROPOSE TO ACCOMPLISH IN PRODUCING THIS COMPLETE, ORGANIZED PIECE OF WRITING?

I see no way in which the framers of Bavli Shebuot signalled an intention to do other than systematically expound the Mishnah, first its language, then its themes or principles or main ideas, as the context may indicate. Apart from a modest effort at broadening the scope of discussion of the oath of testimony to encompass the larger rules of fairness in court procedure, I cannot even find in the composites that fall outside the framework of Mishnah-commentary the slightest interest in reshaping or broadening the topic at hand. The Mishnah-tractate is set forth in a clear and systematic way, and that is precisely what the framers of the Talmud have wished to accomplish. Can we classify the main types of Mishnah-commentary? These seem to me to form a representative sample of the whole:

1. GLOSSING OF THE LANGUAGE OF THE MISHNAH: I.S.1, 2, 3; T. 1; II.F.1; I.1; III.A.1-3; V.B.1; VII.A.1
2. THE SOURCE IN SCRIPTURE OF THE MISHNAH'S RULE: I.J.1+a-e; L.1-3; M.1-2; N.1; R.1; T.4; II.B, G.1, H.4; V.A.1, E.2; VI.A.1+a-b
3. THE NAME OF THE AUTHORITY BEHIND AN ANONYMOUS AND AUTHORITATIVE STATEMENT OF THE MISHNAH: I.T.2-3; T.5+a-c
4. THE FURTHER AMPLIFICATION OF THE MISHNAH'S RULE AND THE PRINCIPLES INHERENT THEREIN: I.B.1, C.1, D.1, E.1 [F.1-4], G.1, H.1, I.1-2, K.1, 2; L.4; N.2. O.1. P.1 [+Q.1-5]; II.A.1-3; C.1, 2; D.1+a, E.1-3, H.1-3 (systematic glossing), H5-8; I.2-5. J.1; K.1 (+L.1-6, topical appendix); M.1-4; III.B.1, C.1, D.1-6 (amplification of what is at issue in the disputes; amplification of the rules; provision of answers to subsidiary problems); IV.A.1, B.1, C.1-3; D.1-3; V.C.1, D.1-2. E.1, 3-6 (plus secondary amplifications); VI.B.1; VII.B.1-6; VIII.A.1; B.1, 2; C.1, D.1; IX.A.1

These four rubrics turn out to encompass every composite, and most of the compositions, of Chapters One through Three. And of them, the one we should predict would constitute the single largest rubric, the fourth, turns out to predominate throughout.

A review of the systematic program of augmentation of the law of the tractate, not only its language, will show that that enterprise not only predominates but also imposes its character upon the tractate as a whole. The Bavli's treatment of Mishnah-tractate Shebuot is highly speculative and theoretical, working within the framework of the rules of the Mishnah-tractate but translating the rules into principles for exploration in their own terms. If I had to define the achievement of the framers of the tractate's compositions and most of its composites, it would identify as principal this transformation of rules into principles and cases into laws. The Talmud is talmudic at just this point, at the fourth of the four rubrics. This tractate defines the Talmud of Babylonia as a commentary to the Mishnah — and little else. But, as others indicate, for that reason it also forms an anomaly in the Talmud.

# XXVI

## The Structure of Babylonian Talmud Abodah Zarah

### Points of Structure

1. Does Babylonian Talmud-tractate Abodah Zarah follow a coherent outline governed by a consistent rules?

In general, our tractate is organized around the Mishnah-tractate of the same name. But as we shall note, it contains numerous, enormous, and important free-standing compositions and composites, which in no way comment on the Mishnah.

2. What are the salient traits of its structure?

Where the Tractate focuses upon the Mishnah, it takes up, ordinarily in this order, the meanings of words and phrases, the scriptural basis for Mishnah-rules, and the name of the authority behind an anonymous passage. It will then proceed to questions of a secondary order, e.g., implications of a statement, possible contradictions, in rule or in principle, between two distinct statements in the Mishnah or in other Tannaite compilations, and, then may come essays on the principle of law or the theme of law of the subject.

3. What is the Rationality of the structure?

The focus upon Mishnah-commentary tells us what enters into the composite, and why one item takes priority over another.

4. Where are the points of irrationality in the structure?

We have to distinguish among the large composites that do not directly address the amplification of the Mishnah between two types. The first is the composite that is tacked on for formal reasons, e.g., more sayings that bear the same attributive formula as the saying that has served the Mishnah, or more information on a subject that the Mishnah treats. The second is the composite that in no way relates to the Mishnah's rules, principles, or authorities. I place the former in parentheses, and catalogue the latter, which then are treated in the proper context: the question of how the intruded ("irrational") composites have affected and drastically changed the re-presentation of the Mishnah-tractate.

These are the composites that diverge from Mishnah-commentary: I.B, C, D,E, F, G, H; I.N (other rulings of Joshua b. Qorha); II.C (other rulings of Nahum the Mede); III.C, E; III.H (other festivals of idolatry); VIII.C, D, E, F, G; IX.B; XIII.B (Appendix on the Symptoms of Various Ailments and their Cures).

### Points of System

1. Does the Babylonian Talmud-tractate Abodah Zarah serve only as a re-presentation of the Mishnah-tractate of the same name?

The Bavli tractate serves not only but mainly as a re-presentation of the Mishnah-tractate of the same name. That is to say, the Bavli-tractate presents the Mishnah-tractate but imparts to the received statement a vast, additional message of its own, one that puts into perspective and imparts depth and significance to the Mishnah-tractate's rules. The full meaning of that statement becomes clear presently.

2. How do the topical composites fit into the Talmud-tractate Abodah Zarah and what do they contribute that the Mishnah-tractate of the same name would lack without them?

Our task is now to survey those large-scale composites that accomplish a task other than that of Mishnah-exegesis. I have already catalogued them above. I omit reference to those items that are mere topical appendices or compilations of sayings in the name of an authority who figures in a Mishnah-comment. These are specified above. The remainder are as follows:

I.B: A Theology of Gentile Idolatry: Its Origins and its Implications for Holy Israel: Why the gentiles rejected the Torah. It was offered to each of them, but they were too much absorbed by their own matters to accept God's will. They did not even carry out the seven commandments of the children of Noah.

I.C: The Critical Importance of Torah-Study for the Salvation of Israel, Individually and Collectively: Why are human beings compared to fish of the sea? To tell you, just as fish in the sea, when they come up on dry land, forthwith begin to die, so with human beings, when they take their leave of teachings of the Torah and religious deeds, forthwith they begin to die.

I.D: God Favors Holy Israel over the Gentiles, Because the Former Accept, Study, and Carry Out the Torah and the Latter Do Not. Therefore at the End of Days God Will Save Israel and Destroy Idolatry: R. Hinena bar Pappa contrasted verses of Scripture: "It is written, 'As to the almighty, we do not find him exercising plenteous power' (Job 37:23), but by contrast, 'Great is our Lord and of abundant power' (Ps. 147:5), and further, 'Your right hand, Lord, is glorious in power' (Ex. 15:6). But there is no contradiction between the first and second and third statements, for the former speaks of the time of judgment when justice is tempered with mercy, so God does not do what he could and the latter two statements refer to a time of war of God against his enemies."

I.E: GOD'S JUDGMENT AND WRATH, GOD'S MERCY AND FORGIVENESS FOR ISRAEL: "It is written, 'You only have I known among all the families of the earth; therefore I will visit upon you all your iniquities' (Amos 3:2). If one is angry, does he vent it on someone he loves?" He said to them, "I shall tell you a parable. To what is the matter comparable? To the case of a man who lent money to two people, one a friend, the other an enemy. From the friend he collects the money little by little, from the enemy he collects all at once."

I.F: BALAAM, THE PROPHET OF THE GENTILES, AND ISRAEL; GOD'S ANGER WITH THE GENTILES BUT NOT WITH ISRAEL: The prophet of the gentiles was a fool, but he did have the power to curse; Israel was saved by God. Said R. Eleazar, "Said the Holy One, blessed be He, to Israel, 'My people, see how many acts of righteousness I carried out with you, for I did not grow angry with you during all those perilous days, for if I had grown angry with you, there would not have remained from Israel a remnant or a survivor.'"

I.G: THE TIME OF GOD'S ANGER IN RELATIONSHIP TO THE GENTILES AND TO ISRAEL; THE ROLE OF IDOLATRY IN GOD'S WRATH AGAINST THE NATIONS: That time at which God gets angry comes when the kings put on their crowns on their heads and prostrate themselves to the sun. Forthwith the Holy One, blessed be He, grows angry.

I.H: THE SINFUL ANCESTOR OF THE MESSIAH AND GOD'S FORGIVENESS OF HIM AND OF ISRAEL: God's forgiveness of David is the archetype of God's forgiveness of Israel. If an individual has sinned, they say to him, 'Go to the individual such as David, and follow his example, and if the community as a whole has sinned, they say to them, 'Go to the community such as Israel. TORAH-STUDY IS THE ANTIDOTE TO SIN: "What is the meaning of the verse of Scripture, 'Happy are you who sow beside all waters, that send forth the feet of the ox and the ass' (Isa. 32:20)? 'Happy are you, O Israel, when you are devoted to the Torah and to doing deeds of grace, then their inclination to do evil is handed over to them, and they are not handed over into the power of their inclination to do evil."

III.C: THE DIVISIONS OF ISRAEL'S HISTORY; THE HISTORY OF THE WORLD IN ITS PERIODS: here we deal with the history of Israel by its periods, with special attention to Israel's relationships with Rome, on the one side, and the point at which the Messiah will come, on the other, ca. 468: When four hundred years have passed from the destruction of the Temple, if someone says to you, 'Buy this field that is worth a thousand denars for a single denar, don't buy it.

III.E: COLLECTION OF STORIES ABOUT RABBI AND ANTIGONUS: Rabbi maintained cordial relationships with the Emperor, in which Rabbi gave the sage advice, and the emperor took it.

VIII.C: THE TRIAL OF ELIEZER B. HYRCANUS. IN THE MATTER OF MINUT: Reference to the idolators' judges' tribunal, scaffold, and stadium, calls to mind the trial of the sage by reason of the charge of Minut, or, in context, Christianity. It is no different in its workings from the state: "the two daughters who cry out from Gehenna, saying to this world, 'Bring, bring.' And who are they? They are Minut and the government."

VIII.D: IDOLATRY AND LEWDNESS: the antidote is Torah-study.

VIII.E: ROMAN JUSTICE, JEWISH MARTYRDOM: Hanina, my brother, don't you know that from Heaven have they endowed this nation Rome with dominion? For Rome has destroyed his house, burned his Temple, slain his pious ones, and annihilated his very best — and yet endures! And yet I have heard about you that you go into session and devote yourself to the Torah and even call assemblies in public, with a scroll lying before you in your bosom.

VIII.F: THE STADIUM, THE CIRCUS, THE THEATER: He who goes to a stadium or to a camp to see the performances of sorcerers and enchanters or of various kinds of clowns, mimics, buffoons, and the like — lo, this is a seat of the scoffers, as it is said, "Happy is the man who has not walked in the counsel of the wicked...nor sat in the seat of the scoffers. But his delight is in the Torah of the Lord" (Ps. 1:12). Lo, you thereby learn that these things cause a man to neglect the study of the Torah.

VIII.G: HAPPY IS THE MAN WHO HAS NOT WALKED IN THE COUNSEL OF THE WICKED, NOR STOOD IN THE WAY OF SINNERS, NOR SAT IN THE SEAT OF THE SCORNFUL. "'Happy is the man who has not walked' — to theaters and circuses of gentiles; 'nor stood in the way of sinners' — he does not attend contests of wild beasts..."

IX.B: COMPOSITE ON THE PROHIBITION OF STARING IN A LASCIVIOUS OR OTHERWISE IMPROPER MANNER

3. CAN WE STATE WHAT THE COMPILERS OF THIS DOCUMENT PROPOSE TO ACCOMPLISH IN PRODUCING THIS COMPLETE, ORGANIZED PIECE OF WRITING?

Clearly, our sages of blessed memory have made a massive and governing transformation of the tractate. We know that is the fact because the topic, idolatry, that emerges from the Bavli is presented in a quite different way from the manner in which the Mishnah has portrayed it. And the shift takes place in the extraneous composites. In this tractate, strikingly, the real re-presentation of the topic takes place in the opening pages, as though the framers wished to make certain we would address the subject of idolatry in the proper context. Here is a fine case of what one may call "re-contextualization.Z"

Specifically, the large and fundamental composites that accomplish other than the exegesis of the Mishnah, many of them standing at the very head of the tractate, place the subject, idolatry, into an entirely new framework, a historical one. Everything is recast in light of our sages' perception of matters, their definition of the context in which we are to discuss this particular subject. Consequently, I doubt that any other tractate has been so thoroughly or profoundly recast into the image, after the likeness, of sages' Judaic system than this one. These strong judgments require ample demonstration, which I shall now provide.

A full grasp of what our sages have accomplished in this tractate requires that we compare the foregoing outline with the outline of the topic as it is set forth in the Mishnah-tractate. The first point to note is that the Mishnah-tractate restates the Written Torah's theology of idolatry and imparts to it a practical and concrete character. We have therefore to examine the three principal stages in the unfolding of the Torah's teachings on idolatry, the Written one, the oral one, and the authoritative re-presentation of the oral one, for Scripture, the Mishnah, and the Talmud, respectively. First comes the relationship of the Mishnah to Scripture.

## A. SCRIPTURE

The tractate devoted to idolatry illustrates that relationship between Mishnah and Scripture in which Mishnah makes concrete and everyday the general conceptions of Scripture. Specifically, what our tractate does is to supply rules and regulations to carry out the fundamental Scriptural commandments about the destruction of idols and all things having to do with idolatry. It follows that while our tractate deals with facts and relies upon suppositions which Scripture has not supplied, its basic viewpoint and the problem it seeks to solve in fact derive from the Mosaic code. Before proceeding, we had best review those general statements which Scripture does make:

Ex. 23:13
> "Take heed to all that I have said to you; and make no mention of the names of other gods, nor let such be heard out of your mouth."

Ex. 23:24
> "When my angel goes before you, and brings you in to the Amorites, and the Hittites, and the Perizzites, and the Canaanites, the Hivites, and the Jebusites, and I blot them out, you shall not bow down into their gods, nor serve them, nor do according to their work, but you shall utterly overthrow them and break their pillars in pieces."

Ex. 23:32-33
> "You shall make no covenant with them or with their gods. They shall not dwell in your land, lest they make you sin against me; for if you serve their gods, it will surely be a snare to you."

Ex. 34:12-16
> The Lord said to Moses, "Come up to me on the mountain, and wait there; and I will give you the tables of stone, with the law and the commandment, which I have written for their instruction." So Moses rose with his servant Joshua, and Moses went up into the mountain of God. And he said to the elders, "Tarry here for us, until we come to you again; and, behold Aaron and Hur are with you; whoever has a cause, let him go to them."
>
> Then Moses went up on the mountain, and the cloud covered the mountain. The glory of the Lord settled on Mount Sinai, and the cloud covered it six days; and on the seventh day he called to Moses out of the midst of the cloud.

Deut. 7:1-5
> "When the Lord your God brings you into the land which you are entering to take possession of it, and clears away many nations before you, the Hittites, the Girgashites, the Amorites, the Canaanites, the Perizzites, the Hivites, and the Jebusites, seven nations greater and mightier than yourselves, and when the Lord your God gives them over to you, and you defeat them; then you must utterly destroy them; show no mercy to them. You shall not make marriages with them, giving your daughters to their sons or taking their daughters for your sons. For they would turn away your sons from following me, to serve other gods; then the anger of the Lord would be kindled against you, and he would destroy you quickly. But thus shall you deal with them: you shall break down their altars, and dash in pieces their pillars, and hew down their Asherim, and burn their graven images with fire."

Deut. 7:25-26
> "The graven images of their gods you shall burn with fire; you shall not covet the silver or the gold that is on them, or take it for yourselves, lest you be ensnared by it; for it is an abomination to the Lord your God. And you shall not bring an abominable thing into your house, and become accursed like it; you shall utterly detest and abhor it; for it is an accursed thing."

Deut. 12:2-3
> "You shall surely destroy all the places where the nations whom you shall dispossess served their gods, upon the high mountains and upon the hills and under every green tree; you shall tear down their altars, and dash in pieces their pillars, and burn their Asherim with fire; you shall hew down the graven images of their gods, and destroy their name out of that place."

## B. From Scripture to the Mishnah

The tractate which proposes to realize these commandments in ordinary life is in three parts, moving form the general to the specific. It turns, first, to commercial relationships, second, to matters pertaining to idols, and, finally, to the very urgent issue of the prohibition of wine, part of which has served as a libation to an idol. There are a number of unstated principles before us. What a gentile is not likely to use for the worship of an idol is not going to be prohibited. What may serve not as part of idolatry but as an appurtenance thereto is prohibited for Israelite use but permitted for Israelite commerce. What serves for idolatry is prohibited for use and for benefit. Certain further assumptions about gentiles, not pertinent specifically to idolatry, are expressed. Gentiles are assumed routinely to practice bestiality, bloodshed, and fornication, without limit or restriction. This negative image of the gentile finds expression in the laws before us. The outline of the tractate follows.

### I. Commercial relationships with gentiles. 1:1-2:7

#### A. Festivals and fairs. 1:1-4

1:1    For three days before gentile festivals it is forbidden to do business with them.
1:2    Ishmael: Three days afterward also.
1:3    These are the festivals of gentiles.
1:4    A city in which there is an idol – in the area outside of it, it is permitted to do business.

#### B. Objects prohibited even in commerce. 1:5-2:2

1:5    These are things which it is forbidden to sell to gentiles.
1:6    In a place in which they are accustomed to sell small cattle to gentiles, they sell them (the consideration being use of the beasts for sacrifices to idols).
1:7    They do not sell them bears, lions, or anything which is a public danger. They do not help build with them a basilica, scaffold, stadium, or judges' tribunal.
1:8-9    They do not make ornaments for an idol, sell them produce which is not yet harvested, sell them land in the Holy Land.
2:1    They do not leave cattle in gentiles' inns, because they are suspect in regard to bestiality.
2:2    They accept healing for property (e.g., animals) but not for a person.

#### C. Objects prohibited for use but permitted in trade. 2:3-7

2:3    These things belonging to gentiles are prohibited, and the prohibition concerning them extends to deriving any benefit from them at all: wine, vinegar, earthenware which absorbs wine, and hides pierced at the heart.
2:4    Skins of gentiles and their jars, with Israelite wine collected in them – they are prohibited, the prohibition extends to deriving benefit, so Meir. Sages: Not to deriving benefit.

2:5   On what account did they prohibit cheese made by gentiles?
2:6-7 These are things of gentiles which are prohibited, but the prohibition does not extend to deriving benefit from them. Milk, bread, oil, etc.
2:7   These are things which to begin with are permitted for Israelite consumption.

## II. Idols. 3:1-4:7

### A. General Principles. 3:1-7

3:1   All images are prohibited, because they are worshipped once a year, so Meir, Sages: Prohibited is only one which has an emblem of authority.
3:2-3 He who finds the shreds of images – lo, these are permitted.
3:4   Gamaliel: What gentiles treat as a god is prohibited.
3:5   Gentiles who worship hills and valleys – the hills or valleys are permitted, but what is on them is forbidden.
3:6   If one's house-wall served also as the wall of a Temple and it fell down, one may not rebuild it.
3.7   There are three states in regard to idolatry: what is built for idolatrous purposes is forbidden. What is improved is forbidden until the improvement is removed. What merely happens to be used for an idol is permitted once the idol is removed.

### B. The Asherah. 3:7-10

3:7   What is an asherah?
3:8-9 Use of an asherah-tree.
3:10  Desecrating an asherah-tree.

### C. The Merkolis. 4:1-2

4:1-2 Three stones beside a Merkolis (= Hermes) are forbidden, so Ishmael.

### D. Nullifying an idol. 4:3-7

4:3   An idol which had a garden or bathhouse.
4:4-6 An idol belonging to a gentile is prohibited forthwith. One belonging to an Israelite is forbidden only once it has been worshipped. How one nullifies an idol.
4:7   If God does not favor idolatry, why does he not wipe it away?

## III. Libation-wine. 4:8-5:12

4:8   They purchase from gentiles the contents of a winepress which has already been trodden out, for it is not the sort of wine which gentiles use for a libation until it has dripped down into the vat.
4:9   Israelites tread a winepress with a gentile, but they do not gather grapes with him.
4:10  A gentile who is found standing beside a cistern of wine – if he had a lien on the vat, it is prohibited. If he had no lien on it, it is permitted.
4:11  He who prepares the wine belonging to a gentile in a condition of cleanness and leaves it in his domain.
5:1   He who hires an Israelite worker to work with him in the preparation of libation-wine – the Israelite's salary is forbidden.

5:2 Libation-wine which fell on grapes – one may rinse them off, and they are permitted. If the grapes were split and absorbed wine, they are prohibited.

5:3-4 A gentile who with an Israelite was moving jars of wine from place to place – if the wine is assumed to be watched, it is permitted. If the Israelite told the gentile he was going away for any length of time, the wine is prohibited.

5:5 The same point, now in the context of eating at the same table.

5:6 A band of gentile raiders which entered a town peacefully – open jars are forbidden, closed ones permitted.

5:7 Israelite craftsmen, to whom a gentile sent a jar of libation-wine as salary, may ask him to pay in money instead, only if this is before the wine has entered their possession. Afterward it is forbidden.

5:8-9 Libation-wine is forbidden and imparts a prohibition on wine with which it is mixed in any measure at all. If it is wine poured into water, it is forbidden only if it imparts a flavor.

5:10 Libation-wine which fell into a vat – the whole of the vat is forbidden for benefit. Simeon b. Gamaliel: All of it may be sold except the value of the volume of libation-wine which is in it.

5:11-12 A stone winepress which a gentile covered with pitch – one dries it off, and it is clean. One of wood, one of earthenware.

The opening unit unfolds in a fairly orderly way, from a prologue on the special problems of fairs, to the general matter of things Israelites may not even buy or sell, as against things they may not use but may trade, I.B, C. The second unit lays down some general principles about images, then presents special ones on two specific kinds of idols, II.B, C, and at the end asks the logical necessary question about how one nullifies an idol entirely. The third unit is a very long essay about libation-wine and its effect upon Israelite-gentile commerce. I do not see any coherent subdivisions of this sizable discussion, which goes over the same ground time and again.

### C. FROM THE MISHNAH TO THE TALMUD

From its initial insertion of a massive account of gentile idolatry, the Talmud reframes issues. The Mishnah asks not a single question of history or theology. it deals only with 1 commercial relationships with gentiles, so far as these are affected by idolatry, 2 idols, and 3 libation wine. So the topic at hand is treated in a routine and commonplace manner. The Talmud transforms and transcends the topic. It transforms it by reframing the issue of idolatry so that at stake is no longer relationships between Israel and idolatrous nations but rather, those between idolatrous nations and God. It then transcends the topic by introducing the antidote to idolatry, which is the Torah. So Israel differs from idolatrous nations by reason of the Torah, and that imparts a special character to all of Israel's everyday conduct, not only its abstinence from idol-worship. In fact, the Talmud makes this tractate into an occasion for reflection on the problem of Israel and the nations.

Predictably, our sages of blessed memory invoke the one matter that they deem critical to all else: the Torah. Israel differs from the gentiles not for the merely negative reason that it does not worship idols but only an invisible God. It differs from them for the positive reason that the Torah that defines Israel's life was explicitly rejected by the gentiles. Every one of them had its chance at the Torah, and all of them rejected it. When the gentiles try to justify themselves to God by appealing to their forthcoming relationships to Israel, that is dismissed as self-serving. The gentiles could not even observe the seven commandments assigned to the Noahides. From that point, the composite that stands at the head of the tractate and imparts its sense to all that will follow proceeds to the next question, that is, from the downfall of the gentiles by reason of their idolatry and rejection of the Torah to the salvation of Israel through the Torah.

Lest we miss the point, the reason for God's favor is made explicit: God favors Israel because Israel keeps the Torah. God therefore is strict with the gentiles but merciful to Israel. This is forthwith assigned a specific illustration: Balaam, the gentiles' prophet, presents the occasion to underscore God's anger toward the gentiles and his mercy to Israel. Bringing us back to the beginning, we then are shown how God's anger for the gentiles comes to the fore when the gentiles worship idols: when the kings who rule the world worship nature rather than nature's Creator. How God forgives Israel is then shown in respect to David's sin, and Torah-study as the antidote to sin once more is introduced. It is difficult to conclude other than that the framers of the Talmud have added to the presentation of the topic the results of profound thought on idolatry as a force in the history of humanity and of Israel. They thus have re-presented the Mishnah's topic in a far more profound framework of reflection than the Mishnah, with its rather petty interests in details of this and that, would have lead us to anticipate.

The next set of free-standing composites present episodic portraits of the matters introduced at the outset. The first involves world history and its periods, divided, it goes without saying, in relationship to the history of Israel, which stands at the center of world history. Rome defines the counterpart, and Israel's and Rome's relationships, culminating in the coming of the Messiah, are introduced. The next two collections form a point and counterpoint. On the one side, we have the tale of how Rabbi and the Roman Emperor formed a close relationship, with Rabbi the wise counsellor, the ruler behind the throne. So whatever good happens in Rome happens by reason of our sages' wisdom, deriving as it does from the Torah, on which the stories predictably are going to harp. Then comes as explicit a judgment upon Christianity in the framework of world-history as I think we are likely to find in the Talmud. The set of stories involves Eliezer b. Hyrcanus and how he was tried for Minut, which the story leaves no doubt stands for Christianity. Now "Minut" and the Roman government are treated as twin-sources of condemnation. And it is in that very context that the stories of Roman justice and Jewish martyrdom, by reason of Torah-study, are introduced. Not only so, but — should we miss the contrast the compilers wish to draw — the very same setting sets forth the counterpart and opposite: the stadium, circus, and theater, place for scoffers and buffoons, as against the sages' study-center, where people avoid the seat of the scornful but instead study the Torah.

The Talmud's associations with idolatry then compare and contrast these opposites: Israel and Rome; martyrdom and wantonness; Torah and lewdness and other forms of sin; probity and dignity and buffoonery; and on and on. The Mishnah finds no reason to introduce into the consideration of idolatry either the matter of the Torah or the issue of world history. The Talmud cannot deal with the details of conduct with gentiles without asking the profound questions of divine intentionality and human culpability that idolatry in the world provokes. And yet, if we revert to the Mishnah's fabricated debates with the philosophers, we see the issue introduced and explored. What the Mishnah lacks is not a philosophy of monotheism in contrast with polytheism and its idols, but a theology of history and a theodicy of Israel's destiny, a salvific theory. These the Talmud introduces, with enormous effect. And, we note, once these propositions have been inserted, the Talmud allows the systematic exposition of the Mishnah to go forward without theological intrusion of any kind. The point has been made.

Now, we wonder, where have our sages learned to interpret the issue of idolatry in a historical and theological framework, rather than in a merely practical and reasonable one, such as the Mishnah's authorship provides? A glance at the verses of Scripture given earlier answers the question. Idolatry explains the fate of the nations, Israel's covenant through the Torah, Israel's. But the verses of Scripture cited earlier hardly serve as source for the reflections on Israel and Rome, the ages of human history, the power of God to forgive, and, above all, the glory of the Torah as the mediating source of God's love and forgiveness. All of this our sages of blessed memory themselves formulated and contributed. Scripture provided important data, the Mishnah, the occasion, but for the theology of history formed around the center of the Torah, we look to our sages for the occasion and the source. And sages' success in meeting the challenge of the topic at hand explains why no tractate more successfully demonstrates how the Talmud's framers' massive insertions transform the Mishnah's statement into one of considerably enhanced dimensions and depth. None more admirably matched their capacities of deep reflection on the inner structure of Israel's history with the promise and potential of a subject of absolutely primary urgency.

# XXVII

## The Structure of Babylonian Talmud Horayot

### POINTS OF STRUCTURE

1. DOES BABYLONIAN TALMUD-TRACTATE HORAYOT FOLLOW A COHERENT OUTLINE GOVERNED BY A CONSISTENT RULES?

We find ourselves able to outline most of the tractate by referring to the Mishnah-tractate's principal statements. The larger composites that do not define their purpose within Mishnah-commentary take up themes called for by the contents of the Mishnah. I find nothing in the tractate that cannot be situated in relationship to the program of the Mishnah.

2. WHAT ARE THE SALIENT TRAITS OF ITS STRUCTURE?

As we review the outline of the tractate, we note that one way or the other every principal allegation of Mishnah-tractate Horayot is subjected to discussion, though at many points a process of selection has guided the framers of this tractate to one set of problems rather than to some other. The main traits of mind that defined the choices are readily inferred from the pattern of results consistently attained. In general three sets of issues predominate: [1] the wording and sense of sentences in the Mishnah; [2] the foundations in the written part of the Torah, or Scripture, and [3] implications of the Mishnah's rule, which may lead to investigating questions provoked but not addressed by the Mishnah, secondary theoretical issues, and other modes of extension and augmentation. The intellectual quest therefore finds its definition in Mishnah-exegesis.

The greater part of the Talmud's system comes to expression in the questions the framers of the Talmud's Mishnah-exegesis address to the Mishnah; what they wished to say, they stated, for the most part, through the questions they brought to a prior document. Since so much of their commentary appears to adhere closely to the main lines of the Mishnah's own statements, it is easy to conclude that the Talmud's system replicated the Mishnah's. But that is deceiving. Not only do the questions of the Talmud — clarify what the Mishnah's authors must have assumed was already clear, identify authority for the Mishnah that the Mishnah's authors did not find need to expose, say more than the Mishnah's authors found sufficient — subvert the Mishnah. Other than Mishnah-exegetical compositions and composites impart to the topic treated by the Mishnah a very different character altogether. The notion that, in the Talmud, we find pretty much what the Mishnah's statements mean but little else — the "plain meaning" in modern parlance, or the historically-determinate meaning initially intended by the Mishnah's writers — proves not only anachronistic but naive, even bordering on the disingenuous. Nothing in the writings before us compels us to imagine that the Talmud's compositions' and composites' writers conceived any meaning to inhere in the words before them except for the meaning they brought to those words — whatever it was.

3. WHAT IS THE RATIONALITY OF THE STRUCTURE?

The upshot is simply put: to the framers of the Talmud, a reasoned reading of the Mishnah defended the logical coherence of the document they proposed to compile. But then, the rationality proves formal, not substantive. But even at the level at which we work — large-scale aggregates and their formal testimonies — we may identify points of violence to the rationality of order and form, and, violating the structure established for the whole, these plunge us into issues of system.

4. WHERE ARE THE POINTS OF IRRATIONALITY IN THE STRUCTURE?

When large-scale composites take shape around topics or propositions not formed in response to statements in the Mishnah, the structure defined by the character of the document overall bears the weight of anomalies. I find these at XIV.B, C, D, E, F; XV.B, and XIX.H.

## POINTS OF SYSTEM

1. DOES THE BABYLONIAN TALMUD-TRACTATE HORAYOT SERVE ONLY AS A RE-PRESENTATION OF THE MISHNAH-TRACTATE OF THE SAME NAME?

Most of the paragraphs of the Mishnah are taken up in one way or another. I noted only a few that were not fully analyzed, and most of these turn out to be secondary expansions of the Mishnah's own generalizations. But we should not fail to note that even when the Talmud devotes itself to an analysis of the Mishnah's statements, it may well go its own way, beyond the limits of what Mishnah-exegesis requires, though still well within the limits of the Mishnah's topical program. This observation directs our attention to a gray area, between Mishnah-exegesis and the presentation of essentially autonomous discourse, such as is taken up in the next rubric. Here, where Mishnah-commentary spells over into free-ranging exploration of problems precipitated by the Mishnah's concerns but far transcending the Mishnah's own program, we enter the framework of independent thought given the form of subordinated commentary. A survey of the entirety of the document will allow a clearer focus upon this gray area. For the moment it suffices to note that in the Bavli's Mishnah-commentary are embedded the marks of much independent reflection.

*Chapter Twenty-seven. The Structure of Babylonian Talmud Horayot*     *157*

2. How do the topical composites fit into the Talmud-tractate Horayot and what do they contribute that the Mishnah-tractate of the same name would lack without them?

The composite in Unit XIV is provoked by the allusion XIV.A to the transformation of a common person into a ruler or high priest. The change in status is marked — it is, after all, the critical focus of our tractate as a whole! — and it is at that point that the condition of the ruler enters in.

XIV.B: the first point remarks upon the enviable society, the ruler of which acknowledges even inadvertent transgression. That is the mark of good government, accounting also for how rare good government is.

XIV.C: At the head of the next sequence is the contrast between the righteous and the wicked, with the certainty of reward and punishment in the world to come underscoring the justice of God in all things.

XIV.D: The first contrast between the good ruler and the bad one is Lot and Abraham, and the point is, the attitude of the ruler makes all the difference. People may do the same thing, but only if the motive is honorable is that deed consequential; if the motive is dishonorable, then the good that one does turns out to yield nothing. The same actions, e.g., Lot and his daughters, can be both good and bad, and the point of differentiation is the attitude of the ones who do said actions.

XIV.E: The same point, contrasting the good and the evil, emerges in the next example. Tamar and Zimri did the same thing, with very different results.

XIV.F: The key point of differentiation therefore is not the action but the attitude that infuses the action. And the right attitude is one of sincerity; this is stated in an extreme way, better the transgression done sincerely ("for its own sake") than the religious duty done insincerely ("not for its own sake"). But this same point is forthwith modulated: doing commandments and study of Torah in an insincere spirit (e.g., for personal gain) gives way to doing them in a sincere spirit.

XV.B: The composite on anointing kings does not vastly change the face of the unit in which it occurs; the Mishnah has dealt with anointing priests, and what the Talmud here contributes is simply a complement to the Mishnah's topic.

XIX.H: The point of the Mishnah, that the sagacity takes priority over hierarchical status, is not vastly transformed by the Talmud. The composite itself appears somewhat unfocused and diffuse; the unit on correct conduct when a sage enters the room and the secondary expansions and glosses thereof bears no proposition I can identify. The contrast between analytical skills and erudition, while interesting, really does not affect the main point, which is the hierarchical point that the Mishnah has stated in so many words. And yet, a second look suggests otherwise. Now we find ourselves deep within the concerns of the Talmud's sages with analytical capacities, not merely knowledge but the power to use knowledge to form fresh knowledge, and that lies beyond the imagination of the hierarchical program of the Mishnah's framers. By introducing the considerations of hierarchization where they do not pertain — learning vs. analytical abilities indeed! — the framers of the Talmud's concluding units place in a different light the very allegations about the status accorded to the sage; that status, while a given, proves only instrumental. It is what one can do with what one learns that makes the difference, and that is not a matter of status at all. In that same context the stories about Simeon b. Gamaliel and Judah the Patriarch and their invocation of their political status in the setting of the superior learning of the sages (also portrayed in an unflattering light, to be sure), form a wry comment on the sages' hierarchical superiority. That sages take precedence in the Talmud proves less weighty than that, among sages, competition for power takes the diverse form of politics, personalities, and preferment.

3. CAN WE STATE WHAT THE COMPILERS OF THIS DOCUMENT PROPOSE TO ACCOMPLISH IN PRODUCING THIS COMPLETE, ORGANIZED PIECE OF WRITING?

The key to Mishnah-tractate Horayot lies in its location, which is in the Division of Damages, rather than in the Division of Holy Things. Since the bulk of the problems finds resolution in whether a given party is obligated to present an offering, and, if so, which offering said party is required to present, the surface of the tractate is studded with issues typical of the fifth division, but rare in the fourth. But the organizer of the Mishnah, laying out the divisions and assigning to them the tractates and therefore the topical expositions they were to receive, had his reasons. The fourth division concerns itself in significant part with the civil administration of the Jews in the Land of Israel. Tractate Sanhedrin, with its account of the tripartite regime of high priest and Temple, king and army, sages and court, set alongside the great pinnacle of the Mishnah, the thirty chapters of Baba Qamma, Baba Mesia, and Baba Batra, with their movement from the abnormal to the normal, form a sustained account of the life of government and secular relationships within the politics of holy Israel. What we learn in Horayot concerns the errors of the civil authorities, apportioning responsibility for the consequences of error, underscoring the obligation of the individual to face the results of his own actions. The real problem of the tractate as the Mishnah presents matters of government proves remarkably contemporary: what does the private person do when the community's officials err.

Faced with an error on the part of the government, what can a person do? If he knows the government errs, he may not find exculpation in the plea that he has merely carried out orders. If the government errs and the individual does not know better and therefore inadvertently has violated the law, then, but only then,

## Chapter Twenty-seven. The Structure of Babylonian Talmud Horayot

the possibility of atoning is raised. So we require, for the process of remission to get underway, both political error and personal inadvertence. Since the issues derive from the right reading of the Torah, right instruction and right action are contrasted with wrong instruction and inadvertent error. That is why the key language throughout invokes the twin criteria, [1] They are liable only on account of something's being hidden (Lev. 4:13) along with [2] an act [of transgression] which is performed inadvertently. The former, in Jaffee's fine translation, concerns a misinterpretation or exegetical error in the law, and the latter involves the mitigating circumstance of a deed in violation of the law done without intent to break the law.

So the principal point of concern of the tractate is that the law be properly known and intentionally observed; if the law is set forth in error by the responsible authorities, the remissive provisions of the law take over. No wonder the tractate reaches its conclusion where it does, with its meditation on the hierarchical inversion accomplished by the sage. For everything in the end depends upon informed government over responsible, critical citizens (to use an anachronistic term). Israel may have its high priest and king, its castes from times of old. But Israel in the end depends upon the sage, whatever his caste, he who can be relied upon not to commit an error of misinterpretation, and who provides the model for those who would avoid inadvertent sin. That explains the order of the exposition of the topic.

The Mishnah's version of Horayot reaches its conclusion when it emerges from the complexities of responsibility for the public interest, the public's stake in the correct administration of law, and the subtle transformation that takes a private person and endows him with the status of embodiment of the community (what happens when one sins and then becomes high priest or ruler being one formulation of matters). Then, laying down the fundamental conviction that hierarchy in this world contrasts with the hierarchy established by the Torah, the Mishnah-tractate makes its final statement on issues of status and responsibility. That is specifically where we confront the Talmud's two striking additional points. Together they accomplish a surprise no less remarkable than the Mishnah-tractate's meditation on hierarchy.

The first treats as altogether null all questions of hierarchy, beginning to end, making the point that it is not the position one holds that matters, or even the acts that one performs in office, but the attitude that characterizes the office holder. This point is hammered home in the contrasts between Lot and Abraham, the two daughters of Noah, Zimri and Tamar, and in the elaborate essay on the centrality of right attitude. When all is said and done, then, we step aside from the Mishnah-tractate altogether, with its concern for error committed inadvertently, with oversight and misinterpretation of the law, by stating that what matters in the end is not what one does but the attitude that one brings to one's action. True, the Mishnah has invited that very point, by its insistence upon the criterion of inadvertence (inadvertently committing an act that is based upon an erroneous reading of the Torah). But inadvertence forms an invitation to the profound thinking on intentionality that the sizable composite the Talmud introduces places on display. The main point of the Mishnah concerns the consequences of inadvertent action, based upon the wrong decision of public authorities. The main point of the Talmud, where it speaks for itself and not in exegesis of the Mishnah, differentiates not actions at all, whether based upon improper government or uninformed sagacity, but rather attitudes by which one and the same action is carried out.

The second treats as null the datum of the tractate, that the sage forms a single and undifferentiated caste in the hierarchy of ruler and ruled, priests, Levites, Israelites, and on down. The sage stands at the apex by reason of learning; the caste of the sages requires no more sustained a process of differentiation than any other, than the priests (but for the high priest), than the Levites, than the Israelites. The main point of the Mishnah is that the sage disrupts all other established modes of hierarchization. The Talmud's treatment of that point subverts that celebration of the sage within the caste system by introducing those tensions of learning versus intellect, mastery of traditions versus power of logic and reason, that impose upon the status of sagacity those variables that the life of intellect generates. The status of "being a sage" no longer carries weight; various modes of sagacity impart complexity and subtle to the simplicities of the Mishnah's uncomplicated conception of hierarchization. Since no one can ultimately determine whether Sinai takes precedence over the one who can pierce mountains, the indeterminacy of intellect upsets all conceptions of hierarchization, and the sages move on into an altogether new and unpredictable plane of being. It would be difficult to point to a more complete, if subtle, subversion of a Mishnah-tractate than the one accomplished by the framers of the Bavli, who here present us with one of their (very many) intellectual masterpieces.

# XXVIII

## The Structure of Babylonian Talmud Zebahim

POINTS OF STRUCTURE

1. DOES BABYLONIAN TALMUD-TRACTATE ZEBAHIM FOLLOW A COHERENT OUTLINE GOVERNED BY A CONSISTENT RULES?

The remarkable consistencies of organization of the Talmud-tractate leave no doubt that the compilers intended to formulate a point-by-point commentary to the Mishnah, explaining, first, the scriptural foundations of the Mishnah's law, and, second, the meanings of words and phrases of the Mishnah; they further raised generalizing questions of inference and principle, yielding the demonstration of the fundamental coherence of the laws to a few, governing principles. The tractate also encompasses a handful of sizable composites that serve as inventories of data deemed relevant supplements to a given topic.

2. WHAT ARE THE SALIENT TRAITS OF ITS STRUCTURE?

Throughout the pattern is simple and uniform: Mishnah-commentary, secondary inquiry into broader, governing principles; tertiary amplification of detail. To underscore the uniformity of the document, we note that at not a single point is the given protocol reversed or even revised; we never find secondary generalization prior to Mishnah-commentary; we never find tertiary amplification of tangential detail prior to the inquiry into inference and coherence.

3. WHAT IS THE RATIONALITY OF THE STRUCTURE?

What dictates to the compilers that a given composition or composite must be located in one place and not in some other then is the requirements of a systematic Mishnah-commentary. And, we must also take note, the Mishnah's statements form the provocation for the analysis of inference and coherence; only if the Mishnah contains no pertinent materials, but the Tosefta does, or, the Tosefta does not, but some other (to us unavailable) compilation of Tannaite formulations does, will the analysis of inference and implicit principle proceed to some other than a Mishnaic or a Toseftan statement. So, it must follow, the generative hermeneutics of the Talmud, so far as that hermeneutics governs the rational organization of the whole, derives from the initial decision to accord to the Mishnah the privileged position. That is to say, the privileging of the Mishnah explains the coherence of the whole not only in a formal, but in a substantive sense. The character of the Mishnah accounts for the program of the Talmud, not only for its formal organization of its completed units of thought. The very character of the larger part of these completed units of thought derives from the initial problematic of the document as a whole: *if the Mishnah* — then why this? or: *if the Mishnah,* then what else? or: *if the Mishnah,* then what about..." This tractate requires us to recognize that the rationality of the structure of the document, which we have seen vividly portrayed by this outline of the whole, infuses the rationality of the thought-processes that generate the document's own compositions and the composites formed thereof.

4. WHERE ARE THE POINTS OF IRRATIONALITY IN THE STRUCTURE?

The stated definition of the document's principles of order and inner coherence must then define as irrational a large and consequential composite that entirely ignores the program and the proposition of the Mishnah. By that criterion I see these at IV.E; IV.I; V.B; VIII.B; XVIII.E; XXIV.B; XXXIII.C; LVII.D; LX.B.

POINTS OF SYSTEM

1. DOES THE BABYLONIAN TALMUD-TRACTATE ZEBAHIM SERVE ONLY AS A RE-PRESENTATION OF THE MISHNAH-TRACTATE OF THE SAME NAME?

This Talmud-tractate ignores a sizable sector of the Mishnah-tractate, the framers not having found themselves constrained to say something about everything. If we could identify traits common to all the ignored segments of the Mishnah, we might formulate an explanation for this somewhat odd fact. But I see no such shared traits, and, as a matter of fact, some of the ignored passages prove weighty and formidable in both size and intellectual substance. That the Talmud is much more, and also much less, than a Mishnah-commentary is therefore the established fact.

2. HOW DO THE TOPICAL COMPOSITES FIT INTO THE TALMUD-TRACTATE AND WHAT DO THEY CONTRIBUTE THAT THE MISHNAH-TRACTATE OF THE SAME NAME WOULD LACK WITHOUT THEM?

But it is a fact that the following data do not permit us to explain. For we shall now see that most of the composites of size and consequence that find their way into our Talmud form mere topical appendices. While themselves quite unrelated to the Mishnah in topic, all the more so proposition (if any), they provide a mass of information congruent with statements that are required for Mishnah-exegesis or amplification. I present at the right hand column those composites that present mere topical composites, relevant to the context in which they are located in the wholly formal way just now suggested. At the left I catalogue those composites that make substantive and original statements of their own.

# Chapter Five. The Structure of Babylonian Talmud Yoma 163

IV.E: Topical Appendix on the
Rules Governing the Priestly Garments
IV.I: Topical Appendix
on the religious duty of
sanctifying hands and feet by washing
V.B: Topical Appendix:
Other Rules on the Collection and
Disposition of the Blood of Sacrificial Beasts
VIII.B: A Topical Appendix:
Forming the Requisite Volume to Incur a Penalty:
The Joining Together of Distinct Half-Olive's Bulks
Subjected to Improper Intentionality

XVII.E: When Do Cases Form a Series:
Systematic Analysis of the proposition that
that which is derived on the basis
of a verbal analogy does not in turn go
and impart a lesson by means of a verbal analogy;
and other principles of the Construction of a Series

XXIV.B: Comparing the Altars at Shilo,
the First Temple and the Second Temple.
The Character of the Second Temple and its Altar

XXXIII.C: Resolving Matters of Doubt
Concerning the Confusion of Permitted and
Forbidden Objects, with Special Attention
to Idolatry and Priestly Rations

LVII.D. The Disposition of the Priests' Food
in a Time of Bereavement:
With a Topical Appendix on the Priesthood of Moses

LX.B. Topical Composite: Keeping Overnight
Bullocks that Are to be Burned
Some Theoretical Problems

The picture is clear. XVII.E forms a powerful and original, sustained and compelling analysis of when cases form series, and how we are to derive from a sequence of cases a general rule. That problem of that composite is framed in terms of the exegetical requirements of a passage of our tractate's Mishnah-commentary, but the critical and generative issue concerns only the rules of sequential exegesis out of which all else flows. The details prove congruent to our tractate, but the fundamental issue vastly transcends it. The upshot is that our tractate is untouched by this magnificent exercise, even though the basic point, that rules derive from proper, that is, serial exegesis of Scripture, is underscored. But, it is clear, that truism (practically a platitude) does not provoke the inquiry, does not sustain it, and does not find important, fresh validation from it. And

XXXIII.C need not detain us, since it is an inquiry common to any number of tractates and important here only because of the particular subject matter that serves as the example for analysis. These two free-standing composites in no way change our understanding of the topic and propositions of our Mishnah-tractate, nor do they vastly revise our grasp of the Talmud's Mishnah-exegesis either. So far as I can see, neither one materially changes the character of our tractate.

3. Can we state what the compilers of this document propose to accomplish in producing this complete, organized piece of writing?

Some tractates say what the Mishnah says and clarify details, exemplified by Bavli-tractate Megillah. Other tractates so revise the topical program attached to the Mishnah-tractate subject to discussion as to impart to the Mishnah an entirely new meaning, to allow the Mishnah to make a quite fresh and profound statement, exemplified by Bavli-tractate Moed Qatan. But here we have a huge tractate that provides little more than a reprise of what the Mishnah says. And yet, the net effect of studying the tractate, beginning to end, defies the claim that all we have is a Mishnah-commentary.

For after all is said and done, our Mishnah-tractate does emerge vastly revised by the Talmud's re-presentation. The Mishnah-tractate has taken on entirely new layers of depth and meaning; it has been shown more profound and more complex in its substrate of thought, in its interior structure of logic and principle, in its interconnection with the written Torah. While the Mishnah-tractate speaks through the Talmud, so that the points that the Mishnah's authors wished to make register once more, the Talmud has so amplified the Mishnah's voice, so refined its timber, so redirected its lines of thought, as to accomplish more than a process of clarification or even expansion. The privileging of the Mishnah, illustrated in a tractate that, as we have seen in this enormous outline, does little more than say again what the Mishnah said before, but say it in a fuller manner, has yielded a statement that, in the end, the Mishnah's own authors will have found jarring. These results open more questions than they settle.

# The Structure of Babylonian Talmud Menahot

### Points of Structure

1. Does Babylonian Talmud-tractate Menahot follow a coherent outline governed by a consistent rules?

Without the Mishnah-tractate before us, we could not account for the order or arrangement of a single composite; with the Mishnah-tractate in hand, we know why a passage takes precedence over another and how the compilers of the whole did their work.

2. What are the salient traits of its structure?

A simple order governs throughout, with comments on the Mishnah-paragraph's propositions — language, sources, authority — coming first, then analysis of more theoretical problems, commonly precipitated by the substance of the Mishnah's proposition, to follow.

3. What is the Rationality of the structure?

The compelling logic of coherence derives from the initial decision to assign to the Mishnah priority in all things. Once the Mishnah's order, sequence, and treatment of the subject matter of meal offerings have been assigned the privileged position, all else follows. Without that decision, a considerable range of choices about the formation and organization of received materials, whether legal, exegetical of Scripture, or exegetical of legal formulations of rules (deriving from whatever source), can have been pursued. Nothing in the topic treated in this tractate (and in no other tractate in a sustained and systematic manner) dictated the order and sequence by which sub-divisions are identified and spelled out; but once the Mishnah-tractate's treatment of the topic, in its own words, had been privileged, then this tractate had to take the form — order of subjects, problematic of hermeneutics — that it does, and no other form was possible.

4. Where are the points of irrationality in the structure?

It follows that the sizable composites that coalesce around some other point of structure and order than the requirement of Mishnah-exegesis diverge from the document's rationality. These are given below.

### Points of System

1. Does the Babylonian Talmud-tractate Menahot serve only as a re-presentation of the Mishnah-tractate of the same name?

Because some Mishnah-paragraphs, e.g., IV.A, L.B, with their talmud for some other purpose than that dictated by the Mishnah-passage, are ignored in the Talmud's exegesis, we must give a partially negative answer, and, further, because important composites are framed for a purpose other than that of Mishnah-exegesis, we must complement that negative answer with another. So while in structure, order, and generative hermeneutics, the Bavli-tractate is a Mishnah-commentary and nearly the whole of the document' definitive characteristics find their source and explanation in that fact, still, even within the premise of a privileged Mishnah, still the tractate cannot be classified as "merely" a commentary to the Mishnah. But nothing in the a-symmetric composites listed in the next unit tells us what else, besides a commentary, the framers may have have in mind.

2. How do the topical composites fit into the Talmud-tractate Menahot and what do they contribute that the Mishnah-tractate of the same name would lack without them?

At the right hand margin I list the items that form mere compilations of information on a topic; these contribute nothing to the design and structure of the tractate. At the left are the items that bear an autonomous and independent, consequential message.

I.B: Testing the Proposition: a wrongful intention that is not obviously wrong is treated by the All-Merciful as an intention that can invalidate an offering, but one that is obviously wrong is treated by the All-Merciful as incapable of invalidating the offering

I:E: The Status of the meal offering of the first sheaf of barley grain, the handful of which one took with the intention of making the offering for some purpose other than that for which it was originally designated

I:F: Other Offerings that are improper but may nonetheless be acceptable: The Status of the Terefah-Beast

II:C: Rules on taking the handful: 1. from a utensil that is lying on the ground; 2 Mixing the Meal with Oil

XIII:C: Any passage in which the words 'Torah' and 'statute' occur in regard to any rite, the meaning is only to signify that that matter is indispensable to the proper performance of the rite

XXI:A: Topical Appendix on the Lampstand and Candlestick

## Chapter Twenty-nine. The Structure of Babylonian Talmud Menahot

XXI:D: Topical Appendix: The Shapes of Letters of the Torah; How the Letters Are Written for Use in the Torah
XXI:F: Topical Appendix: The Tefillin. Rules and Regulations in General
XXII:B: Topical Appendix on the Show-Fringes
XXXVIII:C: How to determine the meanings of unfamiliar words: testimony of native speakers
XLIII:B: Composite of Other Theoretical Questions on the Status of Grain, formed mainly around the name of Rami bar Hama, and Subordinate Questions Secondary to His
LXXX:D: Topical Appendix on the Size of the Cubit Measured in Handbreadths
LXXX:G: A Disciple of a Sage as a Sanctified Utensil
XCVII:C: In that day shall there be an altar to the Lord in the midst of the land of Egypt and a pillar at the border thereof to the Lord

3. CAN WE STATE WHAT THE COMPILERS OF THIS DOCUMENT PROPOSE TO ACCOMPLISH IN PRODUCING THIS COMPLETE, ORGANIZED PIECE OF WRITING?

The number and proportions of the items that contribute more than relevant but inchoate information prove negligible, when compared to the dimensions of the tractate overall; all the more so when compared to the sizable number and substantial dimensions of the informational-composites catalogued at the right. True, the point of emphasis, the governing status of intentionality, captures our attention. But how will the framer of the Mishnah-tractate itself have responded, if not with recognition and satisfaction? For our tractate and its companion, Zebahim, form massive exercises on the theme of intentionality and the cult. The other consequential composites review routine themes for the Talmud, the comparison of the disciple of a sage to a sanctified utensil, a poetic idea that the tractate surely sustains with ease, and the generalized messianic sentiments tacked on at the end. The upshot is simple. The compilers of the document determined to privilege the Mishnah, and everything they did — everything! — comes in consequence of that decision. Negatively stated, they did nothing that vastly changed the character of the Mishnah or imparted to it propositions or even implications that it did not possess prior to the Talmud-compilers' labors. Yet that obvious result of this sustained labor equally obviously contradicts the simple fact that, when we study the Mishnah in the setting provided for it by the Talmud, the Mishnah emerges vastly re-presented indeed. So everything comes down to one thing, and that is, the intellectual context in which the privileging of the Mishnah takes place, the premises that governed, and, above all, the implicit critique that the work conveyed.

# XXX

## The Structure of Babylonian Talmud Hullin

### POINTS OF STRUCTURE

1. DOES BABYLONIAN TALMUD-TRACTATE HULLIN FOLLOW A COHERENT OUTLINE GOVERNED BY A CONSISTENT RULES?

The fact that we can outline nearly the whole of the document simply by following the sequence of Mishnah-paragraphs — with one very important composite formed around a Mishnah-paragraph of another tractate altogether — proves that the Talmud tractate is formulated as a commentary to the Mishnah. The rules of structure and the sequence of problems are consistent and coherent with those of other tractates.

2. WHAT ARE THE SALIENT TRAITS OF ITS STRUCTURE?

The Mishnah's program governs throughout; where the Talmud strikes out on its own, it is nearly everywhere a secondary exploration of a question provoked by Mishnah-commentary, e.g., once we have the source in Scripture of a rule of the Mishnah, we may raise questions about other ways of reading Scripture in the same setting.

3. WHAT IS THE RATIONALITY OF THE STRUCTURE?

What makes sense to the framers is the systematic exegesis of the Mishnah's statements and the secondary expansion of those exegeses. The source of exegesis is a corpus of statements relevant to the statements of the Mishnah but not located in the Mishnah; another source of exegesis is the systematic interrelationship of the Mishnah's with Scripture's statements. A third source of exegesis — and a poor third at that — is the principles of the Mishnah in comparison with the application, in other areas of law, of those same principles; or principles of law pertinent to the Mishnah-tractate's subject-matter at two or more passages.

4. WHERE ARE THE POINTS OF IRRATIONALITY IN THE STRUCTURE?

These are the large-scale composites that define their focus elsewhere than in the exegesis of the Mishnah: I.B [general rules on the correct act of slaughter]; XIX.B [The Scriptural Foundations for Various Rules Governing the Slaughter of

Beasts and Fowl]; XXIV.B [Unconsecrated Food Prepared In Accord with the Regulations Governing Holy Things]; XXV.B [God, Creator of the Wild Beasts]; XXXV.D [The Rules Governing Clean and Unclean Eggs]; XXXV.H [Prohibited Creeping Things]; LVI.B [Abraham answered, Behold, I have taken upon myself to speak to the Lord, I who am but dust and ashes]; LVII.C [Exegesis of the Story of Jacob's Wrestling with the Angel]; LVIII.B [On Authentic Generosity, and the Sending of Gifts]; LVIII.C [Sending the Gift of a Hip to an Israelite]; LXI.C [The Volume of Prohibited Meat On Account of Which One Incurs Liability; The Combination of Small Quantities of a Given Prohibited Substance to Comprise the Prohibited Volume]; LXIII.B [Composite on Washing One's Hands at Dinner with Water]; LXXI.B [The Sources of the Law Governing the Relationship of Attachments, e.g., Handles, to That to Which They are Attached, thus, Hide to Carcass]; LXXIII.A/I.2-4, A Talmud for M. Kel. 28:8].

### POINTS OF SYSTEM

1. DOES THE BABYLONIAN TALMUD-TRACTATE HULLIN SERVE ONLY AS A RE-PRESENTATION OF THE MISHNAH-TRACTATE OF THE SAME NAME?

Most of the statements of the Mishnah — surely in excess of 90% — are subjected to systematic exegetical work; words and phrases, but no large-scale and principal statement, in the Mishnah are everywhere dealt with and seldom ignored. And, as we shall now see, little is added to the work of exegesis of the Mishnah-tractate essentially in its own terms. Therefore it follows that the Talmud-tractate serves only as a re-presentation of the Mishnah-tractate of the same name.

2. HOW DO THE TOPICAL COMPOSITES FIT INTO THE TALMUD-TRACTATE AND WHAT DO THEY CONTRIBUTE THAT THE MISHNAH-TRACTATE OF THE SAME NAME WOULD LACK WITHOUT THEM?

We distinguish once more between those composites that carry forward the proposition or the topic of the Mishnah-exegetical composites where they find their location and those that introduce an essentially fresh topic and so, in one way or another, impose upon the Mishnah a distinct and fresh topical or even propositional program. I indent the former and not the latter.

> I.B [general rules on the correct act of slaughter]
> XIX.B [The Scriptural Foundations for Various Rules Governing
> the Slaughter of Beasts and Fowl]
> XXIV.B [Unconsecrated Food Prepared In Accord with the
> Regulations Governing Holy Things]
> XXV.B [God, Creator of the Wild Beasts]
> XXXV.D [The Rules Governing Clean and Unclean Eggs]
> XXXV.H [Prohibited Creeping Things]

## Chapter Thirty. The Structure of Babylonian Talmud Hullin

LVI.B [Abraham answered, Behold, I have taken upon myself to speak to the Lord, I who am but dust and ashes]
LVII.C [Exegesis of the Story of Jacob's Wrestling with the Angel]
    LVIII.B [On Authentic Generosity, and the Sending of Gifts]
    LVIII.C [Sending the Gift of a Hip to an Israelite] In the context of the Mishnah, these two items fit right in.
    LXI.C [The Volume of Prohibited Meat On Account of Which One Incurs Liability; The Combination of Small Quantities of a Given Prohibited Substance to Comprise the Prohibited Volume]
    LXIII.B [Composite on Washing One's Hands at Dinner with Water] This is secondary to the topic of the Mishnah, which is spelled out here.
    LXXI.B [The Sources of the Law Governing the Relationship of Attachments, e.g., Handles, to That to Which They are Attached, thus, Hide to Carcass]
LXXIII.A/I.2-4, A Talmud for M. Kel. 28:8].

3. CAN WE STATE WHAT THE COMPILERS OF THIS DOCUMENT PROPOSE TO ACCOMPLISH IN PRODUCING THIS COMPLETE, ORGANIZED PIECE OF WRITING?

Only two items fall outside of the framework of the Mishnah's program of principles and rules. Both amplify the origin, among the patriarchs, of some of the rules before us, thus underscoring the claim that even before Sinai Israel kept certain commandments concerning food. That that issue occurs en passant and not by reason of a polemic against a contrary claim is suggest by the paucity of such composites. Not only so, but the point at which the specified items occur remains well within the framework of the Mishnah's own topical program. So the composites are formed around their own topical interest, but inserted here essentially in conformity to what is natural to the Mishnah's. The upshot is simply stated: the framers of the Bavli-tractate have vastly expanded the rules set forth in the Mishnah, but they have done so mainly by collecting and arranging other rules on the same topics, rather than by a systematic reconsideration of principles and problems of a theoretical character. They have clarified, extended, amplified, and otherwise improved upon the Mishnah, all the while recapitulating the Mishnah's own statement. Here is a tractate that, sum and substance, re-presents the Mishnah in the Mishnah's own terms and for the Mishnah's own purposes.

# XXXI

## The Structure of Babylonian Talmud Bekhorot

### POINTS OF STRUCTURE

1. DOES BABYLONIAN TALMUD-TRACTATE BEKHOROT FOLLOW A COHERENT OUTLINE GOVERNED BY A CONSISTENT RULES?

The foregoing outline shows that a few rules instruct the framer of a composite on how to do his work. He undertakes to compose a commentary to the Mishnah. In hand are diverse materials, some of which serve that purpose, some of which do not. He selects those that do and gives them pride of place; then he choose secondary materials, relevant in topic if not in problematic to the Mishnah's statements. And beyond that point, as we have seen, he makes use of very little more.

2. WHAT ARE THE SALIENT TRAITS OF ITS STRUCTURE?

At any Mishnah-passage that is chosen for discussion — and nearly all of them are — a simple logic dictates what comes first, and what questions are postponed to await At the risk of specifying what is already obvious from the results of analysis of prior tractates, we note the simple order: explain the external traits of the Mishnah-paragraph ("why specify all these cases), then explain its language, sources, and the authority behind the anonymous and authoritative statement of the law. The second layer of exegesis will then encompass theoretical questions, analysis of principles present in the rule and comparison of other rules that express those same principles, and the like. Thus, for a fine example, see III.B of the foregoing outline: II:1: what need to specify? II:2: what is the scriptural source? II:3: Tannaite complement. We may say that where all three types of compositions occur, the order will be fixed as above.

3. WHAT IS THE RATIONALITY OF THE STRUCTURE?

On that basis, we may say that to the framers of the Bavli, rationality finds its definition in the Mishnah, and to master the rational rules of thought, one investigates the Mishnah's rules of inquiry, evidence, logical proof, and argument, or more truly, the principles of thought and analysis that come to concrete expression in those manifest exercises of enduring rules.

### 4. Where are the points of irrationality in the structure?

The first point of irrationality is the familiar one: large-scale composites that compare to those serving as Mishnah-commentary in rhetoric and formal traits, but that in fact do not comment on the Mishnah at all. The second point of irrationality (in the sense used here) will be identified presently. Examples of the former are at IV.B, IX.A, XVI.B, C; XXVIII.E, XXXI.B, XLV.B, and LX.B.

## Points of System

### 1. Does the Babylonian tractate Bekhorot serve only as a re-presentation of the Mishnah-tractate of the same name?

Because the Talmud does not treat every Mishnah-passage, and because it contains large composites that do not serve as Mishnah-commentary, the answer is negative. But that fact by itself bears no consequences obvious to me. For it does not tell us what our compilers wished to give us, if it was not simply a Mishnah-commentary; nor does it indicate the dimensions of the real problem, which is not solely to define what the Talmud is, but also to find, within the Talmud itself, guidelines that will indicate to us what the framers of the Talmud chose not to give us: the Talmud that might have been.

### 2. How do the topical composites fit into the Talmud and what do they contribute that the Mishnah-tractate of the same name would lack without them?

While in other tractates the topical (and other) composites that fall outside of the framework of Mishnah-commentary or the amplification thereof vastly change the character of the Mishnah's topic, by requiring us to contemplate that topic in a setting or context quite different from the one that the framers of the Mishnah-tractate defined, that is not the case in Bekhorot. I see nothing in the following composites to change the way in which the subject before us is presented by the Mishnah, no stunning juxtapositions, no insertion of wildly-inappropriate subjects to make us see our subject in some other context or light than we do in the Mishnah's presentation of it.

IV.B: This item is invited by the Mishnah-composition that it follows; once we deal with unclean and clean fish, we ask also about the classification of other fauna.

IX.A: This is Mishnah-criticism of another order, not a free-standing composition; the composition is incomprehensible outside of the framework of the Mishnah's pertinent chapters.

XVI.B: Here we have a topical appendix that takes the subject of the Mishnah — discharges by pregnant beasts or women.

XVI.C: Here is an appendix on a principle, attached because the statement of the Mishnah's authority figures. Both items are little more than random add-ons.

## Chapter Thirty-one. The Structure of Babylonian Talmud Bekhorot

XXVIII.E: This composite is nothing more than a familiar exercise in Mishnah-commentary, given a more-ambitious-than-usual form.

XXXI.B: Here we have further disputes by the same authorities on the same topic.

XLV.B: This amplifies the topic at hand by investigating the theory behind a fact.

LX.B: The topical composite on urinating presents no surprises; it is inserted because of a detail in the foregoing.

None of these composites changes the reading of the Mishnah-passage that is under discussion in context. The topical indices do not impart to their context a vastly different quality from what it would have had in their absence.

3. CAN WE STATE WHAT THE COMPILERS OF THIS DOCUMENT PROPOSE TO ACCOMPLISH IN PRODUCING THIS COMPLETE, ORGANIZED PIECE OF WRITING?

On the strength of our clear picture of what the writers of the Talmud wished to accomplish, we now are able to begin to frame a theory on what the compilers of this Talmud chose not to do. That theory emerges from not an abstract or theoretical picture of other talmuds besides the one we have but from the evidence in hand, and only from that evidence.[1] The data to which I refer are those many compositions and even sizable composites that do not take shape around a problem of Mishnah-commentary or other forms of Mishnah (or Tosefta) exegesis. In this tractate, as in all others, we confront both large-scale exercises in Mishnah-commentary and also large-scale writings that in no way take shape around the amplification of things that the Mishnah says or implies. These other writings take up law in an abstract context, not the Mishnah in all is concrete and specific presence.

To show what I mean, I point to the Bavli's reading of Mishnah-tractate Bekhorot I:21I-K. The opening pericope of that composite asks the familiar question, what is the operative consideration in our ruling, and what further inferences are we to draw therefrom? Secondary and tertiary amplification do not change the picture. The framer has selected from a corpus of materials framed in response to explicit statements of the Mishnah. But then IV.B, as noted just now, goes on to a quite different program. What differentiates that composite of seven compositions (at least, as I analyze the group) and holds it together is a common theme, the classification of the sexual traits of fauna. That theme is not relevant to the Mishnah-paragraph before us. To the contrary, the theme that has led the compiler of these items to group them derives from a quite different program of thought and inquiry from the Mishnah's. It is clear, then, that the framers of the Talmud had access to a corpus of writings that divides sharply into two quite different parts: writings that link to the Mishnah, yielding composites that begin with the Mishnah and augment or amplify its materials; and writings that do not. These other writings form a sizable segment of the Talmud, and that proves that the framers

---

[1] Compare my *The Bavli That Might Have Been: The Tosefta's Theory of Mishnah-Commentary Compared with that of the Babylonian Talmud.* Atlanta, 1990: Scholars Press for South Florida Studies in the History of Judaism.

of the document had access to writings in no way composed or compiled into sets with Mishnah-commentary in mind.

In producing the Talmud, the compilers not only gave to the Mishnah the privilege of defining nearly the entire structure of category-formation. They also subordinated whatever they selected out of the corpus of other-than-Mishnah-centered composites, and they placed in a subsidiary position, within the framework of their commentary to the Mishnah, composites of considerable weight and (proportionate to the whole) enormous dimensions. What the compilers of the Bavli chose not to accomplish was the formation of a vast collection of received writings — writings of considerable intellectual ambition! — into some framework appropriate to them; they reduced them to ancillary and subordinated appendices to a framework decidedly inappropriate to them.

This tractate, among many, not only tells us with clarity and force what the framers wished to accomplish, but also what they did not choose to do at all. And, furthermore, the tractate allows us a more than brief glimpse into the vast array of ready-made writings that the framers of the Bavli used only at the cost of producing a document that was less coherent than their best efforts would have led us to expect. Another glance at unit X, the Bavli's reading of Mishnah-tractate Bekhorot 2:2-3, shows us what might have been, which is, a remarkably cogent and coherent exposition of the Mishnah, with some secondary footnotes, tacked on where needed. But, as we recognize, that magnificent and disciplined presentation hardly exhausts the Bavli's repertoire. Since at some points, what I classify as an appendix or a protracted footnote in volume exceeds what I classify as the document's main statement, the problem becomes clear It is to examine the pre-history of the Bavli.

When this academic commentary has laid out the materials in the proper manner, I therefore shall conduct an initial probe into the Talmud's other-than-redactional compositions and composites, that is, into that vast heritage of writing upon which the Bavli's framers drew, but which, in the nature of things, we cannot imagine their having created. Once we know the full extent, within the Bavli, of this quite other kind of writing, we shall identify its traits, both formal and intellectual, and these will open the way toward the examination of the sources of the Bavli's intellectual program and results — that is, the sources besides the Mishnah, the ones generated by a problematic of thought or inquiry or speculation other than that set forth within the Mishnah's inner dynamics.

# XXXII

## The Structure of Babylonian Talmud Arakhin

### Points of Structure

The outline of the tractate reveals no problems and few mysteries. We are able to account for the inclusion, in its particular location, of every composite of which the Talmud-tractate is comprised, and we also can say very simply that not a single item can sensibly have been located elsewhere than its present position in the tractate. Move a composite to some other position and it loses all intelligibility. That is because most of the composites serve as amplifications, within a limited program of exegesis, of Mishnah-paragraphs. To the compositions that are taken over within composites, the same conclusion pertains in a simple sense. While most of the tractate's compositions may stand wholly on their own, in the setting of the tractate they form an integral part of a cogent and sustained exposition of the Mishnah-tractate's propositions or, at the very least, its themes.

1. Does Babylonian Talmud-tractate Arakhin follow a coherent outline governed by a consistent rules?

The outline before us shows that the structure of the Talmud-tractate is supplied by the Mishnah-tractate. The Talmud forms a systematic commentary to the Mishnah.

2. What are the salient traits of its structure?

The routine inquiry follows this program: [1] examination of the wording of a Mishnah-sentence or paragraph and systematic exposition of its meaning, sense, and implications; [2] determination of the foundation, if any, in Scripture of a statement in the Mishnah; [3] comparison and contrast of laws given by the Mishnah, and their principles, with other laws given by the Mishnah or with prevailing principles of law. The outline further shows that secondary and tertiary materials are located at the end of primary components of the large-scale structures.

3. What is the Rationality of the structure?

Nearly all principal entries — marked by capital letters following the topic-sentences deriving from the Mishnah — address issues of the Mishnah. Hence the structure of the present document is defined by the prior document. Any representation of the Talmud of Babylonia in its defining structure as other than a systematic commentary to the Mishnah is false.

4. WHERE ARE THE POINTS OF IRRATIONALITY IN THE STRUCTURE?

Within the definition just now given, the points of irrationality are these: IV.C; XVII.C, D, E; XXVII.B.

POINTS OF SYSTEM

1. DOES THE BABYLONIAN TALMUD-TRACTATE ARAKHIN SERVE ONLY AS A RE-PRESENTATION OF THE MISHNAH-TRACTATE OF THE SAME NAME?

The Talmud-compilers do not address every word of every sentence of every paragraph of the Mishnah. They deal with the larger part, but not the whole, of the received tractate. The real question is, is that judgment formal or substantive? That is, do the compilers deal with all of the principal allegations of the received tractate, even though they do not take up every word or sentence? Or are there large-scale compositions and even composites of the Mishnah-tractate that elicit not a comment from the Talmud-writers? An examination of the underlined, therefore omitted, sentences of the Mishnah-tractate yields a clear and one-sided answer. While the Talmud-compilers may bypass sentences and even paragraphs, they do address every allegation made in the Mishnah concerning the topic treated by the Mishnah. The Babylonian Talmud does serve as a re-presentation of the Mishnah-tractate. Underlined Mishnah-passages include examples of a generalization, some secondary or peripheral rules, qualifications of generalizations, and the like. A rough rule of thumb is that a sentence beginning with the Hebrew equivalent of a "but" or "if" may be ignored, but the sentence to which that qualifying statement is attached will be treated. The encompassing character of the discussion is shown at Unit XXI, where I claim that the complete exposition is covered by the Talmud; that is so even though we do not have a word-for-word commentary. The treatment forms its perspective out of the entirety of the Mishnah-sentences in hand.

2. HOW DO THE TOPICAL COMPOSITES FIT INTO THE TALMUD-TRACTATE ARAKHIN AND WHAT DO THEY CONTRIBUTE THAT THE MISHNAH-TRACTATE OF THE SAME NAME WOULD LACK WITHOUT THEM?

The system of the Talmud, as distinct from its structure, emerges in the inclusion of subjects not dealt with by the Mishnah. Here the Talmud speaks for its framers — those who made connections not made in the Mishnah, yielding, therefore and consequently, conclusions not set forth by the Mishnah. We have already identified the important candidates for identification with the Talmud's system. They are as follows:

## Chapter Thirty-two. The Structure of Babylonian Talmud Arakhin 179

IV.C: This entry simply adds a rule within the thematic structure defined by the Mishnah, that is, laws governing those who are to be put to death. It forms no important statement outside of the framework of the Mishnah's topical program or principles.

XVII.C: The Mishnah's own topic of tale-bearing, gossip, and other forms of sinning through speech, is expanded here and at the next two items. First comes the power of gossip and slander, with an explanation of why slander is a sin and how Heaven penalizes the sinner. The character of slander as a social, not a personal, infraction is underscored.

XVII.D: There is a difference between slander and legitimate criticism. Rebuke is worthy, slander is despicable. There is a difference between sincere reproof, moreover, and hypocritical restraint.

XVII.E: This item is tacked on. The general theme, how Heaven penalizes sin, accounts for the introduction of XVII.E.1, that is, trivial sufferings that exact a penalty for small-scale sins. II.22-23 then are equally occasional. Without this item, the systematic exposition of XVII.C and D would have yielded precisely the same point. My guess is that something in II.20 explains the addition of II.21, and I suspect that the reference-point of II.22 and 23 is the Mishnah, not the foregoing entries; that is to say, XVII.B has Israel punished by reason of the actions of the spies and leaders in the wilderness, e.g., Miriam and Aaron (through speaking ill of the land and through gossip against Moses, respectively). If that is so, then the final items are meant to draw to a close by a final reference to the theme of the Mishnah this massive composite on the principle, but not the thematic materials, of the Mishnah.

XXVII.B: This is simple a further discussion of the established topic, selling estates.

3. CAN WE STATE WHAT THE COMPILERS OF THIS DOCUMENT PROPOSE TO ACCOMPLISH IN PRODUCING THIS COMPLETE, ORGANIZED PIECE OF WRITING?

The one genuinely important systemic composite introduces a theme on which the Talmud-compilers find much to say: gossip and slander, as well as other forms of anti-social behavior that they deem common among Israelites. Had the Talmud's writers not introduced that topic, the presentation of the Mishnah-tractate in its own terms would have suffered in no way that I can perceive. But by forcing consideration of sins of speech, they have made a striking and interesting comment on the Mishnah-tractate's theme, which is, acts of religious consequence that are carried out through speech. For a statement of pledge of one's own, or another party's, Valuation to the purposes of the Temple and the service of God therein does not demand that we also discuss the very opposite of the use of speech for God's purpose. But once we do consider how an act of speech may destroy, as much as build, the sacred community, our appreciation for the matter of Valuations deepens, and its moral meaning comes to the surface. What our sages of blessed memory in the Talmud add to the Mishnah-tractate, therefore, is the profound statement indeed: through an act of speech, one may sanctify, but through an act of speech one may also destroy, the holy community of Israel. The one — the act of sanctification through an act of speech — devotes to God through the Temple the results of good will. The other — the act of slander through an act of speech — diminishes God's people through the expression of ill will.

What the Talmud's compilers do therefore is make a connection of opposites: sanctification through speech as against sin through speech. In this context we call to mind other connections formed through the juxtaposition of opposites that our sages of blessed memory bring about in Talmud-making. In connection with tractate Moed Qatan, we wondered what the Talmud's principal topical innovation had to do with the Mishnah-tractate's interest: the rules of burial and mourning with the intermediate days of the festival? Precisely what has death to do with the intermediate days of the festival? The principal mode of thought of the Mishnah is that of comparison and contrast. Something is like something else, therefore follows its rule; or unlike, therefore follows the opposite of the rule governing the something else. So as a matter of hypothesis, let us assume that the framers of Talmud-tractate Moed Qatan found self-evidently valid the modes of thought that they learned from the Mishnah and so made connections between things that were alike, on the one side, or things that were opposite, on the other. How do death and mourning compare to the intermediate days of the festival? The point of opposition — the contrastive part of the equation — then proves blatant. Death is the opposite of the celebration of the festival. The one brings mourning, the other, joy. But death and the festival also form moments of a single continuum, one of uncleanness yielding to its polar opposite, sanctification, sanctification yielding to uncleanness. Death, we must not forget, also serves as a principal source of uncleanness, the festival, the occasion for sanctification beginning with the removal of cultic uncleanness and the entry into a state of cultic cleanness. These opposites also take their place on a single continuum of being.

So in establishing the connection, through treating the categories as equivalent and counterpart to one another, between death and the festival's intermediate days, sages make the connection between the one and the other — death and the festival's intermediate days — so as to yield a conclusion concerning the everyday and the here and now. These are neither permanently sanctified nor definitively unclean. Now we find the same mode of thought — finding the opposite of the topic at hand, drawing conclusions from the comparison and contrast of the connection that is made between opposites. And, we also observe, we may point to a systemic conclusion that coheres. Just as death and the Festival form opposites yet stand on the single continuum of life, so speech that consecrates and speech that demolishes stand on the single plane of social being: the community of Israel is sanctified through holy speech or it is diminished through evil speech (the exact equivalent in English to the Hebrew words translated as gossip or slander, *lashon*

## Chapter Thirty-two. The Structure of Babylonian Talmud Arakhin

*hara* ). Tractate Arakhin sets forth how through an act of speech one carries out a deed of sanctification; the Talmud's important and fresh composites explain how through an act of speech one does a deed that is the opposite of sanctification, which is, a deed that is unclean in that it contaminates the holy community.

Temple and holy Israel: these form the comparable components; an act of speech then is the variable, yielding the sanctification of goods and persons to the Temple, or the act of contamination of persons in the holy community. The framers of the Talmud contribute the making of connections in the Mishnah's manner but for a purpose of their own devising, and they therefore set forth an important element of a large-scale system, one that, it becomes clear, the Talmud is meant — in a remarkably subtle manner to be sure — to set forth. As the Bavli's tractates pass in review, the outlines of the Bavli's compilers' system begin to emerge. The method continues the familiar mode of thought that through comparison and contrast identifies like and unlike, something and its opposite. The message emerges from the connection that is made between opposites, the conclusion that is to be drawn from the making of that connection.

# XXXIII

## The Structure of Babylonian Talmud Temurah

### POINTS OF STRUCTURE

1. DOES BABYLONIAN TALMUD-TRACTATE TEMURAH FOLLOW A COHERENT OUTLINE GOVERNED BY A CONSISTENT RULES?

The tractate serves as a commentary to the Mishnah-tractate of the same name. No important initiatives of program or form differentiate the Bavli- from the Mishnah-tractate.

2. WHAT ARE THE SALIENT TRAITS OF ITS STRUCTURE?

We have noted a tendency to treat in an abstract way, by appeal to general principles or intersecting considerations, the concrete rulings of the Mishnah-tractate. But it would be wrong to propose that the Bavli's composition-authors and composite-framers have taken as their task the recasting of the Mishnah's statements into more abstract and general terms, since that is true only part of the time, and not in a predictable pattern, so far as I can discern.

3. WHAT IS THE RATIONALITY OF THE STRUCTURE?

It follows that the reasoned and orderly principle of structure finds its definition in the tractate's devotion to Mishnah-commentary.

4. WHERE ARE THE POINTS OF IRRATIONALITY IN THE STRUCTURE?

The following important composites break up the systematic commentary to the Mishnah by introducing large-scale consideration of propositions not set forth in the Mishnah's own text: II.B; IX.B; IX.C; IX.D; XVIII.B; XIX.B; XXII.B. In the outline of the structure of the tractate, they disrupt the presentation of a systematic commentary upon the topics introduced by the Mishnah. In that sense they represent points of irrationality.

### POINTS OF SYSTEM

1. DOES THE BABYLONIAN TALMUD-TRACTATE TEMURAH SERVE ONLY AS A RE-PRESENTATION OF THE MISHNAH-TRACTATE OF THE SAME NAME?

Sizable passages of the Mishnah receive no Talmudic amplification or comment. I cannot explain why the Talmud should ignore such striking passages at II.A, VII.A, or X.A. We cannot speculate on the character of the materials upon which the Talmud's compilers drew, nor can we form a rough estimate of the contribution of the compilers, as distinct from that of the authors of already-available compositions and framers of completed composites. We therefore cannot form a theory of how the compilers of the Talmud determined which passages of the Mishnah do not require comment of any kind. Such a theory moreover would have to account for the difference between highly articulated and systematic, intellectually weighty compositions, on the one side, and rather routine comments, on the other. In the latter category we identify, e.g., the scriptural source of a rule, the identification of the authority behind an unattributed, therefore authoritative rule, the clarification of the wording of a passage, and the like. In the former are the magnificent composites represented by I.C and its many counterparts throughout the Talmud.[1]

2. How do the topical composites fit into the Talmud-tractate Temurah and what do they contribute that the Mishnah-tractate of the same name would lack without them?

---

[1] Another generation will address precisely the question outlined here: the difference between the Talmud's large-scale, intellectually ambitious composites and its rather routine and everyday ones. In our tractate the classification of Mishnah-commentary within one or the other category proves uncomplicated. What I find puzzling is a somewhat different phenomenon. Where a Mishnah-passage is expounded in a simple manner, e.g., source of a rule in Scripture, meaning of words and phrases, simple logical procedures, intersecting rules that have to be harmonized, and the like, I see a consistent pattern through a chapter or the better part of a chapter of the Mishnah. Where a passage is given a huge and profound essay of a theoretical chapter, I note little interest in the simpler kind of Mishnah-exegesis. As a rough rule of thumb, it appears, where we find Mishnah-commentary of the one sort, we do not find that of the other. Why should we not find a systematic program running throughout, where we first deal with the simple issues of exegesis, then the profound questions of abstract theory, but rather the one or the other, I do not know. Perhaps in another age the source-criticism of the Bavli will take up this question in a systematic way. When it does, this academic commentary will be found helpful in identifying the distinct classes of evidence. I myself could not have raised this question without having conducted the exercise of making outlines of tractates. But it is becoming clear that two (or more) distinct programs of Mishnah-commentary are in operation here, and that is besides the quite separate program of introducing into a Mishnah-tractate the systematic and large-scale treatment of topics that the Mishnah-tractate never raises. These then prove two distinct problems that flow together in the interpretation of the exegetical program of a Talmud tractate, the types of Mishnah-commentary, elaboration, and theoretical inquiry; the transformation of a Mishnah-tractate's topic through the insertion of a large topical composite into the exposition of the Mishnah-tractate's topic, that is, the problem of the massive miscellany systematically worked out in these volumes.

## Chapter Thirty-three. The Structure of Babylonian Talmud Temurah

II.B: Since II.A speaks of the priests' effecting a substitution in the case of what belongs to them, the question raised here, the rights of priests to animals now that the Temple is in ruins, is subordinate and the entire, fairly elaborate exposition, simply flows out of the context in which it is located. I see no "miscellany" here.

IX.B, C, and D: The grape clusters, the laws forgotten during the period of Moses, form a tightly-organized topical essay. That concerns the enormous loss of learning that took place when Moses died. The rules affecting the sin offering of an individual that is not needed for its designated purpose form a centerpiece of the lost laws, and that is the obvious explanation of the insertion of the entire, vast miscellany. What is the upshot of the insertion of this exposition — how our sages of blessed memory know much less than Moses, how much was forgotten when Moses died? It is to underscore the complexity of the law, on the one side, and the difficulty of mastering its details, on the other.

XVIII.B: I find it noteworthy that at issue here is precisely what is subject to concern in the foregoing, namely, a beast designated as a sin offering that was lost, then found, and how we resolved the problem.

XIX.B: This item continues the theme of the beast designated as a sin offering that cannot serve that purpose.

XXII.B: This strikes me as a truly miscellaneous entry, though it does carry forward the question of how we dispose of a beast that is consecrated but cannot be used for its designated purpose.

3. CAN WE STATE WHAT THE COMPILERS OF THIS DOCUMENT PROPOSE TO ACCOMPLISH IN PRODUCING THIS COMPLETE, ORGANIZED PIECE OF WRITING?

The answer to this question depends on what we make of the items in No. 2: the anomalies, the topical expositions that our Mishnah-tractate does not require for a full and complete presentation of its subject-matter. I am struck by the uniform concern of the massive miscellanies of our tractate, which is, the animal that has been designated for a sacred purpose but cannot serve. Now when we realize that such an animal forms the counterpart of the one that has been designated to serve as a substitute for an already-consecrated beast, we perceive how our topic has been broadened. That is to say, a substitute is an animal that has been set aside to replace an already-sanctified beast. That animal is given the status of the beast for which it is supposed to substitute, and the original beast retains its status as to sanctification. The upshot is, the second beast becomes as holy as was the original one: if the one was a sin offering, the other enters that status. Then we deal with a beast that is superfluous, and the classic source of such a problem is, two or more animals that are designated as sin offerings. Only one can serve. The rule is very strict. An animal must be designated for the very particular sin that the sinner discovers he has inadvertently committed. Then another animal entering that same status can be used only for the expiation of that particular sin.

The entire complex of massive miscellanies then investigates a very special problem in connection with the entire process of substitution, namely, the beast offered as a substitute for a sin offering — the one case in which the substitute is given a status of sanctification that will not yield a valid offering. So the effect of the massive miscellanies is vastly to deepen our understanding of the issues of the Mishnah-tractate — issues that Moses mastered, but others could not fully grasp. The upshot is to make a point that the Mishnah-tractate invites but never articulates: when a beast has been substituted for another and takes on its status as to sanctification (a beast substituted for a sin-offering, in the present case), then a vast range of profound issues emerges, which our Mishnah-tractate only adumbrates. The inserted composites, moving so far beyond the limits of the Mishnah-tractate, form a commentary on the topic of the Mishnah, but not on any of its specific propositions — a stimulating and suggestive way of re-opening the closed borders of the Mishnah-tractates presentation of its own topic.

# XXXIV

## The Structure of Babylonian Talmud Keritot

### Points of Structure

The main point may be stated very simply: the structure of our tractate is supplied by the Mishnah-tractate, and the system of the tractate aims at a single goal: to assign a position of privilege to the Mishnah as the source of organization and coherent for whatever the framers wish to say and as the focus of the system they wish to set forth. All Talmud-tractates find exact description in that sentence, but this one, more than most, adheres to it with great punctiliousness. That is why we see only a few free-standing composites bearing propositions not immediately relevant to the Mishnah-paragraph to which they stand adjacent. We should err, however, were we to miss the systemic statement that these compelling facts mean to make. It is not merely to allege and demonstrate that the Mishnah is a flawless code, resting on Scripture, containing no contradictions or repetitions. It is that, beyond Scripture, the Mishnah alone demands, and can sustain, rigorous analysis. The Bavli, as our tractate exemplifies it, accords rigorous analysis of a sustained and structured character to no document but Scripture and the Mishnah, and, as between the two, it self-evidently affords priority to the Mishnah. That point of structure bears within itself also the purpose of the system.

1. Does Babylonian Talmud-tractate Keritot follow a coherent outline governed by a consistent rules?

The kind of commentary that the Mishnah receives is well-defined. It is argumentative and analytical, not merely informative or illuminating. For the framers of our tractate's comments on the Mishnah, it was not sufficient to place on display interesting information relevant to something the Mishnah's statement encompasses. A highly cogent set of programs of an analytical character takes priority.

To underscore the remarkable cogency of our tractate, we point to unit XXXII. That unit shows us a theory of Mishnah-commentary contrary to the one that predominates. It simply takes on a complete composite, a composition bearing its own amplification — with no substantive, programmatic point of relevance to the Mishnah. Rather, the composite is tacked on because at one point it intersects with a fact stated, also, by the Mishnah. This tractate contains only one such presentation of the Mishnah, and the Talmud overall encompasses very few of them; no tractate as a whole comprises only or mainly topical allusions and points of amplification. Every Talmud-tractate is dominated, as this one is, by the program of Mishnah-analysis.

2. WHAT ARE THE SALIENT TRAITS OF ITS STRUCTURE?

What I find most interesting in Bavli tractate Keritot is the intellectually economical character of its analytical program. The framers do not find it necessarily to comment on everything; they pick and choose. Nor does a vast and random program of inquiry guide them. They ask some few questions, and where possible, they ask the same question to a sequence of Mishnah-allegations, yielding a set of fairly coherent treatments of a sequence of discrete units of Mishnah-discourse. The result is that some few problems predominate over a long series of passages.

3. WHAT IS THE RATIONALITY OF THE STRUCTURE?

The points of order and intellectual purpose emerge in a structure that follows a regular order of inquiry. First come comments on the wording of the Mishnah, the scriptural foundations of the Mishnah-rule, or the identity of the authority behind the anonymous (therefore authoritative) Mishnah-statement. Second come points of amplification, e.g., why does a given authority take the initiative that he takes ("what is wrong with X that Rabbi A has produced Y), what argument does a given sage have in mind, why has he not accepted the proposition and argument of his counterpart, and the like. Third in order will be more abstract and theoretical questions, which are not required for an exposition of the Mishnah's rule but are necessary to establish the Mishnah's broader context in thought.

4. WHERE ARE THE POINTS OF IRRATIONALITY IN THE STRUCTURE?

I find myself unable to point to a single passage, other than the concluding one, at which the structure of form and program does not define the character of the document. In general and in detail the tractate is the model of a great piece of Talmud-composition and compilation. And, as we see presently, all of the free-standing composites, out of phase with the program of the Mishnah in particular, find a natural place in the document. None but No. XXXII is parachuted down for essentially formal reasons.

## POINTS OF SYSTEM

1. DOES THE BABYLONIAN TALMUD-TRACTATE KERITOT SERVE ONLY AS A REPRESENTATION OF THE MISHNAH-TRACTATE OF THE SAME NAME?

The negative answer derives from two facts. First, the framers bypass in silence a considerable portion of the Mishnah-tractate. They discuss what they choose to discuss, not what the authors of the Mishnah-tractate have set before them. On the opening list of 36 items, for example, we see that only a few items

## Chapter Thirty-four: The Structure of Babylonian Talmud Keritot

receive attention. The second fact is that we can explain what items in the Mishnah's presentation are investigated and explain why those that are omitted have been bypassed. In that same opening list, the items that are treated have in common the fact that they present the same problem: do they call into question the exact enumeration that defines the presentation as a whole? Some seem to encompass more species than the number 36 permits, some fewer. But only those items on the long list that permit us to test the generalization that the list sets forth — 36 distinct classes of sin or crime that provoke the penalty of extirpation, no more, no less. The framer then omits all of the information he might have assembled on numerous items, vast essays on such topics as sacrificing outside of the Temple court, working on the day of Atonement, and the like. It follows that a program of selection intervenes between the formation of Talmud-composites serving the task of Mishnah-exegesis and the Mishnah-tractate itself. The Mishnah-tractate's framers have not dictated to the Talmud-tractate's writers of compositions or of composites the program that they shall follow. The former have provided to the latter only a large repertoire of possibilities, among which the Talmud's writers made their choices.

The positive answer complements the negative one. The Talmud-tractate's composites will systematically address some few questions among the many before them; where possible, a single pressing issue will define analysis of sequences of Mishnah-statements. That simple fact above all proves decisively the proposition of this academic commentary. It is that the Babylonian Talmud provides not simply a paraphrase and clarification of the received document but sets forth an independent and autonomous statement of its own. Here, in a tractate that is quite remarkable for its adherence to the work of Mishnah-commentary and contains few free-standing compositions outside of the Mishnah's topical or theoretical orbit, we bear witness to the intellectual independence of the writers of the Bavli's compositions for this tractate and the autonomous program that governs the work of the compilers of the Bavli's composites to comprise the tractate. A tractate that appears to limit itself to commentary then shows the full possibility of utilizing the form of a commentary for the presentation of a perspective and a program quite distinct from the text that supports the commentary.

2. HOW DO THE TOPICAL COMPOSITES FIT INTO THE TALMUD-TRACTATE KERITOT AND WHAT DO THEY CONTRIBUTE THAT THE MISHNAH-TRACTATE OF THE SAME NAME WOULD LACK WITHOUT THEM?

The free-standing composites are to be taken up one by one, each in its context. What we wish to know is, first, why has the item been inserted where it stands? and, second, how has the inclusion of the composition affected our understanding of the topic or proposition that defines the primary framework of discussion?

### I.F  THE ANOINTING OIL:

The topic is introduced by the immediately-preceding Mishnah-statement. I see no animating proposition in this compilation of topical information.

### V.C  THE OFFERINGS OF A PROSELYTE:

The reason for the inclusion is obvious: the Mishnah has omitted reference to the proselyte's offerings, and the Talmud has explained why his offerings have been omitted. Then comes a free-standing exposition on the theme. The point is made that the proselyte's offerings really do correspond to the Israelite's. His are different but equivalent, and Scripture is explicit. Just as your forefathers entered the covenant only with circumcision and immersion and sprinkling of blood through the sacrifices, so they [proselytes] will enter the covenant only through circumcision, immersion, and sprinkling of blood on the altar — that is the paramount proposition. The character of the prior list can have left the contrary impression, so a sustained demonstration is required to right matters.

### XIII.B  A PREGNANT WOMAN OR NURSING MOTHER EATS WHAT OTHERS MAY NOT EAT, BUT ONLY IN LIMITED VOLUME:

The immediately preceding discussion sets forth rules governing the eating, in very small volume, of prohibited food. That may take place over a long period of time, so that the requisite volume of food for which culpability is incurred is not consumed in so brief a period as to warrant being taken into account. We then turn to another case in which forbidden food may be eaten; it is the pregnant woman. To her applies the opposite consideration: she may eat only a limited volume of forbidden food, but there is no restriction that requires her to eat it over a protracted period of time. So she enters the picture in order to give a pertinent, but diametrically opposite, case from the one that has been discussed: now not time but volume matter.

### XXVII.B  ACQUIRING OWNERSHIP: WHEN DOES THE INITIAL OWNER GIVE UP HOPE OF RECOVERING PROPERTY AND SO RELINQUISH TITLE?

Including this significant discussion makes a profound point. The superficial intersection is topical. In the immediately preceding discussion, we take up the issue of assigning ownership of an abandoned beast. The topic that now comes forward is abandoning ownership of property in general. But the more profound connection is not to be missed. We have been discussing the attitude of a person who dedicates a beast: is it conditional or unconditional? The premise therefore is this: the man's heart is what has moved him, we assume that he has resolved to dedicate the beast unconditionally. That principle calls to mind other ways in which the owner of property gives up his rights of ownership, and, once more, we are reminded, attitude is all. Just as a person may dedicate something to the Temple without condition or qualification, so he may give up ownership of his property through an act of will. That is, he relinquishes ownership of property that he has lost when he gives up hope of recovering it. It goes without saying that that attitude is not subject to qualification or condition. By including what is in fact a free-standing essay, the framer of the large-scale composite has vastly deepened our grasp of the principle operative in his basic Mishnah-commentary, namely, the matter of condition or stipulation as it affects rights of possession and ownership. Seeing the issue of the status of the animal that has been dedicated in this larger context affords us a perspective on what is at stake, and that, is one's attitude towards one's possessions, whether animals given to the Temple or property of which one has lost possession. On the one side, an act of consecration, on the other, an attitude of despair — these form counterparts. Were I a preacher, I would then formulate a sermon based on the contrast between trust in God contained in an act of unconditional consecration, as against the vagaries of trust in property, which we give up by not an act of consecration and hope, but one of despair and renunciation of hope.

**XXVIII.D  SINS FOR WHICH THE DAY OF ATONEMENT EFFECTS ATONEMENT:**

The context is a reasonable one: the kinds of sin for which the Day of Atonement effects atonement. The principal concern of the thematic composite is precisely the opposite: to specify the matters for which the Day of Atonement does not effect atonement at all. And that comes down to a recurrent point, subject to dispute: is uncleanness a matter of sin at all? This is made explicit in the following language: For all your sins...,' and not 'for all your occasions of uncleanness,' which are not matters of sin in any event, thus eliminating the sin offering brought by the woman after she has given birth, which is a purification rite. That same matter is systematically demonstrated for other categories. The point then is to differentiate sin from uncleanness and to demonstrate that uncleanness concerns access to the Temple and has little bearing on one's moral condition. That too offers an important theological point, and the contrast between the discussion of sins for which the Day of Atonement effects atonement and other considerations altogether — which the composite draws sharply — then sets forward a most fundamental principle.

**XXIX.B  ATTAINING ATONEMENT WITH THE INCREASE IN THE VALUE OF CONSECRATED PROPERTY:**

This theoretical problem is introduced because the Mishnah-passage provides an illustration of how consecrated property may increase in value and the consequence of such an event. But the theoretical issue is quite distinct from the context in which it is discussed. The issue is framed in this language: can a man can attain atonement with the increase in the value of consecrated property? Where his own efforts have led to the increase in value, beyond what is required for the original purpose for which he consecrated a beast, there is a strong case to be made that he may designate that increase in value for some other, also holy purpose, e.g., an offering that he has to make. He has not made secular use of what he consecrated, but he has taken for himself the right to designate, in his own behalf, the particular sacred use to which the increase may be put. The case can also be made that he may not attain atonement with that increase, because the original act of consecration, which has defined the status of the property, e.g., the beast, was not for the purpose that he now has in mind. So, in general terms, the question has been raised: may or may not a person gain atonement through the increase in the value of consecrated property? Introducing the question at just this point is absolutely required, since the Mishnah's case invites precisely this question. But the question is one of theory, and a variety of considerations now enters into the matter: the man's own effort, the conflict between a general act of consecration and an act of consecration for a particular purpose. But the deeper issue circulates throughout: if a person consecrates something, may he make himself a partner with God in the utilization of what he has given to God? Here too, the problem is deepened by what is a theological issue formulated in practical, legal terms of the cult. The problem concerns man's partnership with God in the ownership of the natural world, with special attention to man's right to effect his purposes through what he has donated for God's: is the confluence of interest plausible or inappropriate, sharing or hubris?

### XXXII.B ISSACHAR OF KEFAR BARQAI

This singleton has already been dismissed; it is topically relevant but generates no profound thought.

The upshot is simply stated. Most, though not all, of the free-standing topical composites not only make important points of their own but also impart to the context in which they are located a theological dimension that, without them, would be absent. These points emerge.

[1] The proselyte is fully equivalent to the home-born Israelite. The rules of the cult demonstrate that fact.

[2] Food that is prohibited may nonetheless be utilized if it affords no material benefit, e.g., is eaten over a long period of time, or if it is eaten in such small volume as to provide no nourishment of consequence. Prohibitions, then, are set aside when they mark distinctions between the permitted and the prohibited that really make no difference. Only what makes an important difference, e.g., in sustaining life is subject to the prohibitions of the Torah.

[3] Ownership of property depends upon one's attitude toward the property. If one consecrates the property, God through the Temple becomes the owner. An act of will alienates the rights of ownership. If one relinquishes ownership by reason of despairing of recovering possession of the property, he also loses the rights of ownership. So one may give up property either as a gift to Heaven or as a surrender to bad fortunate. Ownership by itself therefore makes little difference; one's attitude toward one's property, on the one side, and one's disposition of possessions, on the other, govern. One does well, therefore, to hold with open arms; one does better to give up ownership of property to Heaven as an act of donation than relinquish ownership to violence as an act of despair.

[4] Various classifications affect a person, and they are not to be confused with one another. A person finds himself in a variety of grids, each covering a particular territory of life. He may be unclean or clean, with consequences having to do with the Temple. He may do a religious duty or commit a sin, with

consequences having to do with the moral life. The rites of the Temple, where they matter, concern not the cultic life of cleanness or uncleanness but the moral life of sin and atonement. The Day of Atonement — the single most consequence exercise of the cult — makes a difference to the moral condition of a human being, not to his cultic classification. The theological statement that morality takes priority over ritual, and that right — forgiveness of sin and atonement — stands above rite will hardly have surprised the prophets.

When we can explain the connections people make, we also can follow the rationality of the conclusions that they draw. The connections between the topic defined in the context of Mishnah-exegesis and that of the free-standing compositions and composites of a topical character yield the conclusions just now set forth. Generalizations about the system that animates the document as a whole will have to await an examination of the entire repertoire of connections between Mishnah-problems and their exegesis and extra-Mishnaic topics and their exposition. The four points we have identified in Bavli tractate Keritot cannot be taken up in isolation from the rest of the document. The demonstration of a single coherent structure imposes its own logic upon the exposition of what may or may not emerge as a cogent and uniform system.

3. CAN WE STATE WHAT THE COMPILERS OF THIS DOCUMENT PROPOSE TO ACCOMPLISH IN PRODUCING THIS COMPLETE, ORGANIZED PIECE OF WRITING?

If I had to select a single recurrent problem that attracts the interest of the authors of compositions and compilers of composites, it is the theory of classification, specifically, the subdivision of a genus into species, on the one side, and the way in which Scripture teaches us how to accomplish that generative problem of thought, on the other. This problem is in two parts: how does a given action subdivides into two or more classifications; how do two or more actions coalesce into a single classification. A second problem that occurs wherever relevant concerns the relationship of intentionality and culpability. A third recurrent exercise is to demonstrate the scriptural foundations of Mishnah-propositions. A fourth is the proof that authorities rule in a consistent way, so that their opinions prove harmonious. A fifth is the inquiry into how differences of opinion rest upon reasonable, but conflicting, principles; disputes are not irrational (or personal!) but always involve good reason for each side's ruling. A sixth is the introduction of an abstract, theoretical problem into a concrete case, e.g., may a prohibition apply to what is already prohibited? A sixth is the extension to a variety of concrete problems of a single, encompassing conception, e.g., the sin offering atones for a concrete action, done unwittingly and later found out, and is not generalized but highly particular; the complementary conception that the suspensive guilt offering is governed by the same rule and corresponds, in the case of what may or may not have taken place, to the situation of a sin offering presented when knowledge of what has happened is certain and precise. This brief account need not recapitulate the results just now set forth in our consideration of the making of connections in the insertion of topical composites and the drawing of conclusions from the connections that are made.

The whole then points toward a single conclusion. These and other results leave us no reasonable doubt that our tractate exhibits the traits of a rigidly formalized structure, one that supports and sustains a highly systematic program. The tractate in vast detail sets forth a structure in form and a system in analytical interest.

# XXXV

# The Structure of Babylonian Talmud Tractate Meilah

### POINTS OF STRUCTURE

1. DOES BABYLONIAN TALMUD-TRACTATE MEILAH FOLLOW A COHERENT OUTLINE GOVERNED BY A CONSISTENT RULES?
2. WHAT ARE THE SALIENT TRAITS OF ITS STRUCTURE?
3. WHAT IS THE RATIONALITY OF THE STRUCTURE?
4. WHERE ARE THE POINTS OF IRRATIONALITY IN THE STRUCTURE?

The Talmud tractate follows the outline of the Mishnah-tractate. The structure of the Bavli-tractate is dictated by that of the Mishnah-tractate, with the proviso that the framers of the Bavli do not find it necessary to comment on every phrase and sentence of the Mishnah-tractate. I find not a single instance in which a major rubric of the Bavli introduces a topic not deriving from the Mishnah. Only a single story moves beyond the limits of Mishnah-exegesis, and that is carefully linked to the requirements of Mishnah-exegesis, as noted in context.

### POINTS OF SYSTEM

1. DOES THE BABYLONIAN TALMUD-TRACTATE MEILAH SERVE ONLY AS A RE-PRESENTATION OF THE MISHNAH-TRACTATE OF THE SAME NAME?

No, because a fair portion of the Mishnah is not treated. But I have no explanation to account for both what is omitted and what is discussed; I do not discern a large-scale theory of matters that the Bavli's framers wish to introduce into the reading of the Mishnah.

2. HOW DO THE TOPICAL COMPOSITES FIT INTO THE TALMUD-TRACTATE MEILAH AND WHAT DO THEY CONTRIBUTE THAT THE MISHNAH-TRACTATE OF THE SAME NAME WOULD LACK WITHOUT THEM?

This question does not pertain, there being no large-scale topical composites.

3. CAN WE STATE WHAT THE COMPILERS OF THIS DOCUMENT PROPOSE TO ACCOMPLISH IN PRODUCING THIS COMPLETE, ORGANIZED PIECE OF WRITING?

The framers of this document propose to set forth a systematic commentary to the Mishnah.

This result is replicated in Mishnah-tractate Tamid, given only a truncated commentary by the Bavli. In Meilah and Tamid we have no large-scale topical composites; the subjects of the two tractates are not seen in a new perspective or under a fresh light by reason of composites or even compositions that greatly revise our conception of things. The hypothesis presents itself that the difference between shorter and longer Bavli-tractates derives principally from whether or not massive miscellanies are inserted. That hypothesis, which is not pertinent to this academic commentary, raises questions of structure. The problem of discerning the Bavli's, as distinct from the Mishnah's system, will find its solution not in what we do not have, but in what we find here in abundance. Toward the solution of that problem, Bavli-tractates Meilah and Tamid make only a negative contribution. I can think of no ad hoc explanation for why the Bavli-tractates find no occasion in the present topics to make fresh points or to bring about a jarring juxtaposition, such that matters appear in a way that is new and different from the Mishnah's presentation of the same subject. I am inclined to think that only when we have all tractates in hand, analyzed in a single manner, will issues of what we do, and do not, find begin to form a suggestive pattern.

# XXXVI

## The Structure of Babylonian Talmud Tractate Tamid

### POINTS OF STRUCTURE

1. DOES BABYLONIAN TALMUD-TRACTATE TAMID FOLLOW A COHERENT OUTLINE GOVERNED BY A CONSISTENT RULES?

The Talmud for the Mishnah-tractate follows standard patterns. The structure is defined by the Mishnah-sentences that are chosen for discussion, and these are set forth in the order in which they occur in the Mishnah-tractate. Nothing in its content suggests a reason for omitting from Talmudic analysis the larger part of the Mishnah-tractate.

2. WHAT ARE THE SALIENT TRAITS OF ITS STRUCTURE?

The Talmud is a commentary to the Mishnah.

3. WHAT IS THE RATIONALITY OF THE STRUCTURE?

So far as the Talmud for this Mishnah-tractate undertakes the task, the work is done in the conventional way.

4. WHERE ARE THE POINTS OF IRRATIONALITY IN THE STRUCTURE?

The first anomaly is the introduction of paragraphs of Mishnah-tractate Middot, which are subjected to the standard inquiry. But these are introduced in the setting of the paragraphs of Mishnah-tractate Tamid to which they correspond at I.H, I. The one important point of disruption is at V.C, D.

### POINTS OF SYSTEM

1. DOES THE BABYLONIAN TALMUD-TRACTATE TAMID SERVE ONLY AS A RE-PRESENTATION OF THE MISHNAH-TRACTATE OF THE SAME NAME?

The absence of Talmud for more than half of the Mishnah-tractate gives a negative answer to that question, but how the omission of so much of the Mishnah-tractate constitutes a re-presentation of the Mishnah-tractate I cannot say.

2. HOW DO THE TOPICAL COMPOSITES FIT INTO THE TALMUD-TRACTATE TAMID AND WHAT DO THEY CONTRIBUTE THAT THE MISHNAH-TRACTATE OF THE SAME NAME WOULD LACK WITHOUT THEM?

This question is brings us to V.C. While we may discern a thematic thread that leads from V.B to V.C, the unit is so remarkable for its utter independence from its topical context that it must be regarded as a true anomaly. If we ask for any point at which the tale, with its several distinct units, requires us to consider the topic of our tractate in a fresh light, or suggests a perspective that we should not otherwise have formed for our tractate's subject, we find no compelling reply. Here is therefore a fine example of what the Talmud would have set forth were it not organized in the way it is, which is, as a systematic exegesis of the Mishnah's topics and concrete statements concerning those topics. Perhaps V.D's obvious task — to write a suitable homily to conclude the tractate — may be extended to encompass V.C, in which case the theory behind including the story was to show the superiority of our sages' Torah-learning over gentile wisdom, represented by Alexander. But then the story is disproportionate to the task. We have therefore to conclude that the topical composite — Alexander and our sages — in no way forms part of the Talmud's re-presentation of the Mishnah-tractate or of its topic.

3. CAN WE STATE WHAT THE COMPILERS OF THIS DOCUMENT PROPOSE TO ACCOMPLISH IN PRODUCING THIS COMPLETE, ORGANIZED PIECE OF WRITING?

So far as our truncated tractate accomplishes the task of Mishnah-exegesis, the goal of the compilers is clear and unexceptional. The question on the abbreviated character of the tractate need not detain us, since it concerns structure, not system. What we learn about the system that the Bavli's sages bring to the Mishnah derives from two sets of facts, first, the character of the Mishnah-commentary, second, the results of the introduction of compositions and composites that aim at other than Mishnah-commentary. Here the data prove too fragmentary to generate plausible hypotheses; but in due course, they will surely serve in the formation of such hypotheses.

# XXXVII

## The Structure of Babylonian Talmud Niddah

### POINTS OF STRUCTURE

1. DOES BABYLONIAN TALMUD-TRACTATE NIDDAH FOLLOW A COHERENT OUTLINE GOVERNED BY A CONSISTENT RULES?

That the Bavli presents a commentary to selected Mishnah-tractates raises the question, what sort of commentary? The answer comes to us from any Bavli-tractate, since a single program governs all of them, without differentiation by subject-matter, on the one side, or by any other distinctive traits (practical vs. theoretical law, for instance), on the other. If we can define the repertoire of intellectual initiatives characteristic of one tractate, we shall find the same repertoire governing the reading of all others, with the simple qualification that proportions of types of inquiry may vary. The work of differentiating among tractates must await the formulation of the consistent rules that dictate to the compilers of the Talmud to a given Mishnah-tractate how they are to do their work.

2. WHAT ARE THE SALIENT TRAITS OF ITS STRUCTURE?

That the Bavli's reading works its way phrase-by-phrase through numerous Mishnah-paragraphs presents the question, what are the guide-lines — the premises as to right thinking, right formulation, or right point of origination — that dictate to the Bavli's Mishnah-commentators the character of their work? The salient traits of the structure of our Talmud emerge, first of all, from the simple fact that this protracted outline demonstrates beyond all doubt: we can outline the Bavli in the way in which we should be able to outline any well-crafted, analytical and propositional composition. That is, we work our way from topic-sentences, supplied by the Mishnah, to subordinate points made in amplification of those sentences, to secondary and derivative observations, and, finally, to miscellaneous information or ad hoc observations of a low-order. The fact that we may outline the Bavli in such a simple and systematic way — the occasional lapses showing us what might have been — defines the single salient trait of structure, to invent a word: the Bavli's "outline-ability."

3. WHAT IS THE RATIONALITY OF THE STRUCTURE?

The premises of the Bavli encompass not only that the Talmud-tractate follows a coherent outline, but also of what that coherence consists. Here, once more, a brief survey of the lead-entries of twenty-five entries on our outline suffices to show us the deep structure of order and reason that supports the entire composition, beginning to end:

1. Examination of the sense and meaning of the wording of the Mishnah; clarification of the allegations of the Mishnah; provision of details required to grasp the Mishnah's rule, articulation of what is implicit in our Mishnah's rule

I.E.1, I.F.1; II.C.1, II.E.1, II.H.1; III.E.1; IV.A.1, IV.C.1; V.A.1, V.B.1, V.C.1; VI.1.A, VI.B.1, VI.C.1; VII.A.1; X.A.1, X.B.1, X.C.1, X.E.1, X.F.1, X.G.1, X.H.1, X.8.1; XI.B.1, XI.C.1, XI.D.1, XI.E.1; XII.A.1; XIV.A.1, XIV.B.1; XVI.A.1, XVI.C.1; XVII.A.1, XVII.B.1; XVII.C.1; XX.A.1, XX.B.1, XX.C.1; XXII.A.1; XXIII.B.1; XXIV.J.1, XXIV.L.1

2. What is the operative consideration, meaning, the principle that underlies a variety of cases?

I.A.1

3. What is the source in Scripture for a given rule, meaning, the Torah's statement, in its language, of what the Mishnah-framers have set forth in theirs, or the basis in the Torah for the ruling of the Mishnah-framers?

X.D.1; XIX.A.1, XIX.B.1; XX.E.1; XXIII.A.1; XXIII.D.1; XXIV.A.1, XXIV.B.1, XXIV.C.1, XXIV.D.1, XXIV.E.1, XXIV.F.1, XXIV.G.1, XXIV.H.1, XXIV.I.1, XXIV.K.1

4. What other Tannaite opinion addresses the matter taken up by the Mishnah-rule, and how does that opinion square with what the Mishnah tells us? This shades over into the inquiry into the identity of authorities who concur, or who do not concur, with the Mishnah rule

I.B.1, I.C.1; II.A.1, II.B.1, II.D.1, II.F.1, II.G.1; VI.D.1; VIII.A.1; IX.A.1, X.J.1, X.I.1, X.L.1; XII.B.1, XII.C.1; XIII.A.1, XIII.B.1; XVI.B.1XVII.D.1; XIX.C.1; XX.D.1; XXI.A.1; XXIII.C.1; XXV.A.1

5. Further opinion on the matter taken up by the Mishnah-rule, e.g., a complementary rule, or an inference to be drawn from the Mishnah-rule and how that inference squares with the implicit principles in other matters of law altogether?

I.D.1; II.I.1; III.1.A, III.B.1, III.D.1; VI.E.1; XI.A.1; XV.A.1; XVIII.A.1; XXIII.E.1, XXIII.F.1; XXV.B.1

6. How a Mishnah-rule relates to one given in another context altogether; how another Mishnah-passage illuminates, or is illuminated by, our Mishnah's statement

III.C.1; XVII.E.1

We see that every composite attached to a Mishnah-statement begins with that Mishnah-statement and focuses its attention upon the requirements of clarifying the meaning or implications of that statement. It follows that the structure and order of the Talmud-tractate find their definition in the Mishnah-tractate, and the rationality of the Bavli emerges from the Bavli's compilers' definition of the requirement of Mishnah-exegesis, pure and simple.

4. WHERE ARE THE POINTS OF IRRATIONALITY IN THE STRUCTURE?

It follows that large-scale composites that do not respond to the Mishnah's program emerge as not merely asymmetrical to the document that presents them but as beyond the document's own manifest sense of what is rational and orderly. Do these composites call into question the character of the Bavli as a reasoned reading of the Mishnah? These are the compositions or composites that do not respond to statements in the Mishnah: IV.B, VIII.B, XVI.D, XXXV.B, LII.C, D, E, and LIII.F. We have now to ask about the system that the Bavli-tractate's structure sustains and the relationship of the structurally-irrational composites to that system.

### POINTS OF SYSTEM

1. DOES THE BABYLONIAN TALMUD-TRACTATE NIDDAH SERVE ONLY AS A RE-PRESENTATION OF THE MISHNAH-TRACTATE OF THE SAME NAME?

I discern only a few lines of the Mishnah-tractate that the Bavli-compilers fail to address.

2. HOW DO THE TOPICAL COMPOSITES FIT INTO THE TALMUD-TRACTATE NIDDAH AND WHAT DO THEY CONTRIBUTE THAT THE MISHNAH-TRACTATE OF THE SAME NAME WOULD LACK WITHOUT THEM?

The topical and other composites add information but do not vastly revise our picture of the tractate's topic and problematic. An examination of each item leaves no doubt that the compilers of the tractate made no effort by striking intrusions or juxtapositions to impart to the Mishnah-tractate dimensions of meaning not present in the Mishnah's framers' original statement on the subject.

IV.B: The appendix is entirely in order to amplify the topic of the Mishnah-sentence at hand. It does not change but only underscores the point of the prior composite.

VIII.B: The composite on correct conduct of sexual relations is attached to begin with because of the concern of the Mishnah-rule that there be light to see whether or not menstrual blood is excreted; but it is forbidden to have sexual relations by day, and that theme is then expounded at some length.

XVI.D: The Mishnah's statement that the foetus is completed on the forty-first day is amplified with a huge composite on the character of the foetus. The subdivisions of the composite are readily discerned. I see neither in the parts nor in the whole a polemic, let alone an effort to impart to the topic a layer of meaning deriving from the juxtaposition of the compositions that are before us. The composite cannot be classified as merely random, to be sure, but seen in context, none of its parts changes the picture of the theme or much revises the viewpoint of the Mishnah-statement.

XXXV.B: The composite on the obligations of tithing provides information on the Mishnah-sentence's topic, a standard appendix.

LII.C, D, and E: what we have here is a problem in the organization of the Talmud, since VII.E simply carries forward LII.C, and only D is inserted; this is an appendix that supplements VII.C. The set hardly corresponds to the usual appendix of a topical character; it is the only formation of materials in the dozen and a half tractates examined to this point that is not accessible to the simple, topical outline that I have created for the description of the Talmud; the Talmud's components here adhere to a different scheme of organization from the one that governs throughout.

LIII.F: Like XXXV.B, what we have here is a talmud to a Mishnah-paragraph that otherwise has none in the Bavli. The inclusion here is for good and substantial reasons.

The upshot may be stated very simply. Our Talmud-tractate contains not a single composite that imparts to the treatment of the topic, or of any proposition that unpacks the topic, a character or a dimension that the Mishnah's own presentation does not invite or even require. The few asymmetrical composites I have identified prove inert and merely bear information.

3. CAN WE STATE WHAT THE COMPILERS OF THIS DOCUMENT PROPOSE TO ACCOMPLISH IN PRODUCING THIS COMPLETE, ORGANIZED PIECE OF WRITING?

The structure of our tractate is coherent and cogent; it finds its definition in the Mishnah-tractate that is under discussion. The system of the Bavli-tractate's reading of the Mishnah finds its purpose in the character of the Mishnah — the Mishnah's wording, the Mishnah's sense, the Mishnah's implications, and the inferences to be drawn from the Mishnah. I discern in this tractate no other purpose than to present a complete, well-organized explanation of the Mishnah-tractate, its meaning and its practical requirements for the conduct of the holy life of the family in response to the Torah's commandments. Some tractates form only Mishnah-commentaries, while other tractates accomplish the same end while imparting to the Mishnah's topic dimensions of meaning that the Mishnah's presentation of its topic do not clearly define. Bavli-tractate Niddah provides a fine model for what it means, to the compilers of the Talmud and the authors of an important corpus of compositions upon which they drew to comment upon the Mishnah.

How the Mishnah, for its part, dictated the character of its commentary lies beyond the framework of this academic commentary of mine, though the question obviously demands its answer. No one who has devoted close attention to the Bavli can doubt the main outline of the answer, which, I should contend, is intuitively obvious to anyone who has read ten lines of the document: the purpose of the authors of compositions of Mishnah-commentary and of framers of composites of Mishnah-amplification is to say what, in their judgment, the Mishnah means or implies. The consequent, and I think the real task, then, is to analyze the components of that judgment of theirs, to unpack and analyze each of the givens of the rationality and the consequent logic that govern throughout the Bavli. In my view, the raw-materials for such an analysis are contained in this academic commentary of mine.

# South Florida Studies in the History of Judaism

| | | |
|---|---|---|
| 240001 | Lectures on Judaism in the Academy and in the Humanities | Neusner |
| 240002 | Lectures on Judaism in the History of Religion | Neusner |
| 240003 | Self-Fulfilling Prophecy: Exile and Return in the History of Judaism | Neusner |
| 240004 | The Canonical History of Ideas: The Place of the So-called Tannaite Midrashim, Mekhilta Attributed to R. Ishmael, Sifra, Sifré to Numbers, and Sifré to Deuteronomy | Neusner |
| 240005 | Ancient Judaism: Debates and Disputes, Second Series | Neusner |
| 240006 | The Hasmoneans and Their Supporters: From Mattathias to the Death of John Hyrcanus I | Sievers |
| 240007 | Approaches to Ancient Judaism: New Series, Volume One | Neusner |
| 240008 | Judaism in the Matrix of Christianity | Neusner |
| 240009 | Tradition as Selectivity: Scripture, Mishnah, Tosefta, and Midrash in the Talmud of Babylonia | Neusner |
| 240010 | The Tosefta: Translated from the Hebrew: Sixth Division Tohorot | Neusner |
| 240011 | In the Margins of the Midrash: Sifre Ha'azinu Texts, Commentaries and Reflections | Basser |
| 240012 | Language as Taxonomy: The Rules for Using Hebrew and Aramaic in the Babylonia Talmud | Neusner |
| 240013 | The Rules of Composition of the Talmud of Babylonia: The Cogency of the Bavli's Composite | Neusner |
| 240014 | Understanding the Rabbinic Mind: Essays on the Hermeneutic of Max Kadushin | Ochs |
| 240015 | Essays in Jewish Historiography | Rapoport-Albert |
| 240016 | The Golden Calf and the Origins of the Jewish Controversy | Bori/Ward |
| 240017 | Approaches to Ancient Judaism: New Series, Volume Two | Neusner |
| 240018 | The Bavli That Might Have Been: The Tosefta's Theory of Mishnah Commentary Compared With the Bavli's | Neusner |
| 240019 | The Formation of Judaism: In Retrospect and Prospect | Neusner |
| 240020 | Judaism in Society: The Evidence of the Yerushalmi, Toward the Natural History of a Religion | Neusner |
| 240021 | The Enchantments of Judaism: Rites of Transformation from Birth Through Death | Neusner |
| 240022 | Åbo Addresses | Neusner |
| 240023 | The City of God in Judaism and Other Comparative and Methodological Studies | Neusner |
| 240024 | The Bavli's One Voice: Types and Forms of Analytical Discourse and their Fixed Order of Appearance | Neusner |
| 240025 | The Dura-Europos Synagogue: A Re-evaluation (1932-1992) | Gutmann |
| 240026 | Precedent and Judicial Discretion: The Case of Joseph ibn Lev | Morell |
| 240027 | Max Weinreich *Geschichte der jiddischen Sprachforschung* | Frakes |
| 240028 | Israel: Its Life and Culture, Volume I | Pedersen |
| 240029 | Israel: Its Life and Culture, Volume II | Pedersen |
| 240030 | The Bavli's One Statement: The Metapropositional Program of Babylonian Talmud Tractate Zebahim Chapters One and Five | Neusner |

| | | |
|---|---|---|
| 240031 | The Oral Torah: The Sacred Books of Judaism: An Introduction: Second Printing | Neusner |
| 240032 | The Twentieth Century Construction of "Judaism:" Essays on the Religion of Torah in the History of Religion | Neusner |
| 240033 | How the Talmud Shaped Rabbinic Discourse | Neusner |
| 240034 | The Discourse of the Bavli: Language, Literature, and Symbolism: Five Recent Findings | Neusner |
| 240035 | The Law Behind the Laws: The Bavli's Essential Discourse | Neusner |
| 240036 | Sources and Traditions: Types of Compositions in the Talmud of Babylonia | Neusner |
| 240037 | How to Study the Bavli: The Languages, Literatures, and Lessons of the Talmud of Babylonia | Neusner |
| 240038 | The Bavli's Primary Discourse: Mishnah Commentary: Its Rhetorical Paradigms and their Theological Implications | Neusner |
| 240039 | Midrash Aleph Beth | Sawyer |
| 240040 | Jewish Thought in the 20th Century: An Introduction in the Talmud of Babylonia Tractate Moed Qatan | Schweid |
| 240041 | Diaspora Jews and Judaism: Essays in Honor of, and in Dialogue with, A. Thomas Kraabel | Overman/MacLennan |
| 240042 | The Bavli: An Introduction | Neusner |
| 240043 | The Bavli's Massive Miscellanies: The Problem of Agglutinative Discourse in the Talmud of Babylonia | Neusner |
| 240044 | The Foundations of the Theology of Judaism: An Anthology Part II: Torah | Neusner |
| 240045 | Form-Analytical Comparison in Rabbinic Judaism: Structure and Form in *The Fathers* and *The Fathers According to Rabbi Nathan* | Neusner |
| 240046 | Essays on Hebrew | Weinberg |
| 240047 | The Tosefta: An Introduction | Neusner |
| 240048 | The Foundations of the Theology of Judaism: An Anthology Part III: Israel | Neusner |
| 240049 | The Study of Ancient Judaism, Volume I: Mishnah, Midrash, Siddur | Neusner |
| 240050 | The Study of Ancient Judaism, Volume II: The Palestinian and Babylonian Talmuds | Neusner |
| 240051 | Take Judaism, for Example: Studies toward the Comparison of Religions | Neusner |
| 240052 | From Eden to Golgotha: Essays in Biblical Theology | Moberly |
| 240053 | The Principal Parts of the Bavli's Discourse: A Preliminary Taxonomy: Mishnah Commentary, Sources, Traditions and Agglutinative Miscellanies | Neusner |
| 240054 | Barabbas and Esther and Other Studies in the Judaic Illumination of Earliest Christianity | Aus |
| 240055 | Targum Studies, Volume I: Textual and Contextual Studies in the Pentateuchal Targums | Flesher |
| 240056 | Approaches to Ancient Judaism: New Series, Volume Three, Historical and Literary Studies | Neusner |
| 240057 | The Motherhood of God and Other Studies | Gruber |
| 240058 | The Analytic Movement: Hayyim Soloveitchik and his Circle | Solomon |

| | | |
|---|---|---|
| 240059 | Recovering the Role of Women: Power and Authority in Rabbinic Jewish Society | Haas |
| 240060 | The Relation between Herodotus' *History* and Primary History | Mandell/Freedman |
| 240061 | The First Seven Days: A Philosophical Commentary on the Creation of Genesis | Samuelson |
| 240062 | The Bavli's Intellectual Character: The Generative Problematic: In Bavli Baba Qamma Chapter One And Bavli Shabbat Chapter One | Neusner |
| 240063 | The Incarnation of God: The Character of Divinity in Formative Judaism: Second Printing | Neusner |
| 240064 | Moses Kimhi: Commentary on the Book of Job | Basser/Walfish |
| 240066 | Death and Birth of Judaism: Second Printing | Neusner |
| 240067 | Decoding the Talmud's Exegetical Program | Neusner |
| 240068 | Sources of the Transformation of Judaism | Neusner |
| 240069 | The Torah in the Talmud: A Taxonomy of the Uses of Scripture in the Talmud, Volume I | Neusner |
| 240070 | The Torah in the Talmud: A Taxonomy of the Uses of Scripture in the Talmud, Volume II | Neusner |
| 240071 | The Bavli's Unique Voice: A Systematic Comparison of the Talmud of Babylonia and the Talmud of the Land of Israel, Volume One | Neusner |
| 240072 | The Bavli's Unique Voice: A Systematic Comparison of the Talmud of Babylonia and the Talmud of the Land of Israel, Volume Two | Neusner |
| 240073 | The Bavli's Unique Voice: A Systematic Comparison of the Talmud of Babylonia and the Talmud of the Land of Israel, Volume Three | Neusner |
| 240074 | Bits of Honey: Essays for Samson H. Levey | Chyet/Ellenson |
| 240075 | The Mystical Study of Ruth: *Midrash HaNe'elam* of the Zohar to the Book of Ruth | Englander |
| 240076 | The Bavli's Unique Voice: A Systematic Comparison of the Talmud of Babylonia and the Talmud of the Land of Israel, Volume Four | Neusner |
| 240077 | The Bavli's Unique Voice: A Systematic Comparison of the Talmud of Babylonia and the Talmud of the Land of Israel, Volume Five | Neusner |
| 240078 | The Bavli's Unique Voice: A Systematic Comparison of the Talmud of Babylonia and the Talmud of the Land of Israel, Volume Six | Neusner |
| 240079 | The Bavli's Unique Voice: A Systematic Comparison of the Talmud of Babylonia and the Talmud of the Land of Israel, Volume Seven | Neusner |
| 240080 | Are There Really Tannaitic Parallels to the Gospels? | Neusner |
| 240081 | Approaches to Ancient Judaism: New Series, Volume Four, Religious and Theological Studies | Neusner |
| 240082 | Approaches to Ancient Judaism: New Series, Volume Five, Historical, Literary, and Religious Studies | Basser/Fishbane |
| 240083 | Ancient Judaism: Debates and Disputes, Third Series | Neusner |

| ID | Title | Author |
|---|---|---|
| 240084 | Judaic Law from Jesus to the Mishnah | Neusner |
| 240085 | Writing with Scripture: Second Printing | Neusner/Green |
| 240086 | Foundations of Judaism: Second Printing | Neusner |
| 240087 | Judaism and Zoroastrianism at the Dusk of Late Antiquity | Neusner |
| 240088 | Judaism States Its Theology | Neusner |
| 240089 | The Judaism behind the Texts I.A | Neusner |
| 240090 | The Judaism behind the Texts I.B | Neusner |
| 240091 | Stranger at Home | Neusner |
| 240092 | Pseudo-Rabad: Commentary to Sifre Deuteronomy | Basser |
| 240093 | FromText to Historical Context in Rabbinic Judaism | Neusner |
| 240094 | Formative Judaism | Neusner |
| 240095 | Purity in Rabbinic Judaism | Neusner |
| 240096 | Was Jesus of Nazareth the Messiah? | McMichael |
| 240097 | The Judaism behind the Texts I.C | Neusner |
| 240098 | The Judaism behind the Texts II | Neusner |
| 240099 | The Judaism behind the Texts III | Neusner |
| 240100 | The Judaism behind the Texts IV | Neusner |
| 240101 | The Judaism behind the Texts V | Neusner |
| 240102 | The Judaism the Rabbis Take for Granted | Neusner |
| 240103 | From Text to Historical Context in Rabbinic Judaism V. II | Neusner |
| 240104 | From Text to Historical Context in Rabbinic Judaism V. III | Neusner |
| 240105 | Samuel, Saul, and Jesus: Three Early Palestinian Jewish Christian Gospel Haggadoth | Aus |
| 240106 | What is Midrash? And a Midrash Reader | Neusner |
| 240107 | Rabbinic Judaism: Disputes and Debates | Neusner |
| 240108 | Why There Never Was a "Talmud of Caesarea" | Neusner |
| 240109 | Judaism after the Death of "The Death of God" | Neusner |
| 240110 | Approaches to Ancient Judaism | Neusner |
| 240111 | Ecology of Religion | Neusner |
| 240112 | The Judaic Law of Baptism | Neusner |
| 240113 | The Documentary Foundation of Rabbinic Culture | Neusner |
| 240114 | Understanding Seeking Faith, Volume Four | Neusner |
| 240115 | Paul and Judaism: An Anthropological Approach | Laato |
| 240116 | Approaches to Ancient Judaism, New Series, Volume Eight | Neusner |
| 240119 | Theme and Context in Biblical Lists | Scolnic |
| 240120 | Where the Talmud Comes From | Neusner |
| 240121 | The Initial Phases of the Talmud, Volume Three: Social Ethics | Neusner |
| 240122 | Are the Talmuds Interchangeable? Christine Hayes's Blunder | Neusner |
| 240123 | The Initial Phases of the Talmud, Volume One: Exegesis of Scripture | Neusner |
| 240124 | The Initial Phases of the Talmud, Volume Two: Exemplary Virtue | Neusner |
| 240125 | The Initial Phases of the Talmud, Volume Four: Theology | Neusner |
| 240126 | From Agnon to Oz | Bargad |
| 240127 | Talmudic Dialectics, Volume I: Tractate Berakhot and the Divisions of Appointed Times and Women | Neusner |
| 240128 | Talmudic Dialectics, Volume II: The Divisions of Damages and Holy Things and Tractate Niddah | Neusner |

| | | |
|---|---|---|
| 240129 | The Talmud: Introduction and Reader | Neusner |
| 240130 | *Gesher Vakesher:* Bridges and Bonds<br>The Life of Leon Kronish | Green |
| 240131 | Beyond Catastrophe | Neusner |
| 240132 | Ancient Judaism, Fourth Series | Neusner |
| 240133 | Formative Judaism, New Series: Current Issues and Arguments<br>Volume One | Neusner |
| 240134 | Sects and Scrolls | Davies |
| 240135 | Religion and Law | Neusner |
| 240136 | Approaches to Ancient Judaism, New Series, Volume Nine | Neusner |
| 240137 | Uppsala Addresses | Neusner |
| 240138 | Jews and Christians in the Life and Thought of Hugh of<br>St. Victor | Moore |
| 240140 | Jews, Pagans, and Christians in the Golan Heights | Gregg/Urman |
| 240141 | Rosenzweig on Profane/Secular History | Vogel |
| 240142 | Approaches to Ancient Judaism, New Series, Volume Ten | Neusner |
| 240143 | Archaeology and the Galilee | Edwards/McCullough |
| 240144 | Rationality and Structure | Neusner |
| 240145 | Formative Judaism, New Series: Current Issues and Arguments<br>Volume Two | Neusner |

## South Florida Academic Commentary Series

| | | |
|---|---|---|
| 243001 | The Talmud of Babylonia, An Academic Commentary,<br>Volume XI, Bavli Tractate Moed Qatan | Neusner |
| 243002 | The Talmud of Babylonia, An Academic Commentary,<br>Volume XXXIV, Bavli Tractate Keritot | Neusner |
| 243003 | The Talmud of Babylonia, An Academic Commentary,<br>Volume XVII, Bavli Tractate Sotah | Neusner |
| 243004 | The Talmud of Babylonia, An Academic Commentary,<br>Volume XXIV, Bavli Tractate Makkot | Neusner |
| 243005 | The Talmud of Babylonia, An Academic Commentary,<br>Volume XXXII, Bavli Tractate Arakhin | Neusner |
| 243006 | The Talmud of Babylonia, An Academic Commentary,<br>Volume VI, Bavli Tractate Sukkah | Neusner |
| 243007 | The Talmud of Babylonia, An Academic Commentary,<br>Volume XII, Bavli Tractate Hagigah | Neusner |
| 243008 | The Talmud of Babylonia, An Academic Commentary,<br>Volume XXVI, Bavli Tractate Horayot | Neusner |
| 243009 | The Talmud of Babylonia, An Academic Commentary,<br>Volume XXVII, Bavli Tractate Shebuot | Neusner |
| 243010 | The Talmud of Babylonia, An Academic Commentary,<br>Volume XXXIII, Bavli Tractate Temurah | Neusner |
| 243011 | The Talmud of Babylonia, An Academic Commentary,<br>Volume XXXV, Bavli Tractates Meilah and Tamid | Neusner |
| 243012 | The Talmud of Babylonia, An Academic Commentary,<br>Volume VIII, Bavli Tractate Rosh Hashanah | Neusner |

| | | |
|---|---|---|
| 243013 | The Talmud of Babylonia, An Academic Commentary, Volume V, Bavli Tractate Yoma | Neusner |
| 243014 | The Talmud of Babylonia, An Academic Commentary, Volume XXXVI, Bavli Tractate Niddah | Neusner |
| 243015 | The Talmud of Babylonia, An Academic Commentary, Volume XX, Bavli Tractate Baba Qamma | Neusner |
| 243016 | The Talmud of Babylonia, An Academic Commentary, Volume XXXI, Bavli Tractate Bekhorot | Neusner |
| 243017 | The Talmud of Babylonia, An Academic Commentary, Volume XXX, Bavli Tractate Hullin | Neusner |
| 243018 | The Talmud of Babylonia, An Academic Commentary, Volume VII, Bavli Tractate Besah | Neusner |
| 243019 | The Talmud of Babylonia, An Academic Commentary, Volume X, Bavli Tractate Megillah | Neusner |
| 243020 | The Talmud of Babylonia, An Academic Commentary, Volume XXVIII, Bavli Tractate Zebahim A. Chapters I through VII | Neusner |
| 243021 | The Talmud of Babylonia, An Academic Commentary, Volume XXI, Bavli Tractate Baba Mesia, A. Chapters I through VI | Neusner |
| 243022 | The Talmud of Babylonia, An Academic Commentary, Volume XXII, Bavli Tractate Baba Batra, A. Chapters I through VI | Neusner |
| 243023 | The Talmud of Babylonia, An Academic Commentary, Volume XXIX, Bavli Tractate Menahot, A. Chapters I through VI | Neusner |
| 243024 | The Talmud of Babylonia, An Academic Commentary, Volume I, Bavli Tractate Berakhot | Neusner |
| 243025 | The Talmud of Babylonia, An Academic Commentary, Volume XXV, Bavli Tractate Abodah Zarah | Neusner |
| 243026 | The Talmud of Babylonia, An Academic Commentary, Volume XXIII, Bavli Tractate Sanhedrin, A. Chapters I through VII | Neusner |
| 243027 | The Talmud of Babylonia, A Complete Outline, Part IV, The Division of Holy Things; A: From Tractate Zabahim through Tractate Hullin | Neusner |
| 243028 | The Talmud of Babylonia, An Academic Commentary, Volume XIV, Bavli Tractate Ketubot, A. Chapters I through VI | Neusner |
| 243029 | The Talmud of Babylonia, An Academic Commentary, Volume IV, Bavli Tractate Pesahim, A. Chapters I through VII | Neusner |
| 243030 | The Talmud of Babylonia, An Academic Commentary, Volume III, Bavli Tractate Erubin, A. ChaptersI through V | Neusner |
| 243031 | The Talmud of Babylonia, A Complete Outline, Part III, The Division of Damages; A: From Tractate Baba Qamma through Tractate Baba Batra | Neusner |
| 243032 | The Talmud of Babylonia, An Academic Commentary, Volume II, Bavli Tractate Shabbat, Volume A, Chapters One through Twelve | Neusner |

| | | |
|---|---|---|
| 243033 | The Talmud of Babylonia, An Academic Commentary, Volume II, Bavli Tractate Shabbat, Volume B, Chapters Thirteen through Twenty-four | Neusner |
| 243034 | The Talmud of Babylonia, An Academic Commentary, Volume XV, Bavli Tractate Nedarim | Neusner |
| 243035 | The Talmud of Babylonia, An Academic Commentary, Volume XVIII, Bavli Tractate Gittin | Neusner |
| 243036 | The Talmud of Babylonia, An Academic Commentary, Volume XIX, Bavli Tractate Qiddushin | Neusner |
| 243037 | The Talmud of Babylonia, A Complete Outline, Part IV, The Division of Holy Things; B: From Tractate Berakot through Tractate Niddah | Neusner |
| 243038 | The Talmud of Babylonia, A Complete Outline, Part III, The Division of Damages; B: From Tractate Sanhedrin through Tractate Shebuot | Neusner |
| 243039 | The Talmud of Babylonia, A Complete Outline, Part I, Tractate Berakhot and the Division of Appointed Times A: From Tractate Berakhot through Tractate Pesahim | Neusner |
| 243040 | The Talmud of Babylonia, A Complete Outline, Part I, Tractate Berakhot and the Division of Appointed Times B: From Tractate Yoma through Tractate Hagigah | Neusner |
| 243041 | The Talmud of Babylonia, A Complete Outline, Part II, The Division of Women; A: From Tractate Yebamot through Tractate Ketubot | Neusner |
| 243042 | The Talmud of Babylonia, A Complete Outline, Part II, The Division of Women; B: From Tractate Nedarim through Tractate Qiddushin | Neusner |
| 243043 | The Talmud of Babylonia, An Academic Commentary, Volume XIII, Bavli Tractate Yebamot, A. Chapters One through Eight | Neusner |
| 243044 | The Talmud of Babylonia, An Academic Commentary, XIII, Bavli Tractate Yebamot, B. Chapters Nine through Seventeen | Neusner |
| 243045 | The Talmud of the Land of Israel, A Complete Outline of the Second, Third and Fourth Divisions, Part II, The Division of Women, A. Yebamot to Nedarim | Neusner |
| 243046 | The Talmud of the Land of Israel, A Complete Outline of the Second, Third and Fourth Divisions, Part II, The Division of Women, B. Nazir to Sotah | Neusner |
| 243047 | The Talmud of the Land of Israel, A Complete Outline of the Second, Third and Fourth Divisions, Part I, The Division of Appointed Times, C. Pesahim and Sukkah | Neusner |
| 243048 | The Talmud of the Land of Israel, A Complete Outline of the Second, Third and Fourth Divisions, Part I, The Division of Appointed Times, A. Berakhot, Shabbat | Neusner |
| 243049 | The Talmud of the Land of Israel, A Complete Outline of the Second, Third and Fourth Divisions, Part I, The Division of Appointed Times, B. Erubin, Yoma and Besah | Neusner |
| 243050 | The Talmud of the Land of Israel, A Complete Outline of the Second, Third and Fourth Divisions, Part I, The Division of | |

| | | |
|---|---|---|
| | Appointed Times, D. Taanit, Megillah, Rosh Hashannah, Hagigah and Moed Qatan | Neusner |
| 243051 | The Talmud of the Land of Israel, A Complete Outline of the Second, Third and Fourth Divisions, Part III, The Division of Damages, A. Baba Qamma, Baba Mesia, Baba Batra, Horayot and Niddah | Neusner |
| 243052 | The Talmud of the Land of Israel, A Complete Outline of the Second, Third and Fourth Divisions, Part III, The Division of Damages, B. Sanhedrin, Makkot, Shebuot and Abldah Zarah | Neusner |
| 243053 | The Two Talmuds Compared, II. The Division of Women in the Talmud of the Land of Israel and the Talmud of Babylonia, Volume A, Tractates Yebamot and Ketubot | Neusner |
| 243054 | The Two Talmuds Compared, II. The Division of Women in the Talmud of the Land of Israel and the Talmud of Babylonia, Volume B, Tractates Nedarim, Nazir and Sotah | Neusner |
| 243055 | The Two Talmuds Compared, II. The Division of Women in the Talmud of the Land of Israel and the Talmud of Babylonia, Volume C, Tractates Qiddushin and Gittin | Neusner |
| 243056 | The Two Talmuds Compared, III. The Division of Damages in the Talmud of the Land of Israel and the Talmud of Babylonia, Volume A, Tractates Baba Qamma and Baba Mesia | Neusner |
| 243057 | The Two Talmuds Compared, III. The Division of Damages in the Talmud of the Land of Israel and the Talmud of Babylonia, Volume B, Tractates Baba Batra and Niddah | Neusner |
| 243058 | The Two Talmuds Compared, III. The Division of Damages in the Talmud of the Land of Israel and the Talmud of Babylonia, Volume C, Tractates Sanhedrin and Makkot | Neusner |
| 243059 | The Two Talmuds Compared, I. Tractate Berakhot and the Division of Appointed Times in the Talmud of the Land of Israel and the Talmud of Babylonia, Volume B, Tractate Shabbat | Neusner |
| 243060 | The Two Talmuds Compared, I. Tractate Berakhot and the Division of Appointed Times in the Talmud of the Land of Israel and the Talmud of Babylonia, Volume A, Tractate Berakhot | Neusner |
| 243061 | The Two Talmuds Compared, III. The Division of Damages in the Talmud of the Land of Israel and the Talmud of Babylonia, Volume D, Tractates Shebuot, Abodah Zarah and Horayot | Neusner |
| 243062 | The Two Talmuds Compared, I. Tractate Berakhot and the Division of Appointed Times in the Talmud of the Land of Israel and the Talmud of Babylonia, Volume C, Tractate Erubin | Neusner |
| 243063 | The Two Talmuds Compared, I. Tractate Berakhot and the Division of Appointed Times in the Talmud of the Land of Israel and the Talmud of Babylonia, Volume D, Tractates Yoma and Sukkah | Neusner |
| 243064 | The Two Talmuds Compared, I. Tractate Berakhot and the Division of Appointed Times in the Talmud of the Land of Israel and the Talmud of Babylonia, Volume E, Tractate Pesahim | Neusner |
| 243065 | The Two Talmuds Compared, I. Tractate Berakhot and the Division of Appointed Times in the Talmud of the Land of Israel and the Talmud of Babylonia, Volume F, Tractates Besah, Taanit and Megillah | Neusner |

| | | |
|---|---|---|
| 243066 | The Two Talmuds Compared, I. Tractate Berakhot and the Division of Appointed Times in the Talmud of the Land of Israel and the Talmud of Babylonia, Volume G, Tractates Rosh Hashanah and Moed Qatan | Neusner |
| 243067 | The Talmud of Babylonia, An Academic Commentary, Volume XXII, Bavli Tractate Baba Batra, B. Chapters VII through XI | Neusner |
| 243068 | The Talmud of Babylonia, An Academic Commentary, Volume XXIII, Bavli Tractate Sanhedrin, B. Chapters VIII through XII | Neusner |
| 243069 | The Talmud of Babylonia, An Academic Commentary, Volume XIV, Bavli Tractate Ketubot, B. ChaptersVII through XIV | Neusner |
| 243070 | The Talmud of Babylonia, An Academic Commentary, Volume IV, Bavli Tractate Pesahim, B. Chapters VIII through XI | Neusner |
| 243071 | The Talmud of Babylonia, An Academic Commentary, Volume XXIX, Bavli Tractate Menahot, B. Chapters VII through XIV | Neusner |
| 243072 | The Talmud of Babylonia, An Academic Commentary, Volume XXVIII, Bavli Tractate Zebahim B. Chapters VIII through XV | Neusner |
| 243073 | The Talmud of Babylonia, An Academic Commentary, Volume XXI, Bavli Tractate Baba Mesia, B. Chapters VIII through XI | Neusner |
| 243074 | The Talmud of Babylonia, An Academic Commentary, Volume III, Bavli Tractate Erubin, A. ChaptersVI through XI | Neusner |

## South Florida-Rochester-Saint Louis Studies on Religion and the Social Order

| | | |
|---|---|---|
| 245001 | Faith and Context, Volume 1 | Ong |
| 245002 | Faith and Context, Volume 2 | Ong |
| 245003 | Judaism and Civil Religion | Breslauer |
| 245004 | The Sociology of Andrew M. Greeley | Greeley |
| 245005 | Faith and Context, Volume 3 | Ong |
| 245006 | The Christ of Michelangelo | Dixon |
| 245007 | From Hermeneutics to Ethical Consensus Among Cultures | Bori |
| 245008 | Mordecai Kaplan's Thought in a Postmodern Age | Breslauer |
| 245009 | No Longer Aliens, No Longer Strangers | Eckardt |
| 245010 | Between Tradition and Culture | Ellenson |
| 245011 | Religion and the Social Order | Neusner |
| 245012 | Christianity and the Stranger | Nichols |
| 245013 | The Polish Challenge | Czosnyka |
| 245014 | Islam and the Question of Minorities | Sonn |
| 245015 | Religion and the Political Order | Neusner |

# South Florida International Studies in Formative Christianity and Judaism

| | | |
|---|---|---|
| 242501 | The Earliest Christian Mission to 'All Nations' | La Grand |
| 242502 | Judaic Approaches to the Gospels | Chilton |
| 252403 | The "Essence of Christianity" | Forni Rosa |
| 242504 | The Wicked Tenants and Gethsemane | Aus |
| 242505 | Messiah-Christos | Laato |
| 242506 | Romans 9–11: A Reader-Response Analysis | Lodge |